JOHN PAUL II

THE ENCYCLICALS

IN EVERYDAY LANGUAGE

JOHN PAUL II

THE ENCYCLICALS
IN EVERYDAY LANGUAGE

New Updated Edition

Edited by

Joseph G. Donders

ORBIS BOOKS

Maryknoll, New York 10545

The Catholic Foreign Mission Society of America (Maryknoll) recruits and trains people for overseas missionary service. Through Orbis Books, Maryknoll aims to foster the international dialogue that is essential to mission. The books published, however, reflect the opinions of their authors and are not meant to represent the official position of the Society. To obtain more information about Maryknoll and Orbis Books, visit our website at www.maryknoll.org.

Published by Orbis Books, Maryknoll, New York, U.S.A.

Manufactured in the United States of America

Library of Congress Cataloging-in-Publication Data
Catholic Church. Pope (1978- : John Paul II)
    John Paul II : the encyclicals in everyday language / edited by Joseph G. Donders.– New updated ed.
        p.   cm.
    Includes index.
    ISBN 1-57075-374-1 (pbk.)
    1. Encyclicals, Papal.   2. Catholic Church–Doctrines–Papal documents.   I. John Paul II, Pope, 1920-   II. Donders, Joseph G.   III. Title.

BX1378.5 .C37   2001
262.9'1–dc21

                                                                    00-069121

Contents

Abbreviations   vii

Preface   ix

1. **Redeemer of Humankind**
   Redemptor Hominis   March 4, 1979   1

2. **The Mercy of God**
   Dives in Misericordia   November 30, 1980   21

3. **On Human Work**
   Laborem Exercens   September 14, 1981   41

4. **The Apostles of the Slavs**
   Slavorum Apostoli   June 2, 1985   71

5. **Lord and Giver of Life**
   Dominum et Vivificantem   May 30, 1986   80

6. **The Mother of the Redeemer**
   Redemptoris Mater   March 25, 1987   108

7. **On Social Concern**
   Sollicitudo Rei Socialis   December 30, 1987   126

8. **The Mission of the Redeemer**
   Redemptoris Missio   December 7, 1990   143

9. **The Hundredth Year: "New Things" One Hundred Years Later**
   Centesimus Annus   May 1, 1991   173

10. **The Splendor of Truth**
    Veritatis Splendor   August 6, 1993   201

11. **The Gospel of Life**
    Evangelium Vitae   March 25, 1995   242

12. **That They May Be One**
    Ut Unum Sint   May 25, 1995   291

13. **Faith and Reason**
    Fides et Ratio   September 14, 1998   325

Epilogue   358

Index   363

Abbreviations

AG   Vatican Council II, *Ad Gentes,* Decree on the Church's Missionary Activity

CCC *Catechism of the Catholic Church*

DF   Vatican Council I, *Dei Filius,* Dogmatic Constitution on the Catholic Faith

DH   Vatican Council II, *Dignitatis Humanae,* Declaration on Religious Freedom

DM   *Dives in Misericordia,* Rich in Mercy, encyclical of Pope John Paul II, November 30, 1980

DS   Denziger-Schönmetzer, *Enchiridion Symbolorum, Definitionum et Declarationum de Rebus Fidei et Morum,* Manual of Creeds, Definitions, and Declaration on Matters of Faith and Morals, comp. H. Denziger, rev. ed. by A. Schönmetzer

DV   Vatican Council II, *Dei Verbum,* Dogmatic Constitution on Divine Revelation

EN   *Evangelii Nuntiandi,* Apostolic Exhortation of Pope Paul VI, December 8, 1975

GS   Vatican Council II, *Gaudium et Spes,* Pastoral Constitution on the Church in the Modern World

HV   *Humanae Vitae,* On Human Life, encyclical of Pope Paul VI, July 25, 1968

LG   Vatican Council II, *Lumen Gentium,* Dogmatic Constitution on the Church

NA   Vatican Council II, *Nostra Aetate,* Declaration on the Relationship of the Church to Non-Christian Religions

RH   *Redemptor Hominis,* Redeemer of Humankind, encyclical of John Paul II, March 4, 1979

RM   *Redemptoris Missio,* The Mission of the Redeemer, encyclical of John Paul II, December 7, 1990

RP   *Reconciliatio et Paenitentia,* Reconciliation and Penance, Post-Synodal Apostolic Exhortation, December 2, 1984

SA   *Slavorum Apostoli,* The Apostles of the Slavs, encyclical of John Paul II, June 2, 1985

SC   Vatican Council II, *Sacrosanctum Concilium,* Constitution on the Sacred Liturgy

ST   Thomas Aquinas, *Summa Theologiae.*

UR   Vatican Council II, *Unitatis Redintegratio,* Decree on Ecumenism

VS   *Veritatis Splendor,* The Splendor of Truth, encyclical of Pope John Paul II, August 6, 1993

Preface

Encyclicals are the most important and the most authoritative documents a pope writes. In 1745 Pope Benedict XIV wrote the first one, on usury. Since then about three hundred encyclicals have been published. The most famous is probably Pope Leo XIII's *Rerum Novarum* (On New Things) of 1891, on the social problems of his time. Encyclicals are in general no easy reading. The originals are often written in what some call "curial Latin." Because encyclicals are so important, they often are written in a cautious language as well, which does not help an easy understanding. Not all of them are actually written by the popes who — by signing them — make them their own. Often not much is known about their authors and their history. Reading Pope John Paul II's encyclicals, many wish that he would be less abstract, that he would tell a story. Sometimes he does that, as in his latest encyclical on Christian unity.

It is sometimes said that anything an author writes is autobiographical. Maybe this whole series of encyclicals is a story, John Paul II's story. When you compare the themes in John Paul II's encyclicals with what we know of the life of Karol Wojtyla, you will see that might well be the case.

His main theme is the indwelling of God in each human being and consequently in human society. He powerfully experienced this reality himself during the Second World War. Doing forced labor and living under a dictatorial regime as an orphan deprived of practically everything, he began to meditate on the works of the great mystics John of the Cross and Teresa of Avila. It is that spiritual reality of God's indwelling that pervades the twelve encyclicals he wrote. It is the basis of practically all he writes on the role of the Trinity and of Jesus Christ in the life of a human being, on the consequent human rights and the rights of workers, on the distribution of the goods and work in our world, on evangelization and mission, on interreligious dialogue and ecumenism, on the gospel of life and a civilization of love. He stresses that the acknowledgment of this divine presence in every human being is the way the church has to follow. He explains how human beings discover the fullness of their dignity and that of their fellow human beings in their encounter with Jesus Christ.

His approach to these issues shows him not only as a believing pastor but also as a philosopher influenced by the personalism and existential phenomenology of his student days and the signs of the times in which we live as his contemporaries. Reading his encyclicals one can trace a development. Notwithstanding the many categorical statements in his encyclicals, his latest one ends with a question, asking how Jesus' vicar on earth should exercise his authority in our days.

This book contains unofficial versions of John Paul II's encyclicals. We prepared them to make those texts more accessible to the reader. Care has been taken to edit them faithfully in sense lines and in everyday language, while maintaining their message. In any formal discussion of these texts the official texts should be used next to this version.

1

Redeemer of Humankind

Redemptor Hominis

March 4, 1979

John Paul II outlines his pontifical program. He refers to the great jubilee of Jesus' birth in the year 2000. His pontificate will be like an Advent time, expecting Jesus. In the line of the Second Vatican Council he states that looking at Jesus Christ we see who we really are. We are created in God's image and sharers in God's life. This is the good news the church has to preach and respect. It is the foundation of our human rights and of our work for justice and human development. It asks for the reimagining and the restructuring of the world as we know it. It is a truth that begs for interreligious dialogue and Christian unity. It is this truth about the human person that indicates the way the church should go.

I. INHERITANCE

1. At the Close of the Second Millennium

Jesus Christ is the center of the universe and of history.
This time, in which God entrusted to me
the universal service of the Chair of Saint Peter in Rome,
is very close to the year 2000.
2000 will be the year of the great jubilee,
recalling that "the Word became flesh and dwelt among us" (Jn 1:14).
    It is — in a way — a time of a new Advent,
    a season of expectation:
    "in these last days God spoke to us by his Son" (Heb 1:1–2)
    who became man, born of the Virgin Mary.

2. The First Words of the New Pontificate

After the election, when I was asked,
"Do you accept?"

I answered:
"With obedience in faith to Christ, my Lord,
    and with trust in the mother of Christ and of the church,
    in spite of the great difficulties, I accept,"
making the link between the incarnation
and my ministry.
    In the spirit of my predecessor John Paul I,
    I chose the name John Paul II
    to express my love for the unique inheritance
    left to the church by John XXIII and Paul VI.
    I wish to refer to that inheritance as a threshold,
    from which I intend to continue into the future,
    guided by the Spirit Christ promised and sent to his church.

3. Trust in the Spirit of Truth and Love

Thanks to the Second Vatican Council
this inheritance struck deep roots
in the consciousness of the church:
    the "awareness" Paul VI chose as the theme
    in his encyclical *Ecclesiam Suam.*
Let me link myself to Paul VI's encyclical
in this, my first document.
He showed us how the church is conscious of being
    "a sacrament or sign and means of intimate union with God
    and of unity of all humankind" (LG 1).

4. Reference to Paul VI's First Encyclical

This awareness is open to all,
so that all may find in the church
"the unsearchable riches of Christ" (Eph 3:8).
    It is this consciousness that gives the church
    its apostolic, missionary dynamism,
    carrying on what Paul VI called the "dialogue of salvation."
Paul VI knew how to show the true face of the church "ad extra"
in spite of its various internal "ad intra" weaknesses
in the postconciliar period.
    That is how the human family
    has become — it seems — more aware
    of how necessary the church,
    its mission, and its service are to humanity.
The growing criticism within the church
was not always without a sincere love for the church.
    One of its demands was to overcome the tendency
    to what has been called its "triumphalism."

Though it is true that the church
should have humility as its foundation,
and be critical as regards
its human character and activity,
criticism, too, should have its just limits.
Otherwise it ceases to be constructive,
wishing to direct the opinion of others
in accordance with one's own,
in too thoughtless a manner.
> Paul VI, respecting every particle of truth,
> preserved the providential balance
> of the bark's helmsman.

Though not free of internal difficulties and tensions,
the church is at the moment more strengthened
against excesses of self-criticism,
more critical as regards thoughtless criticism,
more resistant to various "novelties,"
more mature in discernment,
better in bringing out its everlasting treasure,
more intent on its own mystery,
and — because of all this —
more serviceable for its mission of the salvation of all.

5. *Collegiality and Apostolate*

This greater awareness of its unity and its service
springs from the principle of collegiality,
mentioned by the Second Vatican Council.
> Christ himself made this principle
> a living part of the Apostolic College of the Twelve
> with Peter at their head,
> renewing it in the ever growing
> College of Bishops over all the earth.

Fulfilling the Council's wish for a permanent organ of collegiality,
Paul VI founded the Synod of Bishops,
giving a new dimension to his pontificate and that of his successors.
> The principle of collegiality,
> chiefly displayed through the synod,
> helped to dissipate doubts
> and to indicate ways for renewing the church.

It found its expression
in the Apostolic Exhortation *Evangelii Nuntiandi*
— so welcome a program for renewal —
and in the last session of the Synod of Bishops on catechesis.
> In this context mention must also be made
> of the national episcopal conferences,

the various diocesan, provincial, and national synods,
the many councils of priests,
the old and new organizations for lay apostolate,
and the lay people committing themselves
to collaborate with pastors and institutes of consecrated life.
This development is much stronger
than the symptoms of doubt, collapse, and crisis.

6. *The Road to Christian Unity*

Pope John XXIII declared the issue of Christian unity
to be the consequence of Jesus' will and prayer:
"I pray . . . Father . . . that they all may be one" (Jn 17:21).
Vatican II responded to this issue
with its Decree on Ecumenism.
Pope Paul VI, availing himself
of the Secretariat for Promoting Christian Unity,
took the first difficult steps on the road to unity.
We have made real and important advances,
together with other Christian churches and communities.
The present historical situation
asks us to seek ways to draw ever closer.
There are people who would like to turn back.
Some even say that these efforts are harmful
to the cause of the Gospel,
that they are leading to further rupture,
causing confusion and ending up with indifferentism.
It is maybe good that these fears are expressed,
but here, too, correct limits must be maintained.
To all who wish to dissuade the church
from seeking the unity of Christians,
the question must be asked:
"Have we the right not to do it?"
Can we fail to have trust
in our Lord's grace?
What we have just said
must also be applied — with due difference —
to our drawing closer
to the representatives of non-Christian religions,
through dialogue, contacts, prayer in common,
and the investigation of the treasures of human spirituality,
not lacking in the members of those religions.
Does not their firm belief
— a belief that is also an effect of the Spirit of truth
operating outside the visible confines of the Mystical Body —
make Christians often feel ashamed?

It is a noble thing to try to understand
persons and systems,
recognizing in them what is right.
This neither jeopardizes
the certitude about one's own faith,
nor weakens the principles of morality.

II. THE MYSTERY OF REDEMPTION

7. *Within the Mystery of Christ*

How should we continue what was begun?
What should we do to bring us closer
to the "Everlasting Father" (Is 9:6)?
    This is the question the new pope
    must ask himself,
    accepting the call Christ gave Peter:
    "Feed my lambs" (Jn 21:15).

The fundamental answer to this question
is to turn toward Christ, our Redeemer.
    In him are "all the treasures of wisdom and knowledge" (Col 2:3),
    the church being his Body.
The church listens to his words,
relives his death and resurrection in its daily life
and unceasingly celebrates the Eucharist,
the fountain of life and holiness.

8. *Redemption as New Creation*

In Jesus Christ the world — subject to futility because of its sin —
recovers its original link with God.
    Is the world of the new age,
    with its immense progress,
    but also with its threat of pollution of the environment,
    its armed conflicts,
    its prospect of atomic self-destruction,
    its lack of respect for the life of the unborn,
    its space flights,
    and its conquests of science and technology,
    not "groaning in travail" (Rom 8:22),
    "waiting eagerly
    for the revealing of the children of God" (Rom 8:19)?
In its analysis of the modern world
the Second Vatican Council expressed the depth of human consciousness
using the word "heart."
Christ is the one who entered that heart.

The mystery of the human being
takes on light in the mystery of the Incarnate Word.
   "Christ, the new Adam, fully reveals
   human beings to themselves,
   and brings to light their most high calling....
   He who is the 'image of the invisible God' (Col 1:15)
   is himself the perfect human being
   who has restored in the children of Adam
   that likeness of God which had been disfigured
   ever since the first sin.
   By his incarnation the Son of God
   united himself — in a way —
   with each human being" (GS 22).

9. *The Divine Dimension of the Mystery of Redemption*

Jesus Christ became our reconciliation with the Father.
   The redemption of the world is — at its deepest level —
   the fullness of justice in the heart of the firstborn Son,
   in order to become justice in the hearts of many human beings.
Jesus "leaving" this world on the cross
is a new manifestation of God's fatherhood,
in Jesus drawing near again to humanity
and to each human being,
giving them the holy "Spirit of truth" (Jn 16:13).
   The *God of creation*
   is revealed as the *God of redemption*,
   — the God who is "faithful" (1 Thes 5:24) —
   and faithful to God's love for humanity and the world.
God's love and mercy,
taking the form and name of Jesus Christ,
are greater than sin.

10. *The Human Dimension of the Mystery of Redemption*

A human being cannot live without love.
That is why Christ fully reveals us to ourselves.
We are "recreated" in the mystery of redemption.
   If we really wish to understand ourselves
   we must appropriate and assimilate
   the whole of the reality of the incarnation and redemption
   and draw near to Christ.
   This process will lead not only to the adoration of God,
   but also to deep wonder at ourselves.
How precious must we be in the eyes of the Creator,
if we "gained so great a redeemer" and if God "gave his only Son,"
in order that we should have "eternal life" (Jn 3:16).

The *name* for that deep amazement
at our worth and dignity
is the Gospel, the good news.
It is also called Christianity.
This amazement determines
the church's mission in the world,
and even more so in the modern world.
It vivifies authentic humanism;
it fixes Christ's place in human history,
leading through cross and death to resurrection.

11. *The Mystery of Christ as the Basis of the Church's Mission and of Christianity*

The church comes to its self-awareness in dialogue,
attentive to the ones it wishes to speak with.
The Second Vatican Council presented the globe to us
as a map of various religions.
It also showed — superimposed on this map —
layers of atheism, beginning with that atheism
that is organized, programmed, and structured
as a political system.
The Council's documents on non-Christian religions
are filled with deep esteem for the great spiritual values,
and for the primacy of the spiritual,
religiously, morally, and culturally
expressed in the life of humankind.
The Council fathers saw in the various religions,
and rightly so, many "Seeds of the Word" (AG 11).
Though the routes taken may be different,
God is the one meaningful goal of human life.
They paid special attention to the Jewish religion
and to the believers of Islam,
whose faith also looks to Abraham (NA 3–4).

All Christians should meet and unite around Christ,
getting to know each other and removing all obstacles
blocking the way to perfect unity.
We must display to the world our unity,
proclaiming the mystery of Christ,
revealing the divine and human dimension
of the redemption,
struggling for the dignity that each human being
has reached and can reach in Christ,
the dignity of the grace of divine adoption
and the inner truth of humanity,

to which the modern world
attaches such a fundamental importance.
We must all share in this mission,
more necessary than ever.
If this mission seems to encounter
greater opposition than ever before,
it is because it is more awaited than ever.
May we be like those "violent people of God"
consciously joining in the great mission
of revealing Christ to the world,
helping everyone to get to know
"the unsearchable riches of Christ" (Eph 3:8)
since they are meant for every individual
and since they are everybody's property.

12. *The Church's Mission and Human Freedom*

Before their full communion is achieved
Christians must first find what unites them.
So that we together can come close
to the magnificent heritage of the human spirit
manifest in all religions (NA 1–2).
It will enable us to approach with esteem
all cultures,
all ideological concepts,
all people of good will.
It is this esteem, respect, and discernment,
that since the time of the apostles
— think of Saint Paul at Athens! —
has marked the missionary attitude,
an attitude that always begins
with a feeling of deep appreciation
for "what is in the human being" (Jn 2:26),
respecting everything that has been brought about
by the Holy Spirit, "which blows where it wills" (Jn 3:8).
Mission is never destruction!
That is why we attach such great importance
to the Second Vatican Council's
Declaration on Religious Freedom.
When Christ and, after him, the apostles
proclaimed the truth that came from God,
they preserved a deep esteem for the people they met,
their intellect, will, conscience, and freedom.
The human person's dignity was part of their proclamation,
an attitude that seems to fit the special needs of our time.
The church is the guardian of this freedom!

Jesus Christ meets everyone with the same words:
"You will know the truth
and the truth will make you free" (Jn 8:32),
　words containing both
　a requirement and a warning:
　the requirement of an honest relationship to truth
　and a warning against every illusory freedom.
Standing before Pilate Jesus said:
"I was born to bear witness to the truth" (Jn 18:37).
All through the centuries he has been standing with those
condemned for the sake of truth.

III. REDEEMED HUMANITY'S SITUATION IN THE MODERN WORLD

13. *Christ United Himself with Each Human Being*

The church wishes to serve this single end:
that each person may be able to find Christ,
so that Christ may walk with each one the path of life.
　Jesus Christ is the chief way for the church,
　our way to the "Father's House" (Jn 14:1),
　and the way to each person.
Nobody can halt the church
on this way on which each person unites with Christ.
　The church cannot remain insensitive
　to whatever serves a person's true welfare,
　any more than it can remain indifferent
　to what threatens it.
It is the church's fundamental solicitude that
"life should conform more to a person's surpassing dignity" (GS 91),
so as to make life ever more human (GS 38).
　And all this not in the abstract,
　but concretely, dealing with each human being,
　because all are included in the mystery of the redemption.
"The human being is the only one on earth
that God willed for itself" (GS 24),
destined for grace and glory.
This is true of each concrete and real human being,
each one of the four billion human beings living on our planet,
all sharing in the mystery of Jesus Christ.

14. *For the Church All Ways Lead to the Human Person*

As human beings are so closely linked to Christ
the church cannot overlook any of them.

Because they are "persons"
they all have their own history of their soul,
through numerous bonds, contacts, situations, and social structures
as regards family, people, and the whole of humanity.
    The human person is the primary route
    the church must travel in fulfilling its mission:
    the human person is the primary and fundamental way
    for the church,
    the way traced out by Christ himself.
Christ is united to human beings,
even when people are unaware of it.
It is human beings in their situations
that the church should be interested in,
aware of their possibilities, but also of the threats
that oppose the task of "making human life more human" (GS 38).

15. *What Modern Humanity Is Afraid Of*

If we read the "signs of the times"
we see that people are afraid of
the result of the work of their hands,
the work of their intellects,
and the tendencies of their wills.
    What all this activity yields
    is not only simply taken away from them,
    but it even turns against them.
Consequently people live increasingly in fear.
They are afraid that part of what they produce
can become the means of an unimaginable self-destruction.
    This state of menace shows itself
    in various ways.
        It shows in the threat to our natural environment.
        Yet it was the Creator's will
        that we should communicate with nature
        as intelligent and noble guardians
        and not as exploiters and destroyers.
    The development of moral ethics
    seems not to keep in step with the progress of technology
    and the development of civilization,
        a progress that cannot
        fail to give rise to disquiet on many counts.
Does such progress make human life really more human?
Are we really becoming better, more spiritually mature,
more aware of the dignity of humanity, more responsible,
more open to others, especially the neediest and the weakest,
and ready to give and to aid all?

These are questions that must be asked by all.
Are we developing and progressing,
or are we regressing and being degraded?
Does good prevail over evil?
The issue of development is on everybody's lips,
it fills newspapers all over the world,
but next to all affirmations and certainties,
it is a subject that also contains questions
and anguished disquiet.
The latter are of no less importance
than the former.

16. *Progress or Threat*

Approaching the end of the second millennium of the Christian era,
we must follow the present-day progress attentively.
What is in question
is not just the multiplying of things,
but the advancement of persons.
It is not so much an issue of *having* more,
but of *being* more.
The danger is that while making advances
in its dominion over things,
humanity might be subjected to the world,
becoming the slave of things,
of the economic system and of production.
A purely materialistic civilization
condemns humanity to such slavery,
even though it might not have been the intention.
If we describe humanity's situation
as far removed from the demands of the moral order,
the exigencies of love, and still more from social love,
then we do that because all this is confirmed
by well-known facts.
The actual situation is marked by many differences,
historically explicable, but ethically uncontrolled.
The rich, highly developed societies have a surplus of goods,
while many other societies are suffering from hunger.
The freedom of one group limits the freedom of others.
We all know this gigantic development
of the parable of the rich banqueter
and the poor man Lazarus.
So widespread is this occurrence that it brings into question
the financial, monetary, and other mechanisms
that support the world economy.
We have here before us a drama that can leave no one indifferent.

The one who profits on one hand
and suffers on the other hand
is always the human person.
   Add to this the misuse of goods by the rich,
   the fever of inflation,
   and the plague of unemployment.
   They are further symptoms
   of the moral disorder in the world
   requiring daring creative steps to preserve
   people's authentic dignity.
This task is not impossible.
The principle of solidarity
asks for appropriate institutions and mechanisms,
whether in trade — where healthy competition may lead the way —
or on the level of a redistribution of riches,
in order that developing peoples may satisfy their needs,
and advance gradually and effectively.
   It is a road that will not be easy
   without a true conversion of mind, will, and heart
   of people who are free and linked in solidarity.
Economic development
must be constantly programmed
within the context of the development of each individual
and each people,
otherwise it gets entangled in its own tensions and excesses.
   It is possible to undertake this duty,
   a duty that is evident when we recall
   — as we always should —
   the scene of the last judgment (Mt 25:31–46):
   "I was hungry and you gave me no food,
   naked, and you didn't cloth me,
   in prison and you did not visit me."
These words become even more charged
when we consider that new states are often offered
means of destruction instead of bread and aid.
   We all know what would happen to misery and hunger,
   if the investments in arms
   would be changed into investments for food.
This consideration may be seen as "abstract,"
it might lead to misunderstandings by both "sides,"
it might provoke new accusations against the church,
but it is our duty — in season and out of season —
to continue demanding:
   "Do not kill,
   respect each one's dignity and freedom."

17. *Human Rights: Letter and Spirit*

This century has been full of great calamities,
not only material ones, but above all moral ones.
    Yet it also gave birth to the United Nations Organization
    with its definition and establishment of human rights.
Human rights are closely linked to the church's mission in the world.
They are the basis of social and international peace.
    What social, economic, political, or cultural program
    that describes itself as "humanistic"
    could fail to bring "the human person" to the fore?
Yet human rights are violated,
undermining these humanistic premises.
    The Declaration of Human Rights
    has as its aim to prevent
    the horrible experiences of the last world war,
    but also to enable the revision
    of programs, systems, and regimes.
    from the point of view of the human person.
If this does not happen, human life is condemned to suffering,
and the peaceful living together of the nations is threatened.
    In the first half of this century the church took a stand
    as regards totalitarian states denying their citizens
    those inviolable human rights.
Sharing the joy of all people of good will
that those rights have been acknowledged and formulated,
the church remains aware that the letter can kill
and only "the spirit gives life" (2 Cor 3:6).
We are often still far from their realization.
The church has always taught states and citizens
the duty to act for the common good:
    a common good that is brought to full realization
    only when all citizens are sure of their rights.
The principle of human rights is bound up with social justice
and it is the measure to test political policies.
These rights include
religious freedom and freedom of conscience,
considered by the Second Vatican Council,
in the document *Dignitatis Humanae,*
not only from a "theological"
but also from a "purely human" point of view.
    The curtailment of those rights
    are in contrast with human dignity.
I appeal to all those who organize social and public life
to respect those human rights.

IV. THE CHURCH'S MISSION AND HUMAN DESTINY

18. *The Church as Concerned for Humanity's Vocation in Christ*

If Christ "united himself with each human person" (GS 22),
the church will find its nature and mission
by entering this mystery, being itself Christ's body
and sharing this mystery with each human person.
    This union with Christ is a mystery,
    by which people are called
    to become partakers of God's life (2 Pet 1:4),
    and "children of God" (Jn 1:12).
    It is humanity's "divine destiny."
The church, living these realities,
looks beyond time but at the same time
is full of care for all that affects human life in time.
    Aware of the never-ending restlessness all this implies,
    the church is the guardian of a great treasure,
    gathering and not scattering (cf. Mt 12:30),
    united with the Spirit of Christ,
    praying with ever growing insistence:
        "Come, Holy Spirit,
        heal our wounds,
        our strength renew,
        on our dryness pour your dew,
        wash the stain of our guilt away,
        bend our stubborn heart and will,
        melt the frozen,
        warm the chill,
        guide the steps that go astray."
This appeal to the Spirit is the answer
to the "materialisms" of our age.
    Is the church alone in this appeal,
    expressed so clearly by the Council,
    when it called the church
    "a sacrament or sign and means of intimate union with God,
    and of the unity of all humankind" (LG 16)?
No, it is not.
Our time is particularly hungry for the Spirit,
because it is hungry for justice, peace, love,
goodness, fortitude, responsibility, and human dignity.
    The human being is the way for the church's daily life,
    in its triple office of priest, prophet, and king (LG 31–36).

19. *The Church as Responsible for Truth*

The church is responsible for the revealed truth,
which is the property of God.
Even the Son living "in the bosom of the Father" (Jn 1:18)
felt the need to stress this himself saying:
  "The word which you hear is not mine,
  but the Father's who sent me" (Jn 14:24).
Christ, concerned for the church's fidelity
promised the assistance of the Holy Spirit,
the gift of infallibility to those mandated to teach that truth (LG 25)
and a special sense of faith to the whole people of God (LG 12, 35).
We are sharers in mission of the prophet Jesus,
responsible for the truth, loving it, and seeking to understand it.
  Seeking that understanding we need theology.
  Theologians are the servants of the divine truth,
  functioning correctly when they seek to serve
  the magisterium entrusted to the bishops
  in communion with Peter's successor,
  when they place themselves at the service of their solicitude
  in teaching and pastoral care and of apostolic commitments
  of the whole people of God.
More than ever before theologians and all people of learning
are called to unite faith with learning and wisdom in all sciences.
  Though this work should be done in manifold ways,
  it can never depart from the fundamental unity
  of faith and morals.
  That is why collaboration with the magisterium
  is indispensable.
  Nobody can make of theology a simple set of personal ideas.
A particular share in this prophetic office
belongs to the pastors of the church
who teach and help to assemble the people of God
around Christ, eucharistically and sacramentally.
  In 1977 the Synod of Bishops
  paid special attention to catechesis.
  Witnessing and teaching go hand in hand.
  This is true in the case of priests,
  but also of religious men and women
  and the many lay people sharing in this responsibility,
  beginning with the catechesis
  given by parents to their children.
The whole people of God shares
in this prophetic responsibility:
scientists, jurists, artists, technicians,

and teachers at all levels,
according to Jesus' words when he said:
   "As the Father has sent me,
   even so I send you....
   Receive the Holy Spirit" (Jn 20:21–22).

20. *Eucharist and Penance*

The entire sacramental life of the church and of each Christian
reaches its summit and fullness in the Eucharist.
   By celebrating and partaking of the Eucharist,
   we unite ourselves with Christ
   interceding for us with the Father,
   through the redeeming act of his sacrifice,
   through which he has redeemed us.
By becoming "children of God" (Jn 1:12)
we also became "a kingdom of priests"
and obtain a "royal priesthood" (Rev 5:10).
   The Eucharist is the sacrament
   in which Christ bears witness
   that each of us has access to the fruits
   of filial reconciliation with God.
The Eucharist builds the church
as the authentic people of God,
commemorating his death on the cross,
the price with which Christ redeemed us.
In it we touch the very Body and Blood of the Lord,
as attested by the words he used at its institution
and we use celebrating the Eucharist.
   Though the church's magisterium
   has been expressing the fullness of this sacrament
   from the most distant time to our own days,
   we are but at the threshold
   of grasping and expressing it.
It is at the same time
a *Sacrifice*-Sacrament,
a *Communion*-Sacrament
and a *Presence*-Sacrament.
   It is the most profound revelation
   of the human brother/sisterhood of Christ's disciples.
   It is not a mere "occasion" for manifesting this relationship.
   Christ is really present and received,
   the soul is filled with grace,
   and the pledge of future glory is given (SC 47).
The liturgical rules should be rigorously adhered to.
Every member of the church should be vigilant

in seeing this sacrament of love
at the center of the life of the people of God,
truly becoming "the life of our souls" (Jn 6:51, 57; 14:6; Gal 2:20).
    And let us never forget Paul's words,
        to examine ourselves before eating the bread
        and drinking the cup (1 Cor 11:28).
This call links the Eucharist and Penance.
The first words of the Gospel of good news was:
"Repent and believe in the Gospel" (Mk 1:15).
The same Christ who calls us to the eucharistic banquet
calls us to penance.
    Without this conversion
    the Eucharist would lack
    its full redeeming effectiveness.
    Christ's self-giving to the Father
    raises in us the need to turn to God
    with a constant, ever more profound conversion.
In recent years much has been done
to highlight the community aspect of penance
in conformity with the most ancient tradition of the church.
    We cannot, however, forget
        that conversion is an act of the individual,
        in which that individual cannot be replaced
    by anyone else.
    Defending individual confession,
        the church is protecting an individual right,
        the right to a more personal encounter
        with the crucified forgiving Christ,
        saying, through the minister:
        "Your sins are forgiven" (Mk 2:5);
        "Do not sin any more" (Jn 8:11).
This is also Christ's right
with regard to every human being
redeemed by him.
    The sacrament of penance
        fits in with the desires of the human conscience
        hungering and thirsting for righteousness (Mt 5:6).
The church gathering in the Eucharist
should have a felt need for penance,
both as regards the sacrament,
but also for what concerns
penance as a virtue.
    The church of the New Advent
        must be the church of the Eucharist and of Penance,
        the church of the Divine Mission.

21. *The Christian Vocation to Service and Kingship*

Among other characteristics of the Christian vocation
the Second Vatican Council highlighted this one:
the sharing in Christ's "kingly function."
  This dignity is expressed in readiness to serve:
  Christ "came not to be served, but to serve" (Mt 20:28).
This is not a question of a mere "social membership";
it is a question of "vocation."
It is a question of responding to Christ's call:
"Follow me" (Jn 1:43).
It shows the "personal" aspect and dimension of this new society,
which — notwithstanding deficiencies — is a community
formed together with Christ,
  a community that — even from a "human" point of view —
  should become more aware of itself,
  of its own life and activity,
  and of how each of its members builds up the Body of Christ.
  It is the principle of "kingly service"
  that the pope, bishops, priests, religious,
  married people, parents, women and men
  in their different professions,
  from the highest to the simplest,
  should apply to themselves.
Each member has a "special gift" (1 Cor 7:7),
serving others, building the church
and the communities in the various spheres of human life on earth.
  Fidelity to one's vocation,
  persevering readiness for "kingly service,"
  has just as much a particular significance
  for married people, faithful to their marriage,
  as for priests faithful in their commitment to celibacy.
By basing ourselves on Christ's example we are able to be "kings,"
producing a mature humanity in each one of us,
a maturity that means full use of the gift of freedom.
  This gift finds its full realization in the unreserved giving
  of the whole of one's person to Christ,
  and with Christ to all.
  This is the ideal of religious life
  undertaken by religious orders, congregations,
  and secular institutes of men and women.
Freedom is not an end in itself;
it is a great gift only when we use it for our true good;
and the best use of freedom is charity,
taking form in self-giving and service.

It is for this freedom that Christ
has set us free.

22. *The Mother in Whom We Trust*

At the beginning of the new pontificate I want to enter
the deepest rhythm of the church's life drawn from Christ,
so that we should have life and life abundantly (Jn 10:10).
    That is why the church is a mother
    and has need of a mother,
    as was so well expressed by the Second Vatican Council
    and proclaimed — at the end of it — by Paul VI
    when he called the mother of Christ
    "the mother of the church."
Mary is the mother of the church
because she gave life to the Son of God,
from whom the whole of the people of God
receives grace and dignity.
    Under the cross Jesus extended his mother's maternity to all
    by designating his beloved disciple as her son.
She remained in the Upper Room
until the day of Pentecost
when the church was born in visible form.
    Later, all the generations of disciples
    took her to their own homes (Jn 19:27).
    We who form today's generation of disciples
    wish to unite ourselves to her in our turn.
    No one else can bring us into the mystery of redemption
    the way Mary can.
    Nobody has been brought into it by God
    as Mary has.
    The mystery of redemption
    took shape beneath the heart of the Virgin of Nazareth,
    a heart that always followed the work of her Son,
    and has gone out to all those Christ embraced.
The Father's love, shown through the Son God gave,
comes close to us through his mother.
Mary must be with us in the church's daily life,
while we feel all the more our need for a profound link
with Christ, apart from whom we can do nothing (Jn 15:5).
    Only prayer can prevent our task
    from becoming a source of crisis
    instead of an occasion for an even further growth
    of the people of God
    marching toward the Promised Land
    at the end of the second millennium.

I want the church to devote itself to this prayer,
together with Mary, the mother of Jesus,
hoping that through this prayer
we shall be able to receive the Holy Spirit,
thus becoming Christ's witnesses
"to the end of the earth" (Acts 1:8).

2

The Mercy of God
Dives in Misericordia

November 30, 1980

Jesus Christ does not only reveal who we are, as stated in the first encyclical; he also reveals God the Father in his love and mercy. Our human dignity cannot be fully understood without reference to God, our common origin. We should share in the love and mercy God shows us in Christ. It should guide our lives. The parable of the prodigal son shows how God will always be faithful to God's parenthood. Mercy is never conquered by evil. Through cross and resurrection Jesus gave witness to God's love for humanity and for each human individual. His program of mercy should be the program of God's people in a world threatened by inequality, injustice, hatred, and anger. Mercy is a source of life. Forgiving is respecting our divine origin, notwithstanding our disfigurement by sin: we are children of the same God.

Part I
HE WHO SEES THE FATHER (cf. Jn 14:9)

1. *The Revelation of Mercy*

Jesus revealed to us God "rich in mercy" as *Father.*
When Philip said "Lord, show us the Father,"
Jesus replied: "He who has seen me,
has seen the Father" (cf. Jn 14:8–9).
    He said this at the Last Supper,
    which was followed by events that confirmed
    that God, rich in mercy, loved us,
    by making us — dead through our sins —
    alive again together with Christ (cf. Eph 2:4–5).

My first encyclical, *Redemptor Hominis*,
was devoted to the fact that the truth about the human person
is revealed to us in Christ.
This time I want to draw attention to the face
of the "Father of Mercies and God of all comfort" (2 Cor 1:3)
revealed in Jesus Christ.
    "Christ fully reveals human persons to themselves...,
    in the very revelation of the Father and of his love" (GS 22).
The dignity of a human person cannot be fully shown
without reference to God the Father.
    This reflection is called for
    by the actual experiences of the church
    and the sufferings and hopes of many human hearts.
    The human being is the way for the church,
    a way we must travel with every individual,
    as Christ traced it out, approaching the Father and his love.
The more the church's mission centers
— *anthropo-centrically* — on the human person,
the more it must be directed
— *theo-centrically* — to the Father.
    Openness to Christ, who reveals who the human being is,
    can be achieved only through an ever more mature reference
    to the Father and his love.

2. *The Incarnation of Mercy*

God speaks to humanity by means of the whole universe,
but this perception of God's power and deity
falls short of a vision of the Father.
    "No one has ever seen God;
    the only Son, who is in the bosom of the Father,
    he has made him known" (Jn 1:18).
Through Christ's actions and words
— and finally through his death and resurrection —
God becomes known in God's love for humanity.
    It is in this way that God becomes visible
    in what the Old Testament already defined as God's mercy.
    Christ gives this term its full meaning in himself:
    he is, in a sense, mercy.
    In him God becomes "visible"
    as the Father "who is rich in mercy."
The present-day mentality seems opposed
to a God of mercy, and in fact to the very idea of mercy.
Humanity's domination of the earth
through science and technology
seems to leave no room for mercy.

On the other hand, "humanity is growing conscious
that the forces it unleashed are in our own hands,
and that it is up to us to control them
or to be enslaved by them" (GS 9).
The world today — and its development —
offers hope in a better future,
but it also reveals many threats,
far surpassing those known up till now.
  The way Christ revealed the "Father of Mercies" to us
  enables us to see God as one who is close to humanity,
  especially when in suffering or under threat.
  That is why many, almost spontaneously,
  guided by their faith, are turning to the mercy of God.
  This effect of the Spirit in human hearts
  is, as it were, a unique appeal addressed to the church.
  In this encyclical I wish to respond to this appeal,
  expressing once more the major anxieties of our time.
  Revelation and faith teach us not only to meditate
  upon God as "Father of Mercies," who "sees in secret" (Mt 6:4)
  and who is always waiting for us,
  but also to have recourse to him in our needs.

Part II
THE MESSIANIC MESSAGE

3. *When Christ Began to Do and Teach*

Before his own townspeople in Nazareth
Jesus said of himself:
"The Spirit of the Lord is upon me,
because he has anointed me to preach good news to the poor . . . ,
to proclaim release to the captives, recovering of sight to the blind,
to set at liberty all those who are oppressed,
to proclaim the acceptable year of the Lord" (Lk 4:18–19).
  This first messianic declaration
  was followed by his actions and words,
  making the Father present in this world.
It is to the poor and oppressed, but especially to sinners,
that the Messiah becomes a sign
of God who is love, a sign of the Father.
  Through his lifestyle and actions
  Jesus revealed that love is present
  in the world in which we live,
  a love particularly noticed in contact
  with suffering, injustice and poverty,

with the "human condition" manifesting
humanity's physical and moral frailty:
the type of love called "mercy."
Christ reveals God as Father, as love (1 Jn 4:16),
as "rich in mercy" (Eph 2:4).
It is Christ's touchstone of his mission as the Messiah.
    Jesus makes mercy
    one of the fundamental themes of his preaching:
    just recall the parables of the prodigal son (Lk 15:11–32),
    the good Samaritan (Lk 10:30–37),
    the good shepherd looking for the lost sheep (Mt 18:12–14),
    the woman looking for the lost coin (Lk 15:8–10),
    and by contrast the parable of the merciless servant (Mt 18:23–35).
        It is especially Luke who treats this theme,
        in his Gospel, called "the Gospel of mercy."
Before we establish the meaning
and the proper content of the concept "mercy,"
we must note that Christ, revealing the love-mercy of God,
demanded from people at the same time
that they too should be guided in their lives by love and mercy.
    Jesus expressed this by giving the commandment,
    which he described as the greatest (Mt 22:38),
    in the form of a blessing:
        "Blessed are the merciful,
        for they shall obtain mercy" (Mt 5:7).
Revealing the Father, who is God "rich in mercy,"
Christ becomes at the same time the model
of merciful love for others,
one of the essential elements of the Gospel ethos.

Part III
THE OLD TESTAMENT

4. The Concept of "Mercy" in the Old Testament

The history of the concept of "mercy" is long and rich.
Jesus addressed people who, as the people of God,
had a special experience of God's mercy.
    When prophets made Israel aware of its infidelity to God
    it appealed to God's mercy.
There are many examples:
the beginning of the history of the Judges (cf. Judg 3:7–9),
Solomon's prayer at the inauguration of the temple (1 Kgs 8:22–53),
the prophetic work of Micah (Mic 7:18–20),
the renewal of the covenant after the exile (cf. Is 1:18).

The prophets relate God's mercy to God's love,
much like the love of a spouse,
pardoning sin, infidelities, and betrayals,
and bringing people back to grace (cf. Jer 31:20).
In this "social" context mercy is correlative
to the experience of individuals languishing in a state of guilt
and enduring suffering and misfortune.
Physical and moral evil cause people
to turn to God asking for mercy.
That is what David does (cf. 2 Sam 11; 12; 24:10)
and Job (Job passim) and Esther (Est 4:17f.).
Their certainty of God's mercy was based on the Exodus experience,
when God saw the affliction of God's people
and decided to deliver them (cf. Ex 3:7f.).
Sin, too, constitutes misery,
as the people experienced when they set up the golden calf.
The Lord triumphed over this infidelity,
declaring "God [to be] merciful and gracious,
slow to anger, and abounding in steadfast love" (Ex 34:6).
All the subtleties of love
were shown to them by God:
God is their Father (cf. Is 63:16),
and Israel is the firstborn son (cf. Ex 4:22);
God is their bridegroom,
calling Israel the "Beloved"
or "the one who obtained pity" (cf. Hos 2:3).
Even when exasperated by their infidelity,
God's tenderness and generous love
overcame anger (cf. Jer. 31:20),
causing the psalmist to break out in hymn and song (Ps 103).
Mercy characterizes the life of Israel;
it is the content of its intimacy,
the content of its dialogue with God.
All the many terms used by the Old Testament
to express God's mercy
converge on one fundamental issue:
the people and the whole of Israel
should appeal for mercy when suffering misfortune
and especially when weighed down by sin.
In this way God's mercy is contrasted with God's justice,
and mercy is shown to be not only the more powerful
but also the more profound of the two.
Though justice is an authentic virtue in the Old Testament,
nevertheless love is "greater" than justice
in the sense that it is primary and fundamental.

Love conditions justice; justice serves love,
a priority that is revealed precisely in mercy.
Mercy differs from justice, but it is not in opposition to it.
We are in the presence of a living God,
who as Creator is linked in love to creation
and "who holds nothing God made in abhorrence" (Wis 11:24).
This brings us back to our beginning,
to our roots, to the mystery of creation
revealing God, who is "love" (1 Jn 4:16).
Connected to this mystery of creation
is the mystery of election, referring to every man and woman,
to the whole of the great human family:
"I have loved you with an everlasting love;
therefore I have remained faithful to you" (Jer 31:3).
"The mountains may depart ... my steadfast love for you
shall not depart from you" (Is 54:10).
This truth applies all through human history,
now and for all time to come (Jon 4:2, 11; Ps 145).

Part IV
THE PARABLE OF THE PRODIGAL SON

5. *An Analogy*

In the beginning of the New Testament
two voices resound in Saint Luke's Gospel,
echoing the Old Testament tradition.
    Mary, entering the house of Zechariah,
    magnifies the Lord for God's mercy
    which is shown "from generation to generation" (Lk 1:49–54).
    And afterward Zechariah blesses the God of Israel
    and glorifies God for the mercy shown (Lk 1:72).
Although the word "mercy" is not mentioned,
Jesus simplifies and deepens its meaning
in the parable of the prodigal son (cf. Lk 15:14–32),
which helps us to understand the very mystery of mercy
as a profound drama played out
between the father's love and the son's sin.
That son, receiving his portion of the inheritance
and squandering it, is the human person of every age,
beginning with the first ones, who lost their original justice.
    The parable touches indirectly
    upon every breach of the covenant of love, on every sin,
    though there is less emphasis on unfaithfulness
    than in the prophetic tradition.

The analogy turns toward the son's interior,
his dignity as a son in his father's house.
Though he complains about having lost his father's goods,
— while his father's servants have enough to eat —
under the surface he implies the tragedy of his lost dignity,
the awareness of a squandered sonship.
     That is why he decides to tell his father:
     "I am no longer worthy to be called your son;
     treat me as one of your hired servants" (Lk 15:18–19).
     These words reveal the real problem.
     Because of his folly and the resulting material situation
     his sense of "lost dignity" had matured.
     There is an awareness of a deeper loss than food.
     It is a great humiliation
     to become a servant in his own father's house,
     but he realizes he has no right any longer
     except to be just that.
          It is with this sense of lost dignity
          that he sets out to his father.
The term "justice" is not used even once in this parable,
just as in the original text the word "mercy" is not used.
But the relationship between justice and love,
which shows itself as mercy, is described with great exactness.
     It shows how love is transformed into mercy,
     when it is necessary to go beyond justice.
The prodigal son, having wasted the received property,
deserves to earn his living as a servant.
Justice would demand this,
not only because he squandered his inheritance,
but also because he had offended his father by his conduct,
which deprived him of his dignity as a son, even in his own eyes.
     This was bound to make his father suffer;
     it was his own son who was involved,
     a relationship that could not be altered.

6. Particular Concentration on Human Dignity

In this simple but penetrating analogy
the figure of the father reveals to us God as Father.
     The conduct of the father enables us to discover
     the Old Testament vision of mercy
     in a new synthesis, full of simplicity and depth.
The father of the prodigal son is faithful to his fatherhood,
faithful to his love for his son.
     This fidelity is expressed not only
     by his readiness to welcome him home,

but even more by his joy in doing so,
a merry-making that provokes the opposition and hatred
of the elder brother,
who had never gone away from his father.
The father's fidelity to himself is expressed with great affection.
When he saw his son returning home,
"He had compassion, ran to meet him,
threw his arms around his neck
and kissed him" (Lk 15:20).
He does this under the influence of a great affection.
but the causes of this emotion lie at a deeper level.
The father is aware that a fundamental good
has been saved: the good of his son's humanity.
Indeed, that humanity has been
— in a way — found again.
That is what the father says to the elder son:
"It was fitting to make merry and be glad,
for this your brother was dead and is alive,
he was lost and is found" (Lk 15:32).
In the same chapter of Luke's Gospel
we read the parables of the sheep
and the coin that were found.
Each time there is an emphasis on that joy
present in the case of the prodigal son.
The father's fidelity to himself
is concentrated upon the humanity
of the lost son, upon his dignity.
The love for the son obliges the father in a way
to be concerned about his son's dignity.
This concern is the measure of his love,
the love the New Testament calls "agape."
This is a love able to reach down to every prodigal son,
to every human misery, and above all to all sin.
A love doing this does not make the person in question
feel humiliated, but rather found again and restored to value.
The father expresses his joy that his son
was "found again" and "returned to life,"
indicating that a good had remained intact.
A son does not cease to be truly his father's son
even if he is prodigal;
a good has been found again,
and the prodigal son returned
to the truth about himself.
We sometimes appraise mercy "from the outside"
as a relationship of inequality

between the one offering it
and the one receiving it,
reasoning that mercy belittles the receiver
and offends his or her dignity.
The parable of the prodigal son shows
that the reality is different.
Mercy is based on the common experience
of the dignity that is proper to a person.
    It is his dignity that makes the son understand
    the truth about himself and his actions;
    it is that refound dignity that is respected by the father
    in a way that he seems to forget all evil done.
This parable expresses the reality of conversion,
the working of love, and the presence of mercy.
    Mercy does not consist in looking at
    moral, physical, or material evil.
    Mercy restores to value;
    it promotes and draws good from evil.
Mercy does not allow itself to be "conquered by evil,"
but overcomes that "evil with good" (cf. Rom 12:21).
Mercy seems particularly necessary for our times.

Part V
THE PASCHAL MYSTERY

7. Mercy Revealed in the Cross and Resurrection

The truth about mercy is revealed at its depth
in the cross and resurrection, the history of our salvation.
The events of Good Friday and Jesus' prayer at Gethsemani
introduce a change in the revelation of love and mercy
as shown in the messianic mission of Christ.
    The one who "went about doing good and healing" (Acts 10:38)
    and "curing every sickness and disease" (Mt 9:35)
    now himself seems to appeal for mercy
    when he is arrested, abused, condemned,
    scourged and crowned with thorns,
    nailed to the cross, and dies tormented (cf. Mk 15:37).
    Deserving mercy from the people to whom he has done good,
    he does not receive it.
    Addressing himself to the Father, he is not spared.
"For our sake God made him who knew no sin to be sin" (2 Cor 5:21).
God's justice is expressed "to God's measure,"
springing from love and accomplished in love;
the love of the Father and the Son,

restores in humanity access
to the fullness of life and holiness coming from God.
  Redemption reveals mercy in its fullness.
  Believer and nonbeliever will be able
  to discover in Christ's solidarity with the human lot
  his dedication to our cause, but also the love of the Father.
  The Father links to humanity by a bond
  even more intimate than that of creation,
  not only creating the human person,
  but enabling us to participate in the very life of God,
  Father, Son, and Holy Spirit.
Jesus on the cross came to give the final witness
to the wonderful covenant of God with humanity
and with every human being,
a covenant as old as the first man and woman,
many times renewed with one single chosen people,
and now open to each and every individual.
  Yet the cross is not yet the final word
  of the God of the covenant.
  That final word is spoken
  when first the women and then the apostles
  hear at the empty tomb the message:
  "He is risen!"
  Yet even in this glorification it is the cross
  that continues to speak of the everlasting love of God the Father,
    "who gave his only Son, that whoever believes in him
    should not perish but have eternal life" (Jn 3:16).
  Believing in the crucified Son means
  "seeing the Father" (cf. Jn 14:9).
  It means believing that love is present in the world
  and that this love is more powerful than evil.
  It means believing in mercy.

8. Love More Powerful Than Death, More Powerful Than Sin

The cross of Christ is also a witness to the power of evil
against the one who was without sin, "even to death" (Phil 2:8).
From the beginning of human history death had been allied to sin.
Death now has justice done to it by the one who was without sin,
and who consequently was the only one
able to inflict death upon death.
  The cross is like a touch of eternal love
  upon the most painful wounds in humanity's earthly existence.
  It is the fulfillment of the messianic program
  that Christ once formulated at Nazareth (cf. Lk 4:18–21),
  using the words of Isaiah (cf. Is 35:5, 61:1–3).

The cross makes us understand the deepest roots of evil.
It is an eschatological sign of the definitive renewal of the world,
foretelling "a new heaven and a new earth" (Rev 21:1),
when God "will wipe away every tear from their eyes,
and when there will be no more death or mourning,
no crying or pain, for the former things have passed away" (Rev 21:4).
  Christ's program of mercy
  becomes the program of his people,
  the program of the church.
  God reveals divine mercy
  when God invites us to have "mercy" on his only Son,
  the crucified one, who tells us:
    "Behold, I stand at the door and knock,
    if anyone hears my voice and opens the door,
    I will come in and eat with him, and he with me" (Rev 3:20).
How could our human dignity be more respected
than by the fact that, while obtaining mercy ourselves,
we are at the same time the ones who show mercy?
Is not this the position of Christ with regard to us
when he says:
    "As you did to one of the least of these . . .
    you did it to me"? (Mt 25:40).
Are the words of the Beatitude:
    "Blessed are the merciful,
    for they shall obtain mercy" (Mt 5:7),
not a synthesis of the whole of the good news?
Do these words not constitute a law
that is simple, powerful, and at the same time easy?
Do they not reveal the deep mystery of God?
  The paschal mystery fulfills Christ's words
  "He who has seen me, has seen the Father."
  The cross and resurrection
  reveal the love that the Father has for him,
  and in him for all people.
    Our faith and hope are for that reason
    centered on the risen Lord,
    who on the evening of that first day of the week
    stood among this disciples in the Upper Room,
    and breathing on them said:
    "Receive the Holy Spirit.
    If you forgive the sins of any,
    they are forgiven!" (Jn 20:22–23).
Here is the one, who in his resurrection
experienced the love of the Father,
revealing himself as the inexhaustible source of mercy.

9. *Mother of Mercy*

At the moment of the incarnation Mary said to Elizabeth:
"His mercy is...from generation to generation" (Lk 1:50),
opening up a new perspective in the history of salvation.

> Since Jesus' resurrection there has been
> a succession of generations
> marked with the sign of the cross
> and "sealed" (cf. 2 Cor 1:21–22)
> with the paschal mystery of Christ.

Mary obtained mercy in an exceptional way,
sharing in the revelation of God's mercy,
standing at the foot of the cross.

> No one experienced the mystery of the cross as she did
> — the "kiss" given by mercy to justice (cf. Ps 89:2) —
> adding her own "fiat."

Mary is the one who has the deepest knowledge of God's mercy,
knowing its price.
That is why we call her the "Mother of Mercy,"
a title expressing the preparation of her whole personality
to perceive the mercy
of which people became sharers
"from generation to generation" (Lk 1:50).

> This title speaks of her
> as the mother of the crucified and risen one,
> called in a special way to bring close to people
> the love that her Son had come to reveal,
> a love that finds its most concrete expression in her love
> for the suffering, the poor, those deprived of their freedom,
> the blind, the oppressed, and sinners,
> a love that is based in her maternal heart,
> reaching all those who accept the merciful love of a mother.

"The motherhood of Mary in the order of grace
lasts without interruption.... By her maternal charity
she takes care of the brothers and sisters of her son
who still journey on earth surrounded by dangers and difficulties,
until they are led into their blessed home" (LG 62).

Part VI
MERCY...FROM GENERATION TO GENERATION

10. *An Image of Our Generation*

Our generation, waiting for the approach of the third millennium,
was included when the mother of God
spoke about the mercy shared "from generation to generation."

The present generation is in a privileged position
scientifically, technologically, socially, and culturally.
　　We have made progress that a few decades ago
　　was even undreamed of.
　　Distances have shrunk
　　through an increased sense of what is universal,
　　a clearer awareness of the unity of the human race,
　　the acceptance of mutual dependency,
　　and the possibility of making contact.
Especially today's young people know
that the progress of science and technology
can produce not only material goods
but also a wider sharing in knowledge.
Progress in the field of information and data processing
and new communication techniques
encourage greater participation in events
and a wider exchange of ideas.
　　The achievements in biological, social, and psychological sciences
　　will help us to understand better the riches
　　of our own being.
Though all this is often still
the privilege of the industrialized countries,
it cannot be denied that the prospect of enabling
every people and every country to benefit
is no longer a utopia
when there is the political will for it.
　　But side by side with all this
　　— or rather as part of it —
　　there are the difficulties
　　that accompany every growth.
There is a sense of unease and powerlessness
as to how to respond.
There is the dichotomy between our untrammeled inclinations
and our thousands of shortcomings.
As the Second Vatican Council noted,
　　"In the face of modern developments
　　there is a growing body of people
　　who are asking the most fundamental questions:
　　What is the human person?
　　What is the meaning of suffering, evil, death,
　　which has not been eliminated by all this progress?
　　What is the purpose of these achievements,
　　purchased at so high a price?" (GS 10).
These tensions and threats have not quieted down
since that Council, on the contrary...

11. Sources of Uneasiness

The feeling of being under threat is increasing.
There is the threat of what human beings can do to each other
through the means provided by military technology;
but there are also the dangers produced by a materialistic society
that accepts the primacy of things over persons,
with the risk that individuals and the environment,
communities, societies, and nations
can fall victim to the abuse of power.
    Our century is full of examples of this,
    and notwithstanding all the declarations
    on the rights of the person,
    we cannot say that these examples belong to the past.
People fear they will fall victim to an oppression
that deprives them of their interior freedom to express
the truth of which they are convinced,
the faith they profess,
or the ability to obey the voice of their conscience.
There is not only the possibility of military conflict,
but also of a "peaceful" subjugation of individuals.
An instance is torture used as a means of oppression
and practiced with impunity.
    All this is happening against the background
    of the gigantic remorse caused by the fact
    that side by side with the wealthy,
    there are those that suffer from hunger.
    Babies are dying under their mothers' eyes;
    there are entire areas of poverty, shortage, and underdevelopment.
    It is a state of inequality that is increasing.
        That is why this moral uneasiness
        is destined to become even more acute.
        There is a defective machinery
        at the root of contemporary economics
        and materialistic civilization
        that does not allow the human family
        to break free from such radically unjust situations.
This uneasiness is experienced not only by those who are deprived
but also by those who live in plenty.
It is an uneasiness that concerns
the fundamental problem of all human existence.

12. Is Justice Enough?

The sense of justice has been reawakening on a vast scale,
giving proof of the ethical character of the tensions in the world—

a desire the church shares with the people of our time
as confirmed during the last century
by the development of Catholic social teaching,
the consequent formation of human consciences,
and individual undertakings, especially in the apostolate of the laity.
    It would be difficult not to notice
    that programs that start from the idea of justice
    sometimes suffer from distortions
    such as spite, hatred, and even cruelty,
    contrasting with the essence of justice,
    which by its nature tends
    to establish equality and harmony.
Jesus challenged the distortion of justice in his time
expressed in the words:
"An eye for an eye, a tooth for a tooth" (Mt 5:38).
Today's forms of justice continue to be modeled on it.
Our experience shows that justice alone is not enough,
that it can even lead to destruction of self,
if that deeper power, which is love,
is not allowed to shape human life:
Summum ius, summa iniuria [extreme law, extreme injustice].
    The church shares the uneasiness of our time.
    One cannot be but worried by the decline of moral values,
    moral permissiveness, the crisis in human relations,
    the loss of the sense of the common good,
    the ease with which this good is alienated,
    and a "desacralization" that turns into "dehumanization"
    of the individual and society.

Part VII
THE MERCY OF GOD IN THE MISSION
OF THE CHURCH

The church, listening to Mary's words
singing of "mercy from generation to generation,"
must become more conscious of the need to bear witness
in its mission to God's mercy.
    The church has the right and duty
    to call upon the mercy of God
    in view of the threats that cloud humanity's horizon today.

13. *The Church Professes the Mercy of God and Proclaims It*

The truth about God's mercy
resounds as a perennial echo in the daily life of the church

through the readings of its liturgy.
People perceive this truth in so many ways
that it would be difficult to list or summarize them.
  Some theologians affirm that mercy
  is the greatest of the attributes and perfections of God.
  It is the way man and woman meet God
  particularly often and closely.
  It is the encounter in which we meet
  "the vision of the Father" Jesus spoke of when he said:
  "He who has seen me, has seen the Father" (Jn 14:9).
    Everything that brings us nearer to Christ
    brings us nearer to the Father
    and the holiness of his mercy.
  The church seems to profess the mercy of God
  in a special way when it addresses itself to the heart of Christ,
  revealing his messianic mission
  and at the same time the merciful love of the Father.
The church lives that mercy authentically
when it professes and claims it,
meditating on the word of God,
participating in the Eucharist
and in the sacrament of penance.
  The Eucharist brings us ever nearer to this love
  that is stronger than death.
  Each one can experience this mercy
  as a love that is more powerful than sin
  in the sacrament of penance.
Because of sin, God who "is love" (1 Jn 4:8)
cannot be revealed otherwise than as mercy,
a mercy that is infinite,
always ready to receive the prodigal children
who return home.
Continually flowing from the sacrifice of the Son,
the readiness and the power to forgive is infinite.
No human sin can prevail over this power
or even limit it.
  It is only the human lack of good will that can limit it,
  the lack of readiness to be converted and to repent,
  opposing grace and truth in the face of the cross.
Conversion consists always in discovering God's mercy,
a "rediscovery" of the Father, who is rich in mercy.
Knowing of God's mercy and seeing God in this way,
every man and woman can live in a state of continuous conversion
during their pilgrimage on earth.
In this way the church does not only teach but lives God's mercy.

The contemporary church is profoundly conscious
that it can carry out its task
only on the basis of the mercy of God,
especially its ecumenical task
of uniting all those who confess Christ.
Only love can bring about that unity
which Christ implored from the Father
and the Spirit never ceases to beseech for us
"with sighs too deep for words" (Rom 8:26).

14. The Church Seeks to Put Mercy into Practice

Jesus taught that one does not only receive mercy,
but that we are called to "practice mercy."
        "Blessed are the merciful,
        for they shall obtain mercy" (Mt 5:7).
The church sees these words as a call to action.
        Practicing mercy is a lifestyle,
        a characteristic of the Christian vocation.
        It is a creative love in which the one who gives also profits,
        and in any case they who show mercy
        can easily find themselves in need of mercy.
When we take Christ as our model
we are able to show mercy to others,
knowing that Christ accepts it
as if it were shown to himself (cf. Mt 25:34–40).
Mercy is not only good done to others;
an act of merciful love is only really such
when we are convinced
that at the same time that we give
we are receiving mercy from those who are accepting it from us.
Without that our actions are not as yet true acts of mercy,
and our conversion to what Christ showed us
by his words, his examples, and the cross,
is not complete.
        The mercy the Beatitude speaks to us about is richer
        than what we find expressed in opinions
        about ordinary human mercy.
        They sometimes see mercy as a unilateral act,
        presupposing and maintaining a distance
        between the one who gives mercy and the one who receives it.
        In this way one fails to see the link between mercy and justice
        as found in the Bible and in the mission of Christ.
        True mercy is the most profound source of justice.
Justice can restore objective goods in an equitable way;
but love, and only love — including that love that is called mercy —

is capable of restoring human persons to themselves
with the dignity that is proper to them,
uniting the giver and receiver in a more profound way.
    Mercy is an indispensable element
    for shaping relationships between people.
    Justice must — so to speak — be corrected
    by the "patient and kind" love
    so characteristic of the Gospel and Christianity
    and so eloquently spoken of
    in the parables of the prodigal son (cf. Lk 15:11–32),
    the lost sheep, and the lost coin (cf. Lk 15:1–10).
    It is indispensable between husbands and wives,
    parents and children, and friends.
Merciful love, however, is not restricted to this.
Paul VI spoke about a "civilization of love"
as the goal for social and political life,
a good that will never be reached if we keep demanding
"an eye for an eye and a tooth for a tooth" (Mt 5:38).
    Society can become ever more human
    only if we do not introduce merely justice,
    but also the "merciful love"
    that is the message of the Gospel.
    Forgiveness shows that love is more powerful than sin.
    It is the condition for reconciliation,
    not only between us and God,
    but also between people.
    Without forgiveness the world would be cold
    from an unfeeling justice,
    human selfishness would transform life
    into a system of oppression of the weak
    and of permanent strife.
The church must consider it one of its principal duties
to proclaim and introduce this mystery of mercy
revealed in Jesus Christ.
Mercy is a source of life.
Christ teaches us to forgive always:
    "Forgive us our trespasses
    as we forgive those who trespass against us" (Mt 6:12) —
        words that say so much to every individual
        about others and about ourselves.
        "Forbear one another in love" (Eph 4:2).
    When Peter asked Jesus how many times
    he should forgive his neighbor,
    Jesus answered "seventy times seven" (Mt 18:22),
    meaning *everyone every time.*

This forgiveness does not do away with justice.
Nowhere in the Gospel does mercy mean
indulgence toward evil, toward scandal,
toward injury or insult.
Reparation for evil and scandal, compensation for injury,
and satisfaction for insult are the conditions for forgiveness.
Thus justice enters into the sphere of mercy.
But mercy adds another dimension
that is most fully expressed in forgiveness.
Over and above the process of "compensation" and "truce"
specific to justice,
love is necessary to affirm the human person as a human person.
    As we noted before,
    analyzing the parable of the prodigal son,
    the one who forgives and the one who is forgiven
    meet each other at an essential point,
    namely, the point of the dignity of the person,
    a point that cannot be lost,
    and the affirmation or rediscovery of which
    is a source of the greatest joy (cf. Lk 15:32).
It is the church's duty to guard this "forgiveness,"
and it does this by guarding its source,
the mercy of God as revealed in Jesus Christ,
"drawing from the wells of the Savior" (cf. Is 12:3),
aware of the Lord's words:
"You received without pay, give without pay" (Mt 10:8).

15. *The Church Appeals to the Mercy of God*

The church proclaims God's mercy,
and it seeks to practice it
seeing it as a condition
for a better and more humane world.
However, at no time
—especially not at a moment as critical as our own—
can the church forget to pray for the mercy of God.
The more the human conscience loses its sense
of the very meaning of the word "mercy,"
the more the church has the duty
to appeal to God for mercy
"with loud cries" (cf. Heb 5:7).
    Those cries should be the mark of the church of our days,
    calling for the love that can free us from the greatest threats,
    threats we have sketched in broad lines above.
Everything said here on mercy
should be transformed into an ardent prayer.

Like the prophets, let us appeal to that love
that has maternal characteristics,
and that, like a mother, follows each of her children,
even if they should number millions
and live in a world that is sinful.
   Let us have recourse to the fatherly love
   revealed to us by Christ;
   let us have recourse to God through Christ,
   thinking of Mary's words that God's mercy
   will be "from generation to generation,"
   asking God's mercy for this generation.
Let us do all this directed by the charity of Christ
planted in our hearts, expressing in this way our love of God,
whom modern humankind has so often called "superfluous":
   "Father forgive them, for they know not
   what they are doing!" (Lk 23:34).
   At the same time mercy expresses our love for people
   without any discrimination,
   without difference of race, culture, language, or world outlook,
   without distinction between friends and enemies,
   desiring the true good for all.
And even if there are some who do not share with me
the faith and hope to ask for God's mercy,
let them at least try to understand my concern.
It is dictated by love for humankind,
according to many contemporaries
threatened by an immense danger
while approaching the end of the second millennium.
   We pray that the love of the Father
   may once again be revealed to the world
   through the work of the Son and the Holy Spirit.
   "Blessed are the merciful, for they shall obtain mercy" (Mt 5:7).
We continue our task of implementing the Second Vatican Council
as a new phase in the self-realization of a church
that is not allowed to withdraw into itself,
but that continues to reveal God the Father,
who allows us to "see" him in Christ (cf. Jn 14:9),
no matter the difficulties and obstacles,
which make this task only the more urgent.

3

On Human Work

Laborem Exercens

September 14, 1981

Created in God's image, human beings share in creation by their work. Work is a human right. It is the activity of a human person; it can never be considered as mere merchandise, as has happened in the past and still happens nowadays. Treating workers as mere tools does no justice to their personal dignity. It belies their nature and has led to the "social question." The workers and their families come first in any consideration of property rights, wages, unions, unemployment, welfare, emigration, pensions, or the workers and their families. These globally valid principles require a restructuring of our world. Jesus was a worker. He gave his life and rose from the dead working at peace and justice, asking us to shoulder his yoke.

PREFACE

Human beings earn their daily bread through work.
Through work they contribute to science and technology
and to the enrichment of the moral and cultural level
of their society.
　　By work we mean any human activity,
　　whether manual or intellectual.
　　Made in the image of God,
　　human beings are placed on earth
　　to have power over it.
　　　　From the beginning
　　　　they have been called to work.
It is work that distinguishes human beings
from other creatures.
They are the only ones capable of work.

Work is something particularly human
done in a community of persons,
a characteristic that marks and, in a sense, constitutes
the very nature of work.

I. INTRODUCTION

1. *Human Work on the Ninetieth Anniversary of* Rerum Novarum

Since it is ninety years ago
that Leo XIII, the great pope of the "social question,"
wrote his encyclical *Rerum Novarum* ("Of New Things"),
I wish to devote this document
to human work and the human worker.
    At the beginning of my papacy I wrote
    "the human being is the primary route
    the church must travel."
We need to return constantly to this way,
showing the riches and the toil
of human existence on earth in all its aspects.
    One of these aspects is work,
    a lasting and fundamental issue,
    always requiring our attention
    and decisive witness.
Fresh questions and new problems roused new hopes,
but also new fears and threats.
    Human life is built up every day from work,
    and graced by it,
    but work also implies toil, suffering, harm,
    and social injustice at the national and international levels.
We eat the bread made by our own hands
(not only the bread to feed our body,
but also the "bread" of science and progress,
civilization and culture),
but we do that
"by the sweat of our face"
in the midst of tensions, conflicts, and crises
that disturb the life of societies and humanity.
    We celebrate this ninetieth anniversary
    on the eve of developments
    in technology, economics, and politics
    that experts say
    will influence the world of work and production
    no less than the Industrial Revolution a century ago.

The introduction of automation,
the increase in cost of energy and raw materials,
the realization that nature's resources are limited
— and that they are being polluted —
next to the demands of peoples up to now subjugated,
who want their rightful place among the nations
and their share in international decision-making;
they all require a reordering of economic structures,
and of the distribution of work.
    For millions these changes may mean unemployment,
    at least for a time, or the need for retraining.
        For the more developed countries
        the changes will probably mean
        lower living standards
        or slower growth of wealth.
    But they also will bring relief and hope
    to the millions who live
    in shameful and unworthy poverty.
It is not for the church to analyze scientifically
the consequences of these changes,
but it is its task to call attention
to the dignity and rights of those who work,
to condemn their violation and to guide these changes
to ensure the true authentic progress
of the individual and society.

2. In the Organic Development of the Church's Social Action and Teaching

Work has been at the center
of the social teaching of the church
for almost a hundred years.
These reflections continue the same tradition.
    Heeding the Gospel word,
    I intend to bring out "new and old."
    "Work" is part of what is as "old" as human life.
    "New" is our present human situation,
    urging the discovery of new meanings of work
    and a reformulating of the tasks
    facing individuals, families, countries,
    the human race, and the church itself.
The social question has never ceased
to engage the church's attention.
The very name
of the Pontifical Council for Justice and Peace
is an indication that the "social question"

calls for a commitment to justice and to peace —
a lesson learned by two world wars
and the threat of self-destruction by nuclear war.
    John XXIII's letter *Pacem in Terris*
    gave us the principles
    of the church's teaching on world peace.
    Up to Pius XI's encyclical *Quadragesimo Anno*
    the church looked mainly at the "labor question"
    within individual countries,
    while more recently it has been calling
    for a just development for all,
    drawing attention to the unequal distribution
    of wealth and poverty among nations and continents.
Our understanding has improved.
While we looked before at the "class" question
now we emphasize the "world" issue,
the building of justice on earth,
not hiding unjust world structures,
but demanding that they be examined and changed.

3. *The Question of Work, the Key to the Social Question*

In the history of the church's social teaching
the issue of work has emerged many times,
finding its source in Scripture, in the book of Genesis,
the Gospels, and the apostles' writings.
It always has been part
of the church's teaching on social morality.
    I return to this question not to repeat,
    but to emphasize more than ever before
    that human work is the key
    to the solution — or rather to the gradual solution —
    of the whole "social question."
    To consider work is of decisive importance
    when trying to make life "more human."

II. WORK AND THE HUMAN BEING

4. *In the Book of Genesis*

The church is convinced that work is a fundamental dimension
of humanity's existence on earth,
a belief confirmed by science and God's revealed word.
    The church believes in humanity,
    not only as shown in history and science
    but as shown first in and by God's word.

The book of Genesis tells how the first human beings,
created "in the image of God,"
before they sin hear the words:
   "Be fruitful and multiply,
   fill the earth and subdue it."
The word "work" is not mentioned
but it must have been meant.
The human being carrying out this order
reflects the very action of the Creator.
Work is an activity that begins in human beings,
and is directed to something outside them.
It presupposes dominion over the earth,
confirming and developing this dominion.
   While the Bible speaks about
   the dominion of the fragment of the universe
   that humanity inhabits,
   today we understand it
   as extending to the whole of the universe.
The biblical words have an immense range.
They never cease to be relevant,
covering past civilizations, modern reality,
and future still unknown and hidden developments.
   Even the acceleration in this process today
   cannot alter the basic meaning
   of that most ancient of biblical texts.
Spreading and confirming its dominion over the world,
humanity continues to do
what was ordered from the very beginning,
reflecting the image of God.
   It is a universal process,
   it embraces all human beings;
   and it takes effect in each human being.

5. *Work in the Objective Sense: Technology*

Work is — objectively — what a human being does
when dominating the earth.
Work has been changing during the ages,
from domesticating animals
and extracting resources from earth and sea,
to cultivating the earth,
transforming, changing, and using its produce.
   Agriculture remains vital
   to economic activity and production.
Industry links the earth's riches with human work,
whether physical or intellectual.

Today much human work has ceased to be manual;
hands and muscles are helped by machinery,
by electronics and micro-processing.
It may seem that it is the machine that "works,"
but it is the human being who works,
and who remains the *subject* of work.
Technology is humanity's ally;
it eases our work,
it perfects, accelerates, and increases it.
Technology sometimes becomes almost an enemy,
supplanting workers,
taking away personal satisfaction, creativity, and responsibility,
causing unemployment,
or making workers mere slaves of the machine.
    Technology is definitely covered
    by the biblical word "subdue the earth,"
    and it has been correctly seen
    as a basic aid to economic progress,
    but it also raises many social and ethical questions
    on how to relate to work and even to each other —
    questions challenging states, governments,
    international organizations, and the church.

6. *Work in the Subjective Sense: The Worker as Subject*

We must pay more attention to the one who works
than to what the worker does.
    The self-realization of the human person
    is the measure of what is right and wrong.
This basic truth has always been
the heart of Christian teaching on human work.
    The ancient world divided people into classes
    according to the type of work people did.
    Manual work was done by slaves
    and considered to be unworthy of free people.
Broadening what the Bible had said
and seeing it in the light of the Gospel,
Christianity changed this idea.
The one who, while being God,
became equal to us in all things
spent most of his life at the carpenter's bench,
showing that the value of work
does not depend on the type of work done,
but on the person who is doing the work.
Human persons and not what they do
determine the dignity of work.

This does away with the division
of people into classes
according to the work they do.
Work can be classified and rated,
but the measure of the value of any work
remains the human being, who is its "subject."
Work is in the first place "for the worker"
and not the worker "for work."
Work itself can have greater or lesser objective value,
but all work should be judged
by the measure of dignity
given to the person who carries it out.
Work has no meaning by itself;
it is always the human being who counts,
even if the work done is the most monotonous or alienating.

7. *A Threat to the Right Order of Values*

This Christian "gospel of work"
had to oppose the *materialistic* and *economist* thought
of the modern age.
Work was understood as "merchandise"
sold by the workers to their employer,
the one who owned everything necessary for production.
These nineteenth-century ideas
have given way to a more human thinking about work,
but the danger of treating work as "merchandise"
— or as an impersonal "work force" —
remains as long as economics is understood
in a materialistic way.
It is this one-sided approach
that concentrates on work as the prime thing,
leaving the worker in a secondary place.
This is a reversal of the order
laid down in the book of Genesis.
The worker is treated as a tool
whereas the worker ought to be treated
as the *subject* of work,
as its maker and creator.
This reversal — whatever other name it gives itself —
should be called "capitalism" —
an economic and social system
that historically has been known
as opposed to "socialism" or "communism."
The error of early capitalism
can be repeated

wherever the worker is treated
as a mere means of production,
as a tool and not as a subject.
To consider work and the worker
in the light of humanity's dominion over the earth
goes to the very heart of the ethical and social question.
It is an insight that should be applied
to all social and economic policy,
within each country, but also internationally,
to the tensions between East and West,
North and South.

8. *Worker Solidarity*

It is useful to recall the changes of the last ninety years.
Although the "worker" remained the same, "work" changed.
New forms of work appeared and disappeared.
  Though this is normal,
  it is necessary to watch out
  for ethical and social irregularities.
It was such an irregularity that gave rise — in the last century —
to the "worker question" or the "proletariat question,"
provoking a great burst of solidarity
among workers, mainly in industry.
  It was a reaction
  against the degradation of the workers, their exploitation
  with regard to their working conditions and security;
  against an unjust system
  that safeguarded the economic initiative of the owners
  but did not pay attention to the rights of the workers.
    This reaction is in line with the church's teaching
    and justified from a social morality point of view.
Worker solidarity has brought profound changes.
Various new systems have been thought out.
Workers often share in running and controlling businesses,
influencing working conditions, wages, and social legislation.
  But new systems have arisen
  that allow old injustices to continue
  and new injustices to appear.
  New developments and communication
  reveal forms of injustices
  more extensive than the ones
  that aroused workers' solidarity
  in the last century,
  not only in industrialized societies
  but also in agricultural countries.

Solidarity movements can also be needed for
social groups not previously mentioned
but who find themselves in a "proletariat" situation.
It can be true of the working "intelligentsia,"
people with degrees and diplomas, who cannot find work —
   a situation that arises
     when education is unsuited to the needs of society,
     or when there is less demand and less pay
     for work that requires education.
We must consequently continue
to study the situation of the worker.
There is a need for solidarity movements
among and with the workers.
The church is firmly committed to this cause,
in fidelity to Christ,
and to be truly the "church of the poor."

9. Work and Personal Dignity

God's original intention for us
— to "work the earth" — was not canceled
when, after the fall, we were told:
   "In the sweat of your face
   you shall eat your bread."
      It meant that work
      would sometimes be a heavy burden,
      a burden known everywhere
      to those who work the land
      or in mines and quarries,
      to steel workers, builders, and construction workers,
      to scientists and thinkers;
      to those who carry responsibilities
      affecting the whole of society,
      to doctors and nurses,
      and to women who bear the daily burden
      of housework and bringing up their children.
But work remains a good thing,
not only because it is useful and enjoyable,
but also because it expresses and increases
the worker's dignity.
Through work we not only transform the world,
we are transformed ourselves,
becoming "more a human being."
Work, however, can also be used to lessen people's dignity,
condemning them to forced labor in concentration camps.

10. *Work and Society: Family and Nation*

Having looked at work as it affects the person,
we must go on to see how it affects the family.
Work is a foundation of family life;
it is a condition making a family possible,
as the family needs earnings
normally produced by work.
  Work affects education in the family,
  for the very reason
    that it makes a person "become a human being,"
  the main purpose of any education.
The family is an important element
shaping the social and ethical order of work,
as the church has always emphasized.
It is a community made possible by work,
and the family is the first school or work.
  The family is part of a wider society,
  a nation, which is through the family
  the great "educator" of everyone,
  providing a history and a culture
  that has been the work of generations.
Everyone is thus a member of a nation
working to increase the common good of their society
and adding in this way to the heritage
of the whole of humanity.
  Person, family, and the wider society
  are always important to human work
  and to the one who works.
  It is the worker who comes first
  and not the work.
  Work is good,
  and it has contributed in recent centuries
  to an immense development,
    yet it should not gain the upper hand,
  taking away the worker's dignity and rights.

III. CONFLICT BETWEEN LABOR AND CAPITAL TODAY

11. *What the Conflict Is About*

The encyclical *Rerum Novarum*
was written in a period,
— by no means over as yet —
when the conflict arose
between "capital" and "labor,"

between the small group of owners
of the means of production
and the larger group of people
who lacked those means
and who share in production
only through their labor.
   The conflict began
   when workers put their powers
   in the hands of the capital owners,
   and these — seeking the highest profit —
   tried to pay the lowest possible wages,
   without further care for the safety,
   the health, or the living conditions
   of the workers and their families.
Some interpreted this conflict
as a class struggle and an ideological conflict
between capitalism and Marxism,
which claims to represent the working class
and the worldwide proletariat.
   In this way the real conflict
   was turned into a systematic class struggle,
   fought not only with ideas
   but also, and mainly, by political means.
We know the history of this conflict
and the demands of both sides.
Marxism believes
that class struggle is the only way
to eliminate class injustices
and classes themselves.
   This will happen, Marxism holds,
   when the means of production
   are transferred from private hands
   to the whole of society,
   thus protecting human labor
   against exploitation.
The goal of the Marxist struggle is to win
power in each society
— by political as well as ideological means —
in order to introduce collective ownership
and to introduce socialism
and, in the final instance, communism
throughout the world.
   There is no need to enter
   into further details on this issue,
   as they are well known.

Let us return to the issue of human work,
an issue that can be fully explained
only by taking into account the context
of our present situation.

12. *The Priority of Labor*

That situation is deeply marked
by the many human conflicts
and the role of technology.
We should not forget
the possibility of a worldwide disaster
caused by a nuclear war.

But above all we must remember
the priority of labor over capital:
labor is the cause of production;
capital, or the means of production,
is its mere instrument or tool.
When the Bible says
that humanity is to subdue the earth,
it speaks about the resources of the earth,
resources that can serve us
only through our work.
To make this work possible
people take ownership
of small parts of these resources.

Whatever we do by way of production,
we do not create the resources;
they are already there,
ready to be discovered and used.
Before we begin our work
there is always this gift
leading us to the Creator.
At the beginning of humanity's work
is the mystery of creation.
This strengthens our conviction
that human work comes before
what we have begun to call capital.
Capital is both the earth's resources
and all the means invented
to help us to use — and to humanize —
those resources.

From the simplest tools
to the most modern ones
— machines, factories, laboratories, and computers —
all are the result of human work.

To be able to use
this enormous collection of modern tools,
we have to master the knowledge
of the people who invented,
planned, built, and perfected them.
> Sharing efficiently in production
> demands ever greater preparation and proper training.
> But even when no training
> or special qualifications are required,
> the human person remains the one who really counts,
> and the whole collection of instruments
> — however perfect —
> is never any more than means
> toward that end.
> This truth has important consequences.

13. *Economism and Materialism*

Capital cannot be separated from labor.
You cannot oppose the two
and still less the people behind these concepts.
> In a just labor system
> their opposition is overcome
> by being faithful to the principle
> that labor comes first,
> whatever the services rendered by the workers.
The opposition of labor and capital
is not caused by the way
labor and capital are organized.
In their organization
the two remain intermingled.
Whatever work one does,
one always enters into two inheritances:
> the resources of nature, given to all,
> and what others have already been doing with them:
> the technology and tools developed to work.
By working the worker always
"enters into the labor of others" (Jn 4:38).
Intelligence and faith tell us
that we are masters of the things of the world,
depending on their Creator
and on the work of those who went before us.
> Capital and tools may "condition" our work.
> They do not make us dependent on them.
This way of looking at things has fallen apart.
Capital and labor became two opposed impersonal forces.

Labor began to be considered
as a merely economic force,
being of greater importance
than the spiritual and the human.
From this "common" and "practical" materialism
thinkers developed a "materialist" philosophy,
and in the final instance "dialectical materialism" —
a faulty way of thinking
because it does not consider the human worker
as the *"subject"* of work and the cause of production,
but as a kind of "outcome" of the way
production is organized.
Treating human work as just another factor in production
was not invented by thinkers in the eighteenth century.
It was the result of how things were done
in the early years of industrialization
when profit was put first,
while the human being should have been in that place.
The worker was treated as a mere tool,
a blow against workers
that caused the social reaction we discussed.
This same error might be repeated again and again.
The only way to overcome it is to change the way
we are thinking and doing things
so that the worker is put first
and labor above capital.

14. Work and Ownership

When we speak about labor and capital,
we are speaking about people,
about those who work
without being the owners of the means of production
and about the entrepreneurs (or their representatives)
who own those means.
That is why "ownership" and "property"
enter into this process.
The church's constant teaching
on the right to private property
and ownership of the means of production
differs radically from the collectivism
proclaimed by Marxism,
but also from the capitalism practiced by liberalism
and the political systems inspired by it.
In the latter case the difference consists in the way
the right to ownership and property is understood.

Christian tradition never upheld this right
as absolute and untouchable.
It has always understood it as subordinated to the fact
that the goods of this world are meant for all.
> Things cannot be owned in a way
> that leads to social conflict.
Property is acquired by work,
in order to serve work.
The means of production
cannot become a separate property,
called capital, as opposed to labor.
> They cannot be owned against labor
> or to exploit labor.
> They cannot be owned
> just for the sake of owning them.
> The only title to their ownership
> —whether private, public, or collective—
> is that they serve labor.
This means that under suitable conditions
the socialization of certain means of production
could be acceptable.
> This is a teaching that goes back as far
> as the writing of Saint Thomas Aquinas.
Confirming once more the church's teaching
that the worker comes first in production and in the economy,
we state that a "rigid" form of capitalism that defends the exclusive right
to own the means of production as a "dogma" is not acceptable.
> The right to this ownership
> must be constantly reviewed.
> Capital is certainly the result
> of the labor of past generations,
> but it also remains true
> that these means of production
> are unceasingly created
> by the labor done with these means of production,
> manually and intellectually.
It is the reason that experts in Catholic social teaching,
popes and bishops,
made many proposals for joint ownership
of the means of production,
sharing by workers in the management
and/or the profits of businesses,
share-holding by labor, etc.
> Whether these proposals can be realized or not,
> it is obvious that putting the worker first

demands adaptation
of the right to own the means of production.
All this is particularly true
in view of the present-day problems
in the "Third World."
Though "rigid capitalism"
must be constantly revised and reformed,
the question is not simply about
the abolition of private ownership.
A satisfactory socialization is not achieved
by transferring ownership
simply from private owners to the state.
People who manage the means of production
in the name of society — without owning them —
may do so properly,
respecting the principle that the worker comes first;
they also may do so badly,
monopolizing the administration of those means
and even offending basic human rights.
True socialization is achieved
only when all persons, on the basis of their work,
can fully consider themselves part owners.
This could be done
by associating — as far as possible —
labor to the ownership of capital
and by creating a range of intermediate associations
with economic, social, and cultural aims,
independent from the public powers
and acting for the common good.

15. The "Personalist" Argument

Labor prevails over capital.
The two are inseparable,
but the ones who use the means of production
also wish the fruit of their work
to be used by themselves and by others.
Workers not only want fair pay,
they also want to share
in the responsibility and creativity
of the very work process.
They want to feel
that they are working for themselves —
an awareness that is smothered
in a bureaucratic system
where they only feel themselves

to be "cogs" in a huge machine
moved from above.
The church has always taught
that work concerns not only the economy,
but also, and mainly, personal values.
    All will profit when these values are respected.
    This was for Saint Thomas Aquinas
    the principal reason
    to favor the private ownership of capital.
While we accept exceptions
to the principle of private ownership
— in our time we see the introduction
of several types of social ownership —
Saint Thomas's "personalist" argument
remains valid both in theory and practice.
    If socialization is to be fruitful,
    it must ensure that workers feel
    that they are working "for themselves."

IV. RIGHTS OF WORKERS

16. *Within the Broad Context of Human Rights*

Work is an obligation;
work is also a source of the workers' rights —
rights that must be seen in the wider context
of the human rights proclaimed by many international organizations
and increasingly guaranteed by states,
    rights that are fundamental to peace today,
    as often has been stated by the church,
    especially since the encyclical *Pacem in Terris.*
Though part of these wider human rights,
the rights given by work are specific.
Work is a duty, because our Creator demanded it
and because it maintains and develops our humanity.
    We must work out of regard for others,
    especially our own families,
    but also because of the society we belong to
    and in fact because of the whole of humanity.
We inherit the work of the generations before us,
and we share in the building of the future
of all those who will come after us.
    All this should be kept in mind
    when considering the rights that come with work
    or the duty to work.

Yet when thinking of the workers' rights,
our first thoughts go out to the relationship
between the workers and their employers,
directly and indirectly.
    The difference between a direct employer
    and an indirect employer is very important.
    Direct employers are the persons or institutions
    with whom one enters directly into a working contract.
    Indirect employers are the many other factors
    that enter the work contract and that can create
    just or unjust relationships in the field of human labor.

17. *Direct and Indirect Employer*

Indirect employers are
the persons and institutions of many kinds,
as well as the collective labor contracts
and the rules of conduct they lay down
that shape the whole economic and social system.
    The indirect employer conditions the conduct
    of the direct employer.
The concept of indirect employer can be applied to every society,
and especially to every state.
    The state must have a just labor policy.
    As everyone knows,
    there are many economic links between states,
    because of import and export, for instance,
    that create mutual dependence.
    Even the most powerful state is not
    completely self-sufficient.
Though in itself normal, this dependence
can easily lead to exploitation and injustice
and influence the labor policies of individual states,
thus affecting the worker who is the proper subject of labor.
    For instance, highly industrialized countries
    and even more "transnational" companies
    fix the highest possible prices for the products they sell,
    while trying to fix the lowest possible prices
    for the raw materials or semi-manufactured goods they buy.
This is one of the causes of the ever growing gap
between the incomes of different countries.
It obviously affects local labor policies
and the situation of the workers in poorer countries.
    In a system thus conditioned
    the direct employer fixes working conditions
    that are below the workers' real needs,

especially when the employer
wishes to obtain the highest possible profits
from the business.
Thus it is clear that society's economic life
— created by all the different forms of dependence —
is enormously extensive and complicated.
　　Yet the workers' rights cannot be doomed
　　to be the mere result
　　of economic systems aimed at maximum profits.
　　The thing that must shape the whole economy
　　is respect for the workers' rights
　　within each country and all through the world's economy.
International organizations, beginning with the United Nations,
the International Labor Organization,
and the Food and Agricultural Organization,
should exercise their influence in this direction.
　　Ministries and social institutions
　　are set up for this purpose
　　within individual countries.

18. *The Employment Issue*

When considering workers' rights
in relation to the "indirect" employer,
the fundamental issue is
finding work for all who are capable of it.
　　Unemployment, either in general or in certain sectors,
　　is the opposite of a just and right situation.
It is the indirect employer's task to act against unemployment,
which is always evil and can become a real social disaster.
　　It is particularly painful when it affects the young,
　　who after their preparation see their wish to work
　　and their readiness to take on their own responsibility
　　sadly frustrated.
The obligation to provide unemployment benefits
is a duty springing from the common use of goods,
or — to put it in a simpler way —
arising from the right to life and subsistence.
　　The indirect employer must engage in planning
　　the different kinds of work by which not only the economic
　　but also the cultural life of a society is shaped,
　　organizing them correctly and rationally.
Though in final analysis this is the state's responsibility,
it should not be unduly centralized,
but done within the framework
of individual and group initiatives.

Action must also be taken internationally,
by means of treaties and agreements,
preserving each society's and each state's sovereignty.
Work is a fundamental right of all human beings,
and the international organizations
have an enormous part to play
in reducing unjust differences of living standards
of workers in different countries,
differences that can be the cause
of violent reactions.
    It is possible to draw up a plan
    for universal and just progress
    following the guidelines
    of Paul VI's encyclical *On the Progress of Peoples,*
    constantly looking at the purpose of human work
    and at the dignity of the human being.
Rational planning and the proper organization of work
should help us to discover
the right balance between different kinds of employment:
work on the land, in industry, in the various services,
and white-collar, artistic, and scientific work,
taking into account individual talents
and the common good of society.
This should be accompanied by a suitable system
of education and instruction.
    When we look at the world,
    we cannot but be struck
    by the huge number of people
    who are unemployed, underemployed,
    and even suffering from hunger,
    while many natural resources remain unused —
        facts that demonstrate
        that there is something wrong with our world.

19. *Wages and Social Benefits*

After all we have said about the indirect employer,
highlighting the place of morality in this question,
the key issue in this matter
is that of just pay for work,
whether work is done
for a private owner of the means of production,
or in a "socialized" system.
    The justice of a social and economic system
    is finally measured
    by the way in which a person's work is rewarded.

According to the principle
of the common use of goods,
it is through the remuneration for work
that in any system most people have access to these goods,
both the goods of nature and those manufactured.
A just wage is a concrete measure
— and in a sense the key one —
of the justice of a system.
The just wage for an adult
responsible for a family
is one that allows the establishment of a family,
its proper maintenance, and provision for the security of its future.
    This can take the form of a "family wage,"
which is a single salary
given to the head of the family for that person's work,
or of other measures such as family allowances
or grants to mothers devoting themselves exclusively
to their families.
Experience confirms that we must reevaluate
the role of the mother in society,
her toil and the need children have
for care, love, and affection.
    It will profit society
to make it possible for a mother
— without curtailing her freedom,
without psychological or practical discrimination,
without handicapping her in any way whatsoever
in regard to other women —
to dedicate herself to the care and education
of her children.
    Having to abandon these tasks
to take up work outside the home
is wrong for society and for the family
when it hinders these main goals
of a mother's mission.
The labor process must be organized in a way
that it respects the needs of all persons
and their roles in life
according to their age and sex.
    In many societies women work
in nearly every sector of life.
They must be able to do so
without discrimination or exclusion from jobs,
and also without having to give up
their specific role in family and society.

Apart from wages, other social benefits
should be available to the worker:
medical assistance,
the right to rest
(at least on Sunday and during annual vacations),
the right to a pension and to insurance for old age
and for accidents at work,
the right to working conditions
that are not harmful to health
or to the workers' moral integrity.

20. Importance of Unions

To secure these rights,
the workers need the right to association
in labor or trade unions.
These organizations should reflect
the particular character
of each work or profession.
   In a sense these unions go back
   to the guilds of the Middle Ages,
   which organized people
   on the basis of their work.
Modern unions differ from these guilds
because they grew from the workers' struggles
to protect their rights
in their relation to the owners
of the means of production.
   History teaches us that organizations of this type
   are an indispensable element in social life,
   especially in industrialized societies.
      This does not mean
      that only industrial workers
      can form these associations.
      Every profession can use them:
      agricultural workers, white-collar workers,
      and employers.
Catholic social teaching does not see unions
as reflecting only a "class" structure,
and even less as engaged in a "class" struggle.
They are indeed engaged in the struggle
for social justice,
but this is a struggle *for* the common good,
and not *against* others.
Its aim is social justice
and not the elimination of opponents.

Work unites people;
its social power builds community.
Those who work
and those who manage or own
the means of production
must in one way or another
unite in this "working" community.
Even if people unite to secure their rights as workers,
their unions remain constructive factors
of social order and solidarity,
impossible to overlook.
Workers' unions should take into account
the economic situation of the country.
They cannot be turned into a kind
of group or class "egoism,"
though they can and should correct
the defects in the system of ownership and management
of the means of production.
The social and economic life
is like a system of "connected vessels,"
and the particular groups
should take that into consideration.
It is not the role of unions to "play politics"
in the sense as it is understood nowadays.
Unions are not political parties;
they should not even have close links with them.
In that case they would soon lose their specific role,
which is to secure the just rights of workers
in the context of the common good
of the whole of society.
They would become instruments
used for other purposes.
One of the methods used by unions
is the strike, or work stoppage —
a means that is recognized by Catholic social teaching
as legitimate under the proper conditions and within proper limits.
Workers should be assured
of the right to strike
without fear of penalty.
The strike is an extreme means
that must not be abused
and definitely not be used for "political purposes."
When essential community services are in question
they must be ensured,
if necessary by means of appropriate legislation.

Abuse of the right to strike
can lead to the paralysis of social and economic life,
contrary to the common good of society.

21. *Dignity of Agricultural Work*

All that has been said so far
about the dignity of human work
can be applied to agricultural work
and the agricultural worker.
Agriculture — providing goods needed to sustain society —
is of fundamental importance.
 The conditions of agriculture
 and agricultural work
 differ from country to country
 according to the level of agricultural development
 and the recognition of the rights of the rural workers.
Agricultural work is difficult,
often physically exhausting,
and sometimes not appreciated
by the rest of society,
to the point that agricultural people
feel that they are social outcasts,
which accelerates the exodus from the countryside
to the cities.
 Added to this are
 the lack of proper training and equipment,
 the spread of individualism,
 and unjust situations.
In certain developing countries
millions of people are forced to work
on land belonging to others.
They are exploited by the big landowners
without any hope
of even a small piece of land of their own.
 They lack legal protection
 for themselves and their families.
 Long days of hard physical work
 are paid miserably.
 Land is abandoned by the owners;
 the entitlement to land cultivated for years
 is disregarded against the "land hunger"
 of more powerful individuals and groups.
Even in technically advanced countries
farm workers are denied their share in decision-making
and refused the right to free association.

In many places radical and urgent changes
are needed to give agriculture and the rural people
their just place in the community.

22. Disabled Persons and Work

Disabled people are fully human in spite of their limitations.
They should be supported so that they can share
in all aspects of social life.
It would be unworthy to admit to work
only those who are fully functional.
This would mean discriminating the healthy
against the weak and the sick.
It would be putting economic gain
above the human person.
Direct and indirect employers
should foster the right of disabled people
to professional training and work.
This poses many practical, legal, and economic problems,
but the community should pool ideas and resources
to offer disabled people work according to their capabilities,
in ordinary, adapted, or "protected" jobs.
Attention must be paid
to ensure them just wages,
promotion possibilities,
and the elimination of obstacles.
Disabled people should feel
that they are not cut off from work,
that they count in society,
and that they are called
to contribute to the progress and welfare
of their families and societies.

23. Work and Emigration

Emigration is an age-old phenomenon,
today widespread because of the complexity of modern life.
Emigration is not without problems.
It means a loss to the country left behind.
Those who could have contributed to its common good
are now offering their efforts to another society
— united by another culture and often speaking another language —
which in a sense, has less right to them than their own.
If emigration is in some aspects an evil,
it is often a necessary evil,
and everything should be done
to prevent even greater moral harm.

Every possible effort should be made
to ensure that it benefits
the emigrants' personal, family, and social lives,
both in their home country
and in the country that receives them.
Just legislation should see to all this.
      Emigrants should not be placed
      at a disadvantage.
      Emigration should not become
      an opportunity for exploitation.
The same criteria should be applied
to immigrant workers as to all the workers in a society,
disregarding differences of nationality, race or religion.
Here too, capital should be at the service of labor,
and not labor at the service of capital.

V. ELEMENTS FOR A SPIRITUALITY OF WORK

24. *A Particular Task for the Church*

Since work is always done by a person,
it follows that the whole person
—body and spirit—is involved,
whether the work is manual or intellectual,
      just as the good news of the Gospel,
      in which we find much about work,
      is addressed to the whole person.
Guided by faith, hope, and love,
we seek to understand the meaning work has
in the eyes of God
and how it is part of our salvation.
      That is why the church considers it its duty
      to speak out on a spirituality of work,
      so that through work people come closer to God,
      participate in their salvation,
      and deepen their friendship with Christ,
      sharing in Christ's threefold mission of
      priest, prophet, and king.

25. *Work Is Sharing in Creation*

Through the centuries people have been working
to better their lives.
For believers there is no doubt that this is God's intention.
Created in God's image
we were given the mandate to transform the earth.

By their work people share in God's creating activity.
We continue — within the limits of our human capabilities —
to develop that activity, advancing in the discovery
of the resources and values in creation.
In the book of Genesis (2:2–3)
God's creative activity is presented in the form of "work,"
done by God for six days, while God "rests" on the seventh day.
This theme is echoed in the last book of Sacred Scripture,
where we read in the book of Revelation (15:3):
"Great and wonderful are your deeds,
O Lord God the Almighty."
Genesis gives us the first "gospel of work."
We should imitate God in working and resting,
created as we are in the image of God.
God's activity continues, as Christ witnessed when he said,
"My Father is working still" (Jn 5:17).
God is working still by sustaining the world
and by working with saving power in our hearts
destined for "rest,"
not only every seventh day,
but for the "rest" the Lord reserves
for his servants and friends (Mt 25:21)
in our "Father's house" (Jn 14:2).
Awareness that our work is a sharing in God's work
ought to permeate even the most ordinary daily activities.
By our labor we are unfolding the Creator's work
and contributing to the realization of God's plan on earth.
The Christian message does not stop us
from building the world
or make us neglect our fellow human beings.
On the contrary
it binds us more firmly to do just that.
The most profound motive for our work
is this knowing that we share in creation.
Learning the meaning of creation in our daily lives
will help us to live holier lives.
It will fill the world with the spirit of Christ,
the spirit of justice, charity, and peace.

26. Christ the Man of Work

Jesus Christ himself showed that to work
is to share in creation.
He not only proclaimed,
but, first and foremost, lived the "gospel of work"
by his deeds.

He was a worker,
a craftsman like Joseph.
Though warning us against too much anxiety
about work and life,
his life shows that he belongs to the working world,
loving it and seeing that to be a worker
is a facet of our likeness with God,
of whom he said:
"My Father is the vinedresser" (Jn 15:1).
The Old Testament mentions many professions
and praises the work of women.
In his parables Jesus speaks about
shepherds, farmers,
doctors, sowers, householders,
servants, stewards, fishermen,
merchants, scholars, and laborers.
He speaks of women's work,
and he compares the task left to the apostles
to the work of harvesters and fishermen.
  Paul echoes these teachings.
  He boasts that he worked like a tent maker,
  and that even as an apostle
  he earned his own living.
  He preached to people "to do their work quietly
  and to earn their own living" (2 Thes 3:12).
  He wrote:
     "If any will not work,
     let them not eat" (2 Thes 3:10)
     and
     "Whatever your task, work heartily,
     as serving the Lord and not people,
     knowing that from the Lord,
     you will receive the inheritance
     as your reward" (Col 3:23–24).
Those teachings have been repeated by the church
as recently as at the Second Vatican Council.
When people work they not only alter things and society;
they develop themselves as well —
a growth that has greater value than technical advances.
  "A person is more precious for what he is,
  than for what he has.
  All that people do to obtain greater justice,
  wider brotherhood,
  and a more humane ordering of social relationships
  has greater worth than technical advances" (GS 35).

27. *Human Work in the Light of the Cross and the Resurrection of Christ*

All work is linked with toil.
The original blessing of work,
sharing in the mystery of creation,
being created in the image of God,
is contrasted with the curse
that sin brought with it.
> "Cursed is the ground because of you,
> in toil you shall eat of it,
> all the days of your life" (Gn 3:17) —
> the toil that announces
> that all human life leads to death.
>> "In the sweat of your face
>> you shall eat bread
>> till you return to the ground
>> for out of it you were taken" (Gn 3:19).

The Gospel's final word on this matter
is the paschal mystery of Christ.
It contrasts his obedience to death
with humanity's disobedience.
It also tells about Christ's return in the resurrection
with the power of the Holy Spirit.
> Their sweat and toil enable the followers of Christ
> to share lovingly his work.
> By enduring the toil of work in union with Christ's suffering
> they collaborate with him in the redemption of humankind.
> They show true discipleship
> by carrying their cross every day.

By dying for all Christ taught us that we, too,
must shoulder the cross that the world places
on those, who work for peace and justice.
> The resurrected Lord, Christ,
> is now at work in people's hearts
> through the power of the Holy Spirit,
> purifying and strengthening them
> in their struggle to make life more human
> and to make the whole earth serve this goal.

The Christian finds in work
something of Christ's cross
and should accept it in the same spirit.
In work, too, thanks to the resurrection
we also find the good news
of the "new heaven and the new earth" (Rev 21:1)

in which we take part precisely
through the toil of our work.
    In this way the cross
    is indispensable to the spirituality of work,
    revealing the good
    that springs from work and its toil.
If work is a small part of the cross,
how does it relate to the resurrection of Christ?
    Vatican II tell us
    that the expectation of a "new" earth
    must not weaken our concern
    for cultivating the world in which we live.
    It must strengthen that concern,
    for it is here that a human family grows,
    foreshadowing the new age.
Earthly progress must be distinguished
from the growth of the kingdom,
but to the extent that it helps
to order human society in a better way,
it is of vital concern to the kingdom of God (GS 39).
    Let Christians realize
    the importance of their work,
    not only in terms of earthly progress,
    but also in the development of the kingdom of God,
    to which we are all called
    through the power of the Holy Spirit
    and the word of the Gospel.

4

The Apostles of the Slavs

Slavorum Apostoli

June 2, 1985

Saint Methodius died over eleven hundred years ago in 885. In 1980 John Paul II named Saints Cyril and Methodius co-patrons of Europe, together with Saint Benedict, the patron of Europe since 1964. The encyclical explains the importance of the two apostles to the Slavs. Though of Byzantine origin, they became missionaries to the Slavs. They translated the Bible into the Slav language, developing a new alphabet (the Cyrillic). They adapted the liturgy to their Slav converts. Because the Slavs belonged to the jurisdiction of the Western church, they went to Rome to have their Bible translation and liturgical texts approved. Overcoming the difficulties they met, they became models of how to link the Eastern and Western churches and to inculturate the good news in a new human context.

I. INTRODUCTION

1. In 1980 I proclaimed the two brothers
   Saints Cyril and Methodius the co-patrons of Europe,
   following in the footsteps of Leo XIII,
   who in 1880 extended the cult of the two saints
   to the whole of the church,
   and of Paul VI, who proclaimed
   Saint Benedict patron of Europe in 1964.

2. The purpose of my 1980 proclamation was
   to draw the attention of all those people of good will
   who have the welfare, harmony, and unity of Europe at heart
   to those three figures as concrete models
   for the Christians of today, especially those of Europe.

It was also linked to the eleventh centenary
of Pope John VIII's approval
of the use of the Old Slavonic language in the liturgy in 880;
the first centenary of the letter *Grande Munus* of Leo XIII,
and the beginning of the theological dialogue
between the Catholic and the Orthodox churches
on the Island of Patmos in 1980.

3. A hundred years after the letter of Leo XIII,
   in different circumstances,
   the first pope called from a Slav nation
   wants to remind the church of those two saints.
   Their special charisms have become
   better understood in the experiences of our own times.
   In the light of the Second Vatican Council
   we can look in a new, more mature and profound way
   at these two, now separated from us by eleven centuries.

II. BIOGRAPHICAL SKETCH

4. Methodius and Cyril (also named Constantine)
   were born in Salonika around 815–820.
   Both of them retired from public life and became monks,
   and both of them were included in a delegation
   sent to the Khazars as cultural and religious experts.

5. The event that determined the rest of their lives
   was when in 863 they were chosen to go
   to the subjects of Prince Rastislav of Greater Moravia
   to "explain the true Christian faith in their own language."
   They devoted the rest of their lives to that mission,
   amid journeys, privations, sufferings, persecution,
   and — in the case of Methodius — even imprisonment.
   They carried with them the texts of the Sacred Scriptures
   translated by them into the Old Slavonic language,
   written in a new alphabet
   adapted to the sounds of that language.
   Their mission activity was successful,
   though not without difficulties
   because of the preceding Christianization
   carried out by Latin churches.
   In 866 they set out for Rome,
   discussed their new mission approach in Venice,
   and were cordially received by Hadrian II,
   who approved their Slavonic books

and their ordination to the priesthood.
Unfortunately Cyril died shortly afterward in Rome.

6. Methodius remained faithful
to what his brother had told him on his deathbed:
"Listen, my brother, we have shared the same destiny,
plowing the same furrow. . . .
I know your love for your Mountain (monastery)
but do not for the sake of the Mountain
give up your work of teaching.
For where can you better find salvation?"
Ordained archbishop of Pannonia
and papal legate for the "Slav peoples,"
he reestablished the episcopal see of Sirmium.
Arrested, he spent two years in prison
and was set free on the personal intervention of Pope John VIII,
which, however, did not end the hostility to the Slavonic liturgy
and the doubts about his orthodoxy.
Called to Rome in 880,
he obtained the publication of the Bull *Industriae Tuae,*
which restored the privileges granted by Hadrian II.
He received a similar recognition
from the Byzantine emperor and patriarch.
The last years of his life he spent
making further translations of sacred books.
He died on April 6, 885.

7. After his death the work of the brothers
suffered a grave crisis;
their followers had to leave their missionary field.
But their sowing of the Gospel seed did not cease to bear fruit,
and their pastoral attitude
of bringing the revealed truth to new peoples,
while respecting their cultural originality,
remains a living model for the church
and for all missionaries.

III. HERALDS OF THE GOSPEL

8. Byzantine in culture, Cyril and Methodius
succeeded in becoming apostles of the Slavs.
Separation from one's homeland, when accepted in faith,
is always a mysterious and fertile precondition
for the development and growth of God's people.
Abraham was asked to leave his country;
Paul was asked to go to Macedonia.

Asked to go to the Slavs,
Cyril and Methodius gave up the contemplative life
to enter a long pilgrimage in the service of the Gospel.

9. When Prince Rastislav complained:
   "Many Christian teachers have reached us
   from Italy, from Greece, and from Germany...
   but we Slavs have no one to direct us toward the truth
   and instruct us in an understandable way,"
Cyril and Methodius were asked to go there.
They went, while Cyril said:
"However tired and physically worn out,
with joy I depart for the sake of the Christian faith."
They obeyed Christ's words:
"Preach the Gospel to the whole of creation" (Mk 16:15),
wishing to become part of those peoples
and to share their lot in everything.

10. They found it natural to take a clear stand
    in the conflicts that were disturbing those societies,
    organizing themselves, defending their identity,
    and resisting forms of life they felt to be foreign to their mission.
    Even in the growing differences
    between Eastern and Western Christianity,
    they succeeded in maintaining perfect orthodoxy,
    paying consistent attention to tradition
    and to the culture of the peoples they evangelized.
       They translated Sacred Scripture into the Slav language,
       understanding and faithfully expressing
       the human values expressed therein.

11. In order to translate the Gospel into a new language,
    they had to grasp the interior world of those
    to whom they intended to proclaim the Word of God
    in images and concepts familiar to them.
    It was a question of a new catechetical method,
    carefully scrutinized by Popes Nicholas I and John VIII.
       Developing a new alphabet,
       identifying with the people's life and traditions,
       Cyril and Methodius are true models
       for all missionaries
       who become all things to all people
       in order to redeem them all,
       and especially to those missionaries
       who labor to translate the Bible
       into the living languages of the various peoples they serve.

Perfect communion in love
preserves the church from particularism, ethnic exclusivism,
racial prejudice, and any nationalistic arrogance.

IV. THEY PLANTED THE CHURCH

12. Cyril and Methodius built the church in a peaceful way.
    Though thought to be "Slavs at heart" by their Slav Christians,
    they remained men of Hellenic culture and Byzantine training.
    They used the Slavonic language in liturgy
    and made it into an effective instrument
    for bringing the divine truths to those who spoke it.
    They did this without any spirit of superiority,
    but out of love of justice and with a clear apostolic zeal.
    As Western Christianity had united migrating new peoples,
    extending to them the same Latin language, culture, and liturgy,
    it is understandable that it sometimes
    regarded differences as a threat.

13. It was unusual and admirable that the two holy brothers
    did not seek to impose their Greek language and Byzantine culture
    or the customs and ways of life of their more advanced society.
    They adapted their Byzantine liturgy
    and the Greco-Roman law
    to the Slavonic language and customs.
    Doing this, they remained faithful to their mission,
    and though subjects of the Eastern Empire
    and the patriarchate of Constantinople,
    they gave an account of their missionary work
    to the Roman pontiff.
    They submitted the doctrine they taught
    and the liturgical books they had written
    to his judgment, approaching the Apostolic See of Rome,
    the visible sign of the church's unity,
    in order to obtain its approval.
    In this way they established the church
    with an awareness of its universality
    as one, holy, catholic, and apostolic.
    Jesus' priestly prayer — "that they may be one" — was their motto:
    "Praise the Lord, all nations!"
    Their apostolate is an invitation to restore
    the unity that was damaged after the time of Cyril and Methodius.
    According to their conviction
    each local church enriches
    the catholic "fullness."

14. Saints Cyril and Methodius are
    the authentic precursors of ecumenism.
    Their solicitude to preserve unity
    between the churches of Constantinople and Rome
    and the Slavonic churches
    will always remain their great merit,
    in particular because of the critical years
    that they exercised their mission.

15. Methodius did not hesitate to face even persecution
    rather than to betray his faithfulness to Byzantium, Rome,
    and the church growing among the Slavs;
    he relied on dialogue, remaining a teacher for all those
    who, in whatever age, seek to eliminate discord
    by respecting the manifold fullness of the church.

V. CATHOLIC SENSE OF THE CHURCH

16. Their catechetical and pastoral method
    merits particular emphasis:
    allowing people to hear
    the Sacred Mysteries celebrated and proclaimed
    in their native language fitted to their own mentality
    and respecting the conditions of their own life.
        During the Second Vatican Council
        — called together to reawaken the church's self-awareness,
        and initiating a period of springtime —
        the assembly drew a similar conclusion:
            "In virtue of this catholicity each individual part of the church
            contributes through its special gifts to the good
            of the other parts and of the whole church" (LG 13).

17. This vision corresponds in a particular way
    to the theological and pastoral vision of Cyril and Methodius.
        Saint Cyril defended this point of view in Venice
        against those who held a rather narrow idea of the church,
        showing that many peoples in the past had already introduced
        liturgies in their own languages.
        He asked whether they were not ashamed to decree and allow
        only three languages (Hebrew, Greek, and Latin),
        deciding that all other people should remain blind and deaf.
            "Let every tongue confess that Jesus Christ is Lord,
            to the glory of God the Father."

18. The church is catholic because it is able to present
    the revealed truth in every human context,

bringing it into contact with the thoughts and expectations
of every individual and people,
forming an immense many-colored living mosaic of the Pantocrator,
who will manifest himself in his total splendor
only at the moment of the parousia.
    The Gospel does not lead to impoverishment or extinction
    of the realities individuals, peoples, and nations offer;
        instead it assimilates, develops, and perfects them.
    Catholicity is not something static,
    through the power of the Holy Spirit
    it wells up and develops every day as something new.

19. All individuals, all nations, cultures, and civilizations
    have their own part to play and their own place
    in God's mysterious plan
    and in the universal history of salvation.
        This was the thought of the two holy brothers:
            "God, merciful and kind,
                waiting for all people to repent
                so that all may be saved" (cf. 1 Tim 2:4).

20. Thanks to the missionary efforts of both saints
    the Slav peoples were able to realize for the first time
    their own vocation to share in the design of the Most Holy Trinity.
    They were able to feel that
    — together with the other nations of the earth —
    they too were descendants and heirs of the promise
    made by God to Abraham (cf. Gn 15:1–21).

VI. THE GOSPEL AND CULTURE

21. The evangelization the two brothers carried out
    contains a model both of what today is called "inculturation"
    and of how to introduce cultures into the life of the church.
        By incarnating the Gospel into them
        Saints Cyril and Methodius
        formed and developed those cultures.
        All the cultures of the Slav nations owe their "beginning"
        or development to the work of those two brothers,
        creating an alphabet and making their language
        an official, liturgical, and literary language
        used up to today in so many liturgies.

22. Their language played a role equal to that
    of the Latin language in the West,
    and it lasted longer than Latin.

VII. THE SIGNIFICANCE AND INFLUENCE OF THE CHRISTIAN MILLENNIUM IN THE SLAV WORLD

23. The missionary activity of Saints Cyril and Methodius
    can be considered as the first effective evangelization of the Slavs.
        In the *Life of Methodius* we find
        the most ancient reference to one of the Polish tribes,
        though insufficient data exist to link this information
        to the institution of a Slav Rite church there.

24. The baptism of Poland in 966
    took place through the Bohemian church
    reaching back to the Latin Rite in Rome,
    but in a way the beginning of Christianity
    is linked to the work of the two brothers.
        In the Balkans their work bore fruit
        in a more visible way.
        Christianity was consolidated in Croatia
        and developed in Bulgaria,
        passing through Romania,
        reaching the ancient Rus' of Kiev
        and then spreading east from Moscow.

25. The family of the Slav peoples rightly considers
    Saints Cyril and Methodius
    as the fathers of both their Christianity and their culture.
    Their work is an outstanding contribution
    to the formation of the common Christian roots of Europe,
    roots that by their strength and vitality
    are solid points of reference, which no one can ignore
    when attempting to reconstruct the unity of the continent.
        Both Christian traditions
        — the Eastern deriving from Constantinople
        and the Western deriving from Rome —
        arose in the bosom of the one church,
        in different cultures.

26. Characteristic of the two brothers
    is their love for the communion of the universal church
    both in the East and the West,
    and within the universal church
    their love for the particular Slav churches.
    It is in this way that they invite us *to build communion together.*
        Yet it is in the field of "inculturation"
        that the example of Cyril and Methodius
        is of even greater value to missionary activity.

Carrying out their mission,
they not only respected the culture they found
but promoted and extended it.

27. Cyril and Methodius are the connecting links
between the Eastern and Western traditions,
which both come together
in the one great tradition of the universal church.
  For full catholicity, every nation, every culture
  has its own part to play in the universal plan of salvation.
  Every particular tradition, every local church
  must remain open and alert to the other churches
  and at the same time to the catholic communion.
Being Christians in our days means
being builders of communion in church and in society.

VIII. CONCLUSION

28. It is fitting that we celebrate how eleven centuries ago
the Slav peoples accepted the Gospel message
from Saints Cyril and Methodius.
I share this celebration with great joy,
being the first son of the Slav race
to occupy the episcopal see of Saint Peter.

29. "Into thy hand I commend my spirit,"
were the last words of Saint Methodius
when he died in 885.

30. O great God, One in Trinity,
I entrust to you the heritage of the faith of the Slav nations.
Preserve and bless this work of yours!
  Grant to the whole of Europe, O Most Holy Trinity
  — through the intercession of the two holy brothers —
  to feel the need for religious and Christian unity
  and for a communion of all its peoples.

31. The pope of Slav origin thanks you
for calling the Slav nations into the communion of the faith.
May it never fail, may it never fade!

32. The future! We trustfully place it in your hands,
Heavenly Father,
invoking the intercession of the mother of your Son,
your apostles Peter and Paul,
Saints Benedict, Cyril and Methodius, Augustine and Boniface,
and all the other evangelizers of Europe.

5

Lord and Giver of Life

Dominum et Vivificantem

May 30, 1986

In Jesus Christ — conceived from the Holy Spirit — a new humanity was born. The Holy Spirit given to us at creation was renewed. The Holy Spirit in us teaches us about sin, righteousness, and the fact that evil has been overcome on the cross and in the resurrection. Denying or resisting this presence of God's Spirit in ourselves or in others is the ultimate sin. In the year 2000 we will celebrate the great jubilee of this renewal of the Holy Spirit in humanity, of which the church is a sign and instrument.

INTRODUCTION

1. Instructed by the words of Jesus,
   the church has proclaimed its belief in the Holy Spirit
   from its earliest days.

2. This faith needs to be constantly reawakened,
   as has been done several times in the last hundred years.
   In our own age we are called anew
   to draw near to the Holy Spirit as the giver of life.
   In this we are helped by the heritage we share
   with the Oriental churches.
   My previous encyclicals
   Redemptor Hominis and *Dives in Misericordia*
   drew their inspiration from Saint Paul's words:
   "The grace of our Lord Jesus Christ,
   and the love of God,
   and the fellowship of the Holy Spirit
   be with you all" (2 Cor 13:14).
   And so does this one on the Holy Spirit.

This letter has been drawn from the heart of the heritage
of the Second Vatican Council.
    It responds to the deep desires
    discernible in people's hearts today,
    a fresh discovery of God,
    the hope of finding a new creation and a giver of life.
The church feels this to be its mission,
while approaching the end of the second millennium after Christ.
    The following will not be exhaustive,
    nor will it answer questions that still remain open;
    it only hopes to develop the church's awareness
    of being "compelled by the Holy Spirit" (LG 17).

Part I
THE SPIRIT OF THE FATHER AND OF THE SON GIVEN TO THE CHURCH

1. *Jesus' Promise and Revelation at the Last Supper*

3. When Jesus' time came to leave this world
   he spoke to the apostles about "another counselor" (Jn 14:16) —
   another counselor because Jesus is the first one (1 Jn 2:1),
   a counselor to continue the work of the good news of salvation.

4. Some time after this prediction Jesus adds:
   "The counselor, whom the Father will send in my name,
   will teach you all things, and bring to remembrance
   all that I have said to you" (Jn 14:26).
      This means that the Holy Spirit will help us on our mission
      and in our understanding of the truth
      that will remain always the same
      in the midst of changing conditions.

5. The apostles will be associated with the Holy Spirit in a special way.
   The human witness of those direct eyewitnesses
   will find its strongest support in the witness of the Spirit of truth,
   guaranteeing its continuation
   among the generations of Christian disciples
   succeeding one another throughout the ages.

6. Jesus adds further
   that the Spirit "will guide you into all truth,"
   referring to what the apostles "cannot bear now" (Jn 16:12f.).
      This "guiding you in all truth"
      refers not only to "the scandal of the cross"
      but to everything Christ "did and taught" (Acts 1:1).

The "guiding into all truth" is achieved in faith,
and in that faith the Holy Spirit is
humanity's supreme guide and light.
   This holds true not only for the apostles,
   but for all Christians accepting and confessing
   the mystery of God at work in human history.

7. There is an intimate bond between the Holy Spirit and Christ,
   as Christ attested:
      "[The Spirit of truth] will glorify me,
      for he will take what is mine and
      declare it to you" (Jn 16:14).
      What is of Jesus is the Father's:
      "All that the Father has is mine" (Jn 16:15).
      The Holy Spirit taking what is "mine"
      draws from what is the Father's.
   Those words "he will take"
   can also explain those other words of Jesus:
      "It is to your advantage that I go away,
      for if I do not go away
      the counselor will not come to you;
      but if I go I will send him to you.
      And when he comes,
      he will convince the world
            concerning sin,
            righteousness,
            and judgment" (Jn 16:7f.).

2. Father, Son, and Holy Spirit

8. In John's Gospel the Father, the Son, and the Holy Spirit
   are called persons.
   Speaking of the Spirit Counselor
   Jesus uses several times
   the personal pronoun "he,"
   revealing at the same time the bonds
   that unite the Father, the Son, and the Paraclete to one another.
      "The Holy Spirit . . . proceeds from the Father" (Jn 15:26),
      the Father "gives the Spirit" (Jn 14:16),
      the Father "sends" the Spirit in the name of the Son (Jn 14:26),
      the Spirit "bears" witness to the Son (Jn 15:26),
      while the Holy Spirit is also sent by the Son:
      "If I go, I will send him to you."
         The Holy Spirit will come
         insofar as Christ will depart through the cross,
         not only *afterward,*

but *because* of the redemption accomplished by Christ,
through the will and action of the Father.

9. The farewell words at the Last Supper
   are the high point of the revelation of the Trinity,
   leading up to Jesus' final words:
   "Go therefore and make disciples of all nations,
   baptizing them in the name of the Father,
   and of the Son, and of the Holy Spirit" (Mt 28:19) —
   words that express the life-giving power of the sacrament,
   bringing about the sharing in the life of the triune God.

10. "God is love" (1 Jn 4:8, 16).
    The love shared by the three persons
    is the Holy Spirit as the Spirit of the Father and the Son.
    In the Holy Spirit the life of the triune God
    becomes totally gift.
    The Holy Spirit is the personal expression
    of this self-giving from which all giving of gifts derives:
    the gift of existence to all things through creation,
    the gift of grace to human beings through salvation.
    "God's love has been poured into our hearts
    through the Holy Spirit,
    which has been given to us" (Rom 5:5).

3. *The Salvific Self-giving of God in the Holy Spirit*

11. In John's Gospel we find
    the divine "logic" of God's saving mystery.
    The redemption accomplished by the Son
    in his departure through cross and resurrection,
    is transmitted to the Holy Spirit,
    the one who "will take what is mine" (Jn 16:14).
    It is the beginning
    of the new salvific self-giving of God
    in the Holy Spirit.

12. It is a *new* beginning in relation to the original beginning
    of God's self-giving in creation,
    when "the Spirit of God
    was moving over the face of the waters" (Gn 1:1f.).
    This creation includes not only the calling into existence of creation,
    but also the presence of God's self-giving Spirit.
    "Let us make the human being in our image,
    in our likeness" (Gn 1:26).
    Does the use of the plural "Let us make"
    already suggest the Trinitarian mystery?

13. Jesus' description of his "departure"
    as a condition for the new beginning
    links it to the mystery of redemption —
        a new beginning needed
        because sin had intervened.

14. The "departure" of Christ through the cross
    has the power of the redemption,
    and it also means a *new* presence
    of the Spirit of God in creation.
    The Spirit of God's Son cries in us: "Abba" (Gal 4:6).
    The Holy Spirit comes at the price
        of Christ's departure on the cross,
        a departure that caused sorrow,
        a sorrow that turned into joy (Jn 16:20).

4. The Messiah, Anointed with the Holy Spirit

15. Christ is the "Anointed One,"
    "the one anointed with the Holy Spirit,"
    words that go back to Isaiah
        — sometimes called the Gospel of the Old Testament:
        "There shall come forth a shoot
        from the stump of Jesse,
        and a branch shall grow out of his roots.
        And the Spirit of the Lord shall rest upon him" (Is 11:1–3).
    This is an important text,
    linking the ancient biblical concept of "spirit"
    understood as "a charismatic breath of wind"
    to the "Spirit" as a person and as a gift,
    a gift for the person.

16. The Messiah is anointed by God,
    possessing the fullness of the Spirit of God
    and sent with the Spirit of the Lord.
    He is also the Servant of the Lord,
    the man of sorrows,
    the one who suffers for the sins of the world.
    "He will bring forth justice for the nations" (Is 42:6).
        The Prophet presents the Messiah
        as the one who comes in the Holy Spirit,
        the one who possesses the fullness of this Spirit in himself,
        and at the same time for others,
        for Israel, for all nations,
        for all humanity.
    Simeon sensed this,
    but even more so Mary,

who "had conceived by the Holy Spirit" (Lk 2:25–35),
pondering in her heart these mysteries.

17. The "Spirit of the Lord"
who rests upon the future of the Messiah
is a gift of God for the servant of God.
    In the Old Testament
    the personality of the Holy Spirit
    remained hidden
    in the revelation of the one God.

18. Jesus makes reference to this prediction
when he reads from the book of Isaiah:
    "The Spirit of the Lord is upon me,
    because he anointed me," adding:
        "Today this Scripture has been fulfilled
        in your hearing" (Lk 4:16–21f.)
He is the one who marks the "new beginning."

5. Jesus of Nazareth, "Exalted" in the Holy Spirit

19. John the Baptist foretells the Messiah-Christ
not only as the one who "is coming"
but also as the one who "brings the Holy Spirit,"
as Jesus will reveal more clearly in the Upper Room.
    At the sight of him John proclaims:
    "Behold the Lamb of God,
    who takes away the sins of the world" (Jn 1:29),
    an expression no less significant
    than Isaiah's "Servant of the Lord."
Though rejected by his own fellow-citizens at Nazareth,
John exalts him before the eyes of Israel
as the Messiah, "the Anointed One" —
    a testimony corroborated
    when "heaven was opened,
    and the Holy Spirit descended upon him
    in bodily form as a dove" (Lk 3:21)
    and a voice from heaven said at the same time:
    "This is my beloved Son" (Mt 3:17).
This is a Trinitarian theophany;
it touches the mystery of
the very person of the Messiah: "my Son."

20. This theophany at the Jordan
would be gradually revealed and confirmed
by what Jesus "did and taught" (Acts 1:1),
"rejoicing in the Holy Spirit" (Lk 10:21).

He rejoices at God's fatherhood,
and because it had been given to him
to reveal God's fatherhood:
"All things have been delivered
to me by my Father;
no one knows who the Son is except the Father,
or who the Father is except the Son,
and anyone
to whom the Son chooses to reveal him" (Lk 10:22).

21. What came at the Jordan
"from outside" comes here "from within,"
from the depths of who Jesus is.
What he says of the Father and of himself
flows from that fullness of the Spirit
that is in him, pervading his own "I,"
inspiring his actions from the depths "within,"
being the Son of the same substance.

6. The Risen Christ Says: "Receive the Holy Spirit"

22. In the Old Testament the Spirit of God
was in the first place "breath";
Isaiah presents him as a "gift" to the Messiah;
at the Jordan Jesus is the one who comes
"in the Holy Spirit."
It is at the Last Supper
that the Holy Spirit is revealed
in a new and fuller way.
He is not only the gift to the Messiah;
he is a Person-gift, another counselor,
who will lead the apostles "into all truth" (Jn 16:13).

23. The paschal events
are the time of the new coming of the Holy Spirit,
the time of the "new beginning."
The Holy Spirit is given to the apostles and to the church
in a new way,
and through them to humanity and the whole world.

24. This happened on the day of the resurrection,
when the risen Jesus, "full of power,"
does two things:
— fulfilling God's promise,
"a new heart I will give you,
and a new spirit I will put within you,
my spirit" (Ez 36:26f.),

— and fulfilling his own promise,
"If I go,
I will send him to you" (1 Jn 16:7).
"On the evening of that day...
Jesus came and stood among them and said:
'Peace be with you.'
When he said this,
he showed them his hands and his side.
He said to them again
'Peace be with you.'
And when he said this,
he breathed on them and said to them,
'Receive the Holy Spirit'" (Jn 20:19-22).
In this key text the Risen Christ "brings"
to the apostles the Holy Spirit
at the price of his own "departure,"
through the wounds of his crucifixion.
There is no sending of the Holy Spirit
— after original sin —
without the cross and resurrection.
The redemption is carried out by the Son
and at the same time
constantly carried out in the history of the world
by the Holy Spirit, the "other counselor."

7. *The Holy Spirit and the Era of the Church*

25. On the day of Pentecost
the Holy Spirit sanctified the church forever.
The Second Vatican Council calls Pentecost
the day of the church's birth.
What had happened on Easter Sunday
inside the Upper Room,
"the doors being shut,"
is now manifested in public.
"Doubtless, the Holy Spirit
was already at work in the world
before Christ was glorified.
Yet on the day of Pentecost,
he came down upon the disciples
to remain with them forever.
On that day the church was publicly revealed
to the multitude,
and the Gospel began to spread among the nations
by means of preaching" (AG 4).

The era of the church began.
The Holy Spirit, transmitted in the episcopal ordination,
the sacraments of orders and confirmation,
dwelling within the church
as in a temple (1 Cor 3:16),
guides it in the fullness of truth (cf. LG 4).

26. The Second Vatican Council
confirmed the presence of the Holy Spirit,
making the Spirit newly "present"
in our difficult age.
    The church opening itself to the contemporary world
    must carefully "discern"
    what comes from the Holy Spirit.

Part II
THE SPIRIT WHO CONVINCES THE WORLD CONCERNING SIN

1. Sin, Righteousness, and Judgment

27. According to Jesus' words, the Spirit
"will convince the world concerning
sin, righteousness, and judgment" (Jn 16:7).
    Jesus explained his words:
        — *concerning sin,*
            because they do not believe in me;
        — *concerning righteousness,*
            because I go to the Father,
            and you will see me no more;
        — *concerning judgment,*
            because the ruler of this world is judged (Jn 16:7).
"Sin" here means the unbelief
Jesus meets among "his own,"
the rejection of his mission.
"Righteousness" seems to be
the definitive justice and glory
the Father will give to him;
and "judgment" means
that the world will be shown guilty of his death.
    Yet Jesus did not come to condemn the world,
    but to save it,
    a truth that is emphasized
    by saying that "the prince of this world"

— that is, Satan —
will be shown to be condemned.

28. The Holy Spirit's mission
is to "convince the world concerning sin,"
against the background of Jesus' salvific work among us,
showing that sin has definitively been judged and condemned.

29. All this became part of the era of the church.
One can see this in the way the Second Vatican Council
understands the "world" as fallen in sin,
    yet emancipated by Jesus,
    to be fashioned anew according to God's design
    and to reach its fulfillment (cf. GS 2).
Sin includes here all the sin in the history of humankind.
In a way it is as if Jesus restricts sin
to those who reject his mission,
but because that mission is universal, every sin in the world
is related to the cross of Christ.

2. The Testimony of the Day of Pentecost

30. What Jesus had foretold the Holy Spirit would do
— "convince *the world* concerning sin" —
was confirmed on the day of Pentecost,
when filled with the Holy Spirit,
    "They began to speak in other tongues" (Acts 2:4),
    "bringing back to unity the scattered races" (Saint Irenaeus).
Under the influence of the Holy Spirit
Peter does something
he certainly had not the courage to do before;
he bears witness to Christ crucified and risen,
"convincing the world concerning sin,"
the sin of the rejection of Jesus.

31. This convincing the world of sin
is linked with the mystery
of the crucified and risen one,
revealing his saving dimension.
    To the question "What shall we do?"
    Peter answers:
    "Repent, and be baptized every one of you,
    in the name of Jesus Christ,
    for the forgiveness of sins,
    and you will receive the gift of the Holy Spirit" (Acts 2:37).
Conversion includes the interior judgment of the conscience,
and at the same time a new beginning, receiving the Holy Spirit.

"Convincing concerning sin"
is a double gift:
    the gift of conscience
    and the gift of redemption.
Peter bears witness to victory over sin,
a victory achieved in a certain sense
through the greatest sin ever committed:
the killing of Jesus.
    The sin of Good Friday
    and of every human sin
    was matched
    by the oblation of supreme love,
    conquering all sins.
At the Easter Vigil the church of Rome
does not hesitate to sing: "O happy fault!"

32. The Holy Spirit "searches the depths" of God,
    and from them draws God's response to sin.
        By convincing the world
        concerning the sin of Golgotha
        — as happens on the day of Pentecost —
        the Holy Spirit shows
        the evil of sin, of every sin
        in relation to the cross of Jesus.
    Humanity is ignorant
    of the "mystery of iniquity" (2 Thes 2:7) hidden in sin
    apart from the cross of Christ,
    just as humanity is ignorant
    of the "mystery of devotion" (1 Tim 3:16)
    apart from the cross of Christ.
        And humanity cannot be convinced
        of these dimensions
        except by the Holy Spirit,
        the Counselor,
        searching the depths of God.

3. The Witness concerning the Beginning: The Original Reality of Sin

33. The dimension of sin
    as described in the book of Genesis
    is the principle and root of all other sin.
    In it the "mystery of iniquity" has its beginning,
    but also the "mystery of devotion,"
    as Saint Paul noted, contrasting the disobedience of the first Adam,
    with the obedience of the second one: Christ.

Sin in its beginning is human "disobedience,"
a rejection, a turning away from the truth
contained in the Word of God,
who was with God, who was God,
without whom "nothing has been made"
since "the world was made through him" (Jn 1:1f.).
When Jesus speaks on the eve of his passion
of those "who do not believe in him"
there is — as it were — a distant echo of that sin
already obscurely described
in the mystery of creation.
    The disobedience in the beginning
    relates to the "nonfaith"
    in the paschal mystery.
They both are a rejection,
or at least a turning away from the truth
contained in the Word of the Father,
a rejection that is the result of the temptation
that comes from the "father of lies" (Jn 8:44).
    At the root of human sin is the lie,
    the rejection of the truth contained in the Word,
    expressing the omnipotence and love
    "of God the Father, Creator of heaven and earth."

34. The Spirit of God is not only the witness of
the mutual love between the Father and the Word-Son;
he himself is this love, the eternal uncreated gift.
    In the Holy Spirit is the source and beginning
    of every giving of gifts to creatures.
Humanity is created from nothing.
Creating means to give existence.
The world is created for and given to humanity,
which receives as a special gift the being created
in the "image and likeness" of God.
    This means not only that humanity
    is rational and free,
    but also that it has the capacity
    of a personal relationship with God,
    of having a mutual covenant,
    and a call to friendship.

35. The Holy Spirit,
knowing from the beginning
the secrets of the human being (cf. 1 Cor 2:10f.),
is the only one who can convince the world concerning sin
and concerning what happened at the beginning.

The Holy Spirit knows how sin was caused
in the will of humankind by the "father of lies,"
who has already been judged.
The Holy Spirit convinces the world of sin,
guiding it toward the righteousness
revealed by Jesus' obedience on the cross.
   The sin of the human beginning
   consists in untruthfulness
   and in the rejection of the gift and the love
   that determine the beginning of the world and humanity.

36. In the book of Genesis
    sin in its original form is understood
    as "disobedience," a transgression of a prohibition
    laid down by God.
       The roots of this disobedience
       are to be sought
       in the real situation of the human being.
    The human being — man and woman —
    is a creature.
    "The tree of knowledge of good and evil"
    was to remind humanity of this limit
    impassable for a created being.
    The temptation was to go beyond that limit,
       "When you eat of it . . . you will be like God
       knowing good and evil" (Gn 3:5).
          God the Creator is
          the source of moral order in the world;
          human beings cannot decide by themselves
          what is good and what is evil.
       Humanity cannot
       "know good and evil like God."
    God decides about good and evil
    in the reflection of the Word, the eternal Son.
    The Holy Spirit gives humanity the gift of conscience,
    so that in this conscience the human being
    — the image of God —
    may reflect its model.
       Disobedience means the rejection of this source.
    The Holy Spirit does not cease
    to convince the world of this sin
    relating it to the cross of Christ.

37. Called to share in God's love and life
    humanity has separated itself
    from this sharing.

To what degree?
Not to the degree of Satan
who "already has been judged" (Jn 16:11).
Nevertheless humanity turned away from God
and opened up in a way to the "father of lies."
The truth about humanity and about God is falsified;
there is now an anti-truth and an anti-Word.
God is placed in a state of suspicion,
of accusation.
The "genius of suspicion" enters human history,
falsifying Good itself.

38. The spirit of darkness (Eph 6:12)
is capable of showing God as an enemy of God's own creature,
a source of danger and threat to humanity.
Humanity is pressed by the "father of lies"
to reject God even to the point of hating God:
"Love of self
to the point of contempt for God,"
as Saint Augustine puts it.
We see this confirmed in the modern age
when atheistic ideologies seek to root out religion,
holding that religion causes the radical "alienation" of humanity.
The rejection of God
reached the point of declaring God's "death,"
a death that is more a threat to humanity than to God.
"Without the Creator the creature would disappear.
When God is forgotten
the creature itself becomes unintelligible" (GS 36).

4. The Spirit Who Transforms Suffering into Salvific Love

39. Invoked through the cross of Jesus to convince the world of sin,
will the Holy Spirit not also have to reveal suffering?
Sin is an offense against God.
What corresponds in God to this offense?
Certainly God's perfection excludes any pain.
Yet in the "depths of God" there is a Father's love
that in the words of the Bible reacts, saying:
"I am sorry that I have made them" (Gn 6:7).
But more often the Bible speaks to us
of a Father who feels compassion for humanity,
as though sharing its pain.
It is this pain that will bring about
the wonderful economy of redemptive love
in Jesus Christ,

so that love can reveal itself as stronger than sin,
and the "gift" may prevail.
> For a human being
> mercy means sorrow and compassion
> for the misfortunes of one's neighbor.
> In God, the Spirit-love, it is expressed
> in a fresh outpouring of saving love.

Whereas sin, by rejecting love,
has caused the suffering of humanity
and the whole of creation (Rom 8:20–22),
the Holy Spirit will enter this human and cosmic suffering
with a new outpouring of love,
which will redeem the world.
> Jesus would say: "I have pity" (Mt 15:32, Mk 8:2),
> manifesting the eternal love full of mercy.

"Convincing the world of sin"
becomes for the Holy Spirit
the good news that sin is conquered
through the sacrifice of the Lamb of God.

40. The letter to the Hebrews,
recalling the sacrifices of the old covenant, adds:
> "How much more shall the blood of Christ,
> who through the eternal spirit
> offered himself without blemish to God,
> purify your conscience from dead works
> to serve the living God" (Heb 9:13f.).

This text invites us to reflect
on the presence of the Spirit
in the sacrifice of the Incarnate Word.
> There is here the connection
> between the sacrifice and "the purification of conscience,"
> between the spirit and the power to "convince concerning sin."

The text also indicates that the Holy Spirit is present
in the sacrifice of Jesus,
just as the Spirit was present in Jesus' conception
and in his hidden and public life.
> According to the same Letter to the Hebrews
> Jesus opened himself totally to the action
> of the Spirit-Paraclete in his humanity
> at Gethsemani and on Golgotha.
> > "He learned obedience through
> > what he suffered" (Heb 5:7f.).

Thus there is a *new humanity*.
Jesus Christ, as a human being,

enabled the Holy Spirit to transform that humanity
into a perfect sacrifice.
    He offered himself "through the eternal Spirit,"
    which means that the Holy Spirit acted
    in a special way in the absolute self-giving of the Son of Man.

41. The Holy Spirit is the "fire from heaven"
at work at the depth of the mystery of the cross.
    In Christ there suffers a God
    who has been rejected by God's own creature,
    but from this suffering the Spirit draws in new measure
    the gift made to humanity
    from the beginning.
The Spirit comes down
into the very heart of the sacrifice on the cross;
Jesus receives the Holy Spirit in such a way
that he — alone with God the Father —
can "give him" to the apostles,
the church, and humanity.
    He alone
    sends the Spirit from the Father (Jn 15:26),
    breathing on them in the Upper Room.
We express this truth daily
in the Roman liturgy:
    "Lord Jesus, Son of the living God,
    by the will of the Father,
    and the work of the Holy Spirit."

5. The Blood That Purifies the Conscience

42. At Easter the Holy Spirit is revealed in a new way
when Jesus says to the apostles: "Receive the Holy Spirit."
He is now revealed as the one
who is to continue the salvific work rooted
in the sacrifice of the cross.
    This work is entrusted to the apostles,
    to the church;
    but the Holy Spirit remains
    the agent of the accomplishment of this work
    in the history of the world,
    the Spirit who
    "blows where he wills" (Jn 3:8).
Jesus' words stress in a special way
the presence of the Holy Spirit
who will convince the world
of sin, righteousness, and judgment.

It is in relation to this presence
that he added:
"If you forgive the sins of any,
they are forgiven;
if you retain the sins of any,
they are retained" (Jn 20:22).
    This power to grant forgiveness
    presupposes and includes
    the saving action of the Holy Spirit.
Becoming "the light of their hearts"
he makes people realize their own evil
and directs them to what is good.
    Thus conversion is brought about
    by the influence of the Counselor,
    entering by virtue of the redemption
    through the blood of the Son of Man
    the sanctuary of human consciences.

43. The *conscience* is the secret core and sanctuary
of human beings,
where they are alone with God,
whose voice echoes in their depths.
The conscience speaks to the heart:
"Do this, shun that."
The conscience is the main characteristic
of the personal subject.
    At the same time a person detects
    in the depths of his or her conscience a law,
    which one does not impose upon oneself,
    but which holds to obedience (GS 16).
The conscience is not an independent
and exclusive capacity to decide
what is good and what is evil.
    Imprinted upon it
    is a principle of obedience,
    vis-à-vis the objective norm,
    the commands and prohibitions
    that are at the basis of human behavior.
It is precisely in this sense
that the conscience is the "secret sanctuary"
in which "God's voice echoes."
    The conscience is "the voice of God"
    even when someone considers it nothing more
    than the principle of the moral order
    without any direct reference to the Creator.

The Gospel's "convincing concerning sin"
can be accomplished in no other way
except through the upright conscience.
 The upright conscience calls good and evil
 by their proper names:
   "— whatever is opposed to life itself,
       such as any type of murder, genocide,
       abortion, euthanasia, or willful self-destruction;
   — whatever violates the integrity of the human person,
       such as mutilation,
       torments inflicted on body or mind,
       attempts to coerce the will itself;
   — whatever insults human dignity,
       such as subhuman living conditions,
       arbitrary imprisonment, deportation,
       slavery, prostitution,
       the selling of women and children,
   — as well as disgraceful working conditions,
       where people are treated
       as mere tools for profit,
       rather than as free and responsible persons . . .
 all these things and others of their kind
 are infamies indeed.
 They poison human society,
 but they do more harm to those who practice them,
 than to those who suffer from injury.
 Moreover they are a supreme dishonor
 to the Creator" (GS 27).
In this way all of life, whether individual or collective,
is involved in the
   "dramatic struggle between good and evil,
   between light and darkness" (GS 13).

44. Calling sin by its right name
 is not all the Holy Spirit works out
 in the human conscience.
   The Holy Spirit also demonstrates
   that the imbalances in the modern world
   are rooted in the basic imbalance
   in the heart of the human being.
 The Holy Spirit always does this
 in relation to the cross of Christ.
 Humanity is not fatally ensnared in sin,
 but wrestling constantly — with the help of God's grace —
 to cling to what is good.

45. This effort of conscience
    determines the paths of human conversion:
    turning one's back on sin
    and restoring truth and love in our hearts.
        Recognizing evil in ourselves
        demands a great effort.
        It is the source of remorse,
        a suffering that is, as it were, a distant echo of
            "the repentance
            at having created the human being,"
        in the "heart" of the Trinity,
        and expressed on the cross
        in Jesus' obedience unto death.
    Sharing in that suffering is redemptive,
    leading to perfect contrition;
    it is the "metanoia" found in the Gospel.
        The giver of this saving power is the Holy Spirit,
        filling "the depths of the human heart,"
        opening them to forgiveness,
        to the remission of sins.
    The Holy Spirit "comes" by virtue of Christ's "departure"
    in the paschal mystery, in each concrete case
    of conversion-forgiveness.

6. The Sin against the Holy Spirit

46. Against this background,
    Jesus' words on "unforgiveness"
    become easier to understand.
        In the three synoptic Gospels
        Jesus speaks about
        "blasphemy against the Holy Spirit."
    It consists in the refusal to accept the salvation
    that God offers through the Holy Spirit.
    Such a refusal excludes:
        "the elements through which the forgiveness of sin
        takes place" (ST, IIa–IIae, q. 14, a. 3).
    Rejecting "the convincing concerning sin,"
    one also rejects the "coming of the Holy Spirit"
    together with the power of Christ's cross.
        The "nonforgiveness" Jesus speaks about
        is linked to "nonrepentance,"
        to the radical refusal to be converted.
    Blasphemy against the Holy Spirit is the sin
    committed by the person
    who claims the "right" to persist in evil.

One closes oneself up in sin,
which means spiritual ruin.

47. In such a person the action of the Holy Spirit
meets an interior resistance,
the "hardness of heart" (Ps 81:13),
or maybe in the words of our time: "the loss of the sense of sin."
    That is why the church constantly prays,
    that the integrity of human consciences
    may not be lost,
    that their healthy sensitivity
    will not be blunted,
    and that there will be no increase
    but a decrease in the world
    of the sin the Gospel calls
    "blasphemy against the Holy Spirit."
    "Do not quench the Spirit" (1 Thes 5:19).

48. Being convinced of sin, righteousness, and judgment
marks the mystery of piety
opposed to the mystery of iniquity.
    Those who let themselves be convinced
    concerning sin and righteousness
    and who are converted
    through the action of the Holy Spirit
    are also led out of the range of "judgment."
They are led into the righteousness
that the Father gives to the Son
and to all those united with him
in truth and love.
    The Holy Spirit is in this way
    revealed as the Spirit of eternal life.

Part III
THE SPIRIT WHO GIVES LIFE

1. Reason for the Jubilee of the Year 2000: Christ Was Conceived by the Holy Spirit

49. The coming of Jesus Christ
into this world approaches a great jubilee,
the third millennium
of what Saint Paul called "the fullness of time" (Gal 4:4).
    Since then human history has been wholly permeated
    by the "measurement" of God,
    a transcendent presence of the "eternal *now*."

"When the time had fully come
God sent forth his Son,
born of a woman...
so that we might receive adoption as children" (Gal 4:4f.).
   Luke and Matthew, the two evangelists
   to whom we owe the narrative of the birth of Jesus,
   express the mystery of the incarnation
   making reference to the Holy Spirit.
As the Apostles' Creed says:
"He was conceived by the power of the Holy Spirit,
and born of the Virgin Mary."
   This is what happened when
   "the fullness of time had come."

50. The great jubilee is the celebration
   of the birth of Jesus Christ, "by the power of the Holy Spirit."
     The conception and birth of Jesus Christ
     are the greatest work of the Holy Spirit
     in the history of creation and salvation.
     It brings about the mystery of the "hypostatic union,"
     the union of the divine nature and the human nature
     of the divinity and the humanity
     in the one Person of the Word-Son.
   "The Word became flesh" (Jn 1:14).
   The incarnation of God the Son
   signifies the taking up into unity with God,
   not only in human nature, but in *this* human nature,
   everything that is "flesh,"
      the whole of humanity,
       the entire visible and material world.
   The incarnation has a cosmic dimension.
   The "firstborn of all creation" (Col 1:15)
   unites himself in some way with the entire human reality,
   and in this reality with all flesh, with the whole of creation.

51. All this is part of the great jubilee to come.
   The church cannot prepare for the jubilee
   in any other way than in the Holy Spirit.
   It is only by the Spirit that what was accomplished
   "at the fullness of time" can be remembered.
     It was the same Holy Spirit
     that made Mary's heart in faith obedient
     to the self-communication of God.
   Elizabeth greeted her with the words:
   "Blessed is she who believed" (Lk 1:45),
   contrasting her with all those

about whom Christ will say,
that they do not believe (cf. Jn 16:9).
    Mary entered the history of salvation
    through the obedience of faith,
    in the openness of her heart to the Holy Spirit,
    giving her the fullness of freedom.
    "Where the Spirit of the Lord is,
    there is freedom" (2 Cor 3:17).

2. Reason for the Jubilee: Grace Has Been Made Manifest

52. The incarnation opens in a new way
the source of divine life
in the history of humankind.
    The Word, the "firstborn of all creation,"
    becomes "the firstborn of many brethren" (Rom 8:29).
    He becomes the head of the Body, which is the church,
    and in the church the head of humanity.
        "All who are led by the Spirit
        are children of God" (cf. Rom 8:14).
This birth, or rebirth,
happens when God the Father
"sends the Spirit of his Son into our hearts" (Gal 4:6),
crying, "Abba, Father" (Rom 8:15).
    He who at creation gives life
    to humanity and the cosmos
    renews this life through the incarnation.
In this way there begins in the heart of all human beings
the gift by which they become
"partakers of the divine nature" (cf. 2 Pet 1:4).

53. Celebrating this jubilee we need to go further back
to even before the Christ
if we want to embrace the whole of the action
of the Holy Spirit throughout the world.
    For this action has been exercised
    in every place and at every time,
    indeed in every individual,
    also "outside the visible body of the church,"
    as the Second Vatican Council reminds us,
    speaking precisely of:
        "all people of good will
        in whose hearts grace works in an unseen way.
        For, since Christ died for all,
        and since the ultimate vocation of the human being
        is in fact one, and divine,

we ought to believe that the Holy Spirit
in a manner known only to God
offers to every human being the possibility
of being associated with the paschal mystery" (GS 22, LG 16).

54. The jubilee should be for everyone
an occasion to meditate on God's presence in the intimacy
of the human being, in mind, conscience, and heart.
God is "closer than my inmost being."
    But in Jesus Christ this divine presence
    has been made manifest in a new way,
    through the power of the Holy Spirit.
    The salvific "hidden God" (cf. Is 45:15)
    "fills the universe" (cf. Wis 1:7)
    as love and gift.

3. *The Holy Spirit in One's Inner Conflict: "For the desires of the flesh are against the Spirit, and the desires of the Spirit are against the flesh"*

55. Unfortunately the Spirit meets
resistance and opposition in our human reality.
    This opposition has its origin in the fact
    that world and God differ radically:
    materiality and Spirit.
Because of sin this opposition
becomes conflict and rebellion.
    There exists in us,
        as being made up of body and spirit,
        a certain tension, well described by Paul,
    who speaks about "works of the flesh"
            —like impurity, drunkenness, enmity,
        strife, jealousy, anger, and the like—
    but also about "the fruits of the Spirit"
            —love, joy, peace, patience, kindness,
        goodness, faithfulness, and gentleness (cf. Gal 5:22).
Paul is not against the body;
he is speaking of good or bad works,
    dispositions, virtues and vices.
    Paul's contrast leads to another one,
    that between "life" and "death":
        "If you live according to the flesh
        you will die;
        but if by the Spirit you put to death
        the world of the flesh
        you will live" (Rom 8:6, 13).

56. The resistance to the Holy Spirit Paul speaks about
is to be found in every period of history.
     In our days it takes its clearest form
     in *materialism,*
     which is the core of Marxism,
     and which does not accept God's existence,
     being essentially and systematically *atheistic.*
     Atheism is the striking phenomenon of our time.
     You cannot talk about it in a univocal way,
     nor should it be restricted to the theory of materialism.
A true and proper materialism is atheistic,
though it might sometimes speak
of "spirit" in the fields of culture and morality,
since according to this system
matter is the one and only form of being.
     Against this background so characteristic of our time
     we must emphasize the "desires of the Spirit,"
     preparing for the jubilee in this new time of advent,
     at the end of which "all will see the salvation of God" (Lk 3:6).
This is a possibility and hope
the church entrusts to the men and women of today.

57. Materialism accepts death
as the definitive end of human existence.
Life is then nothing but
an "existence in order to die."
     On the horizon of contemporary civilization
     the signs and symptoms of death
     have become particularly present and frequent.
One has only to think of the arms race,
the danger of nuclear self-destruction,
the taking of lives before they are born
or before they reach the natural point of death,
the new wars that have broken out,
and the attacks on human life by terrorism
organized at an international scale.
     This is only a partial sketch
     of the picture of death in our age.
Does there not arise from all this
a more or less conscious plea
to the life-giving Spirit?
     "We groan inwardly as we wait for..."
     the redemption of our human essence,
     but we do that in unflagging hope,
     because it is to this human being

that God has drawn near,
sending his own Son:
the Son who breathed over them,
   saying: "Receive the Holy Spirit,"
   the Spirit who helps us
   in our weakness (Rom 8:26).

4. The Holy Spirit Strengthens the "Inner Person"

58. "He who raised Christ from the dead
will give life to your mortal bodies also
through the Spirit who dwells in you" (Rom 8:11).
   The church serves this life that comes from God,
   making the human person "the way of the church."
It is under the influence of the Holy Spirit
that a person matures and becomes strong.
   In this Spirit the triune God opens God's very self
   to the human spirit.
   A new life is brought about and
   the person becomes a "dwelling place" of the Holy Spirit,
   "a living temple of God" (cf. Rom 8:9, 1 Cor 6:19),
   living in God and by God.

59. Humanity's intimate relationship with God
will enable people to understand themselves in a new way
as the image and likeness of God—
   rediscovering themselves in Christ
   in their gift to others,
   precisely by reason of their divine likeness.
This is a truth that has always to be rediscovered.
It is in this way that the triune God
—remaining transcendent—
transforms the human world from within,
from inside hearts and minds,
making it ever more human (GS 38, 40),
until God will be "all in all" (cf. 1 Cor 15:28).
   As the year 2000 draws near
   the issue is to ensure
   that an ever greater number of people
   "may fully find themselves...
   through a sincere gift of self."
May the action of the Spirit-Paraclete
accomplish a growth in our world,
both in individual and community life.
   Jesus prayed to the Father,
   "that all may be one...

as we are one" (Jn 17:21–22),
implying "a certain likeness
between the union of the divine persons
and the union of the children of God
in truth and charity" (GS 24).
These words sum up
the whole of Christian anthropology.

60. People discovering this divine dimension
are able to free themselves of the various determinisms,
conditionings, and pressures due to our materialistic society.
   The year 2000 contains in this way the promise of liberation
   by the power of the Holy Spirit:
      a freedom and human dignity that shine especially
      in times of persecution,
      but that manifest themselves
      also in the ordinary conditions of society,
      every time we work together
      — in obedience to the Holy Spirit —
      at the "renewal of the face of the earth."

5. The Church as the Sacrament of Intimate Union with God

61. At the Last Supper Jesus spoke about his new "coming":
   "I will not leave you desolate, I will come to you" (Jn 14:18).
   And when he ascended to heaven he told his disciples:
      "I am with you always
      to the close of the age" (Mt 28:20).
      This new coming of Christ
      by the power of the Holy Spirit
      and his constant presence
      are accomplished sacramentally.

62. The departure and coming of Christ
   are most completely expressed in the Eucharist.
      It is through the Eucharist
      that individuals and communities are strengthened.
      The Eucharist reveals the union of God's children
      and teaches us to share in the sacrifice of Christ,
      "finding ourselves through the gift of ourselves,"
      in communion with God,
      and with others, our brothers and sisters.
   From the earliest days Christians devoted themselves
   to the breaking of bread and prayers, forming a community
   united by the teachings of the apostles (cf. Acts 2:42).
      And so it has always been, though we have to acknowledge
      at the end of this millennium

the great separation between Christians,
which we should overcome by following the Holy Spirit.

63. Through creation
we all "live and move and have our being" in God (Acts 17:28).
Through redemption we are taken up in a double rhythm:
    the mission of the Son
    and the mission of the Holy Spirit,
    both finding their source in the Father.
    The Holy Spirit came through the departure of the Son,
    but the one who has gone away in the paschal mystery
    comes to us and is with us
    through the power of the Holy Spirit.
Through the individual sacraments
the church's ministry brings with it
this departure and this coming
through the action of the Holy Spirit.
The church is the visible dispenser
and the Holy Spirit acts as the invisible dispenser.
Together with the Spirit Jesus is present and acting.

64. The church is the sacrament of intimate union with God;
the church is the sign and instrument
of the presence and action of the Spirit.
    The church is also
    "a sacrament...of the unity of all humankind,"
    a unity rooted in the mystery of creation
    and the mystery of redemption.
        God who created all
        "wishes all to be saved" (1 Tim 2:4).
The church is "a sacrament that is sign and instrument"
of this unity at the very roots of the human race,
trying to restore and strengthen it,
    a task in which the Holy Spirit
    is present and at work.

6. The Spirit and the Bride Say: "Come!"

65. The simplest way in which the Holy Spirit
makes itself felt is in prayer.
Wherever a prayer is offered in the world
the Holy Spirit is breathing in the human heart.
    Prayer remains the voice of the voiceless,
    crying to God.
    The Holy Spirit is the one
    who guides us in prayer,
    giving it a divine dimension.

Our age has a special need of prayer.
Recent years have seen
a growth in the number of people
who are giving first place to prayer.
    This is a comforting sign
    in an age in which humanity feels threatened,
    notwithstanding all the rapid
    technological and scientific progress.

66. The church remains faithful to its birth,
persevering in prayer in the Upper Room
together with Mary.
"Lord Jesus Christ: Come!" (cf. Rev 22:17).
The church perseveres in hope of the eternal kingdom
that is brought about by participation
in the life of the Trinity.
    "Lord Jesus Christ: Come" —
    a prayer that is filled with eschatological significance
    in this time leading up to the great jubilee.

CONCLUSION

67. The way of the church passes
through the heart of the human person,
because here is the hidden place
where we meet the Holy Spirit,
Counselor, Intercessor, Advocate,
Guardian of hope,
Father of the poor, Giver of gifts,
Light of hearts, the sweet Guest of the soul.
    The church keeps professing its faith in a Spirit
    that is an uncreated gift, filling the universe.
It implores from the Holy Spirit,
the joy that "no one will be able to take away" (cf. Jn 16:22)
and a peace that can only pass through love
and that it will never cease to serve.
    Before this Spirit-love, this Spirit of peace,
    I implore for all of us the blessing and grace
    that I desire to pass on to the church
    and to the whole human family.

6

The Mother of the Redeemer

Redemptoris Mater

March 25, 1987

The year 2000 directs our attention to the mother of Jesus, who was here on earth before him. "Full of grace," she joined Jesus in his struggle to overcome evil, expressing her maternal care for all of us, a motherhood confirmed by Jesus from the cross when he entrusted — in the person of John — the whole of humanity to her. As the mother of the church Mary urges all of us: "Do whatever he [Jesus] tells you," mediating in this way between him and us.

INTRODUCTION

1. I wish to begin my reflection on the role of Mary
with Paul's words:
    "When the time had fully come, God sent forth his Son
    born of a woman, born under the law,
    to redeem those who were under the law
    so that they might receive adoption as children.
    And because you are children,
    God has sent the Spirit of his Son into our hearts
    crying: 'Abba, Father'" (Gal 4:4–6).
These words celebrate the love of the Father,
the mission of the Son, the gift of the Spirit,
the role of the woman from whom the Redeemer was born,
and our own divine filiation in the fullness of time.
    This fullness of time marks the moment
    when the Father sent the Son,
    the Holy Spirit formed Christ in Mary's womb,
    time became "salvation time,"
    and the church began its journey in Mary of Nazareth

anticipating in her Immaculate Conception,
the saving grace of Easter.
Mary uttering her first *fiat* to Christ
— the church's Lord and Head —
prefigures the church's condition as spouse and mother.

2. On its journey through time to meet the Lord who comes,
the church proceeds on the path already trod by the Virgin Mary,
"who advanced in her pilgrimage of faith,
and loyally persevered in her union
with her Son unto the cross" (LG 58).

3. The prospect of the year 2000,
the bimillennial jubilee of Jesus Christ's birth,
directs our gaze toward his mother.
Mary appeared on the horizon of salvation history before Christ.
When he appeared, his mother already existed on earth,
a fact reflected every year in the liturgy of Advent.
If we compare the years that are bringing us closer
to the end of the second millennium after Christ,
to the period of the historical expectation of the Savior,
it becomes understandable that we think especially of her
who in the "night" of the Advent expectation began to shine like
a true "morning star."
As "morning star" and "dawn" precede the rising of the sun,
so Mary preceded the rising of the "Sun of Justice"
in the history of the human race.
It is with good reason then
that we feel the need to emphasize
the mother of Christ's presence
in these years leading up to the year 2000.

4. If it is true that the mystery of the human being
takes on light only in the mystery of the Incarnate Word,
then this must be true in a particular way of the woman
who became the mother of Christ.
Mary's mystery is made fully clear
only in the mystery of Christ.
That is why it was such a great joy for Christians
that Mary was declared the "Mother of God"
at the Council of Ephesus (431).
This dogma of the divine motherhood of Mary
was in turn a seal upon the dogma of the incarnation.

5. Being the mother of Christ,
Mary is in a particular way united with the church,
"which the Lord established as his own body" (LG 52).

The Second Vatican Council relates this truth
about the church being the Body of Christ
to the truth that the Son of God was born of the Virgin Mary.
The reality of the incarnation finds a sort of extension
in the mystery of the church — the Body of Christ.
   In these reflections I wish to consider primarily
   "Mary's pilgrimage of faith."
It is not just the Virgin Mother's personal life-story,
but because of her bond with Christ and with the church,
it is also the story of the whole people of God,
of all those who take part in the same "pilgrimage of faith."
   Mary has gone before; she is the model of the church.
   She is the virgin pledged to her Spouse,
   who became herself a mother.

6. Mary accomplished all this in a process
   that can be compared to a journey,
   the pilgrimage of faith, that is the story of all human beings.
      First we wish to concentrate on the present,
      within which Mary continues to "go before" the people of God.
   Mary accomplished her journey;
   she is glorified at the side of her Son in heaven,
   but she does not cease to be the "Star of the Sea"
   for all those who are still on their journey of faith.

Part I
MARY IN THE MYSTERY OF CHRIST

1. *Full of Grace*

7. "Blessed be the God and Father of Our Lord Jesus Christ,
   who has blessed us in Christ, with every spiritual blessing
   in the heavenly places" (Eph 1:3).
      Everyone is included in this divine plan of salvation,
      fully revealed to us in the coming of Christ,
      but it reserves a special place for the woman
      who is his mother —
         a woman foretold to our first parents
         after their fall into sin (Gn 3:15).

8. The angel's words
      "Hail, full of grace, the Lord is with you" (Lk 1:28)
   introduced Mary definitively into the mystery of Christ.
      The words "full of grace" refer to the blessing
      poured out through Jesus Christ upon all people,

but in a special and exceptional degree on Mary.
Elizabeth greeted her as "blessed among women."

The messenger calls Mary "full of grace" as if it were her real name.
What does this name mean?
  "Grace" means a special gift, which has its source
  in the Trinitarian life of God's very self,
  God who is "love" (1 Jn 4:8).
Being named "full of grace" refers to a special blessing
among all the spiritual blessings in Christ.
  Even before the creation of the world,
  she is the one whom the Father has chosen
  as mother of his Son in the incarnation.
  And together with the Father, the Son has chosen her,
  entrusting her eternally to the Spirit of holiness.
In a special way Mary is united to Christ
and eternally loved in this beloved Son,
who is one in being with the Father.
  At the same time, she is and remains open
  to this "gift from above" (Jas 1:17),
  standing out among those who await and receive
  salvation from the Lord (LG 55).

9. "Full of grace" refers first of all to the election of Mary
   as mother of the Son of God.
   Hence the uniqueness of her place
   in the mystery of Christ.
     God's giving of God's very self
     in some way to all creation,
     but directly to human beings,
     reaches one of its high points
     in the mystery of the incarnation.
   The incarnation is indeed a high point
   among all gifts of grace
   in the history of humanity and the universe.
   It is in Mary that the incarnation of the Word
   — the hypostatic union of the Son of God with human nature —
   is accomplished and fulfilled.
     Mary is the mother of the Son of God;
     she far surpasses all creatures,
     in heaven and on earth,
     because of this gift of sublime grace.

10. This glory of grace means that she had been redeemed
    "in a more sublime manner" (LG 53);
    she was preserved from the inheritance of original sin.

From the first moment of her conception or existence,
she belonged to Christ.
Mary receives life from him to whom she herself
gave earthly life as a mother.
The liturgy calls her "Mother of her Creator"
and in the words of a poet: "Daughter of your Son."
That is why the angel called her "full of grace."

11. And so there comes into the world
the seed of a woman who will crush the evil of sin,
but not without a hard struggle,
a struggle that is to extend
through the whole of human history.
Mary, Mother of the Incarnate Word,
is at the very center of that struggle,
remaining a sign of sure hope.

2. Blessed Is She Who Believed

12. Told by the angel that Elizabeth, her kinswoman,
had conceived a son in her old age,
Mary, moved by charity, goes to help her.
Elizabeth, filled with the Holy Spirit,
greets Mary with a loud cry:
"Blessed are you among women,
and blessed is the fruit of your womb" (Lk 1:40–42) —
words that became part of the Hail Mary,
one of the church's most frequently used prayers.
Still more significant are the words Elizabeth adds:
"And why is it granted me
that the mother of the Lord
should come to me?" (Lk 1:43),
proclaiming Mary the Mother of the Lord.
And her final words
would seem to have fundamental importance:
"And blessed is she who believed
that there would be fulfillment
of what was spoken to her by the Lord" (Lk 1:45) —
words that refer to the "fullness of grace"
announced by the angel, the gift of God.
Mary's faith, proclaimed by Elizabeth,
indicates how the Virgin of Nazareth
responded to this gift.

13. The obedience of faith,
by which someone gives himself or herself freely to God,
found perfect realization in Mary.

At the Annunciation Mary responded
with all her human and feminine "I."
By her response Mary was to become "Mother of the Lord."
This fiat of Mary — let it be done to me —
was decisive, on the human level,
for the accomplishment of the divine mystery.
Mary uttered her fiat in faith, conceiving in her mind
— as the fathers of the church teach —
before she conceived in her womb.

14. Mary's faith can be compared to that of Abraham.
Abraham's faith is the beginning of the old covenant;
Mary's faith is the beginning of the new covenant.
It was the culminating point of Mary's faith in awaiting Christ,
and at the same time the point of departure
of her journey toward God.

15. At the Annunciation Mary hears
that the Lord God will give her Son
— to be named Jesus (which means Savior) —
"the throne of his father David"
and "a kingdom to which there will be no end" (Lk 1:32–33).
Though living in the midst of the expectations of her people,
could Mary guess, at the moment of the Annunciation,
the significance of the angel's words?
How is one to understand that "kingdom"
which will have "no end"?
Mary professed above all the "obedience of faith,"
leaving the meaning of all this to God.

16. Forty days after Jesus' birth in conditions of extreme poverty
Mary hears other words, those uttered by Simeon in the temple.
His words confirm the truth of the Annunciation,
"For my eyes have seen your salvation,
which you have prepared in the presence of all peoples,
a light for the revelation to the Gentiles,
and for the glory of your people Israel" (Lk 2:30–32).
But he also says:
"This child is set for a sign that is spoken against,"
and referring to Mary he adds:
"A sword will pierce through your own soul also" (Lk 2:34–35).
These words that tell her — like a second annunciation —
of the actual situation in which her son is to accomplish his mission.
Her motherhood will be sorrowful; after the visit of the Magi
Mary together with the child and Joseph flee into Egypt,
where they have to remain till Herod's death.

17. Once they have returned to Nazareth,
    the long period of the hidden life begins.
    Mary's life is "hid with Christ in God through faith."
    She remains blessed, because she believed day after day.
        It is not difficult to see that in that beginning
        there is heaviness of heart, a sort of "night of the faith,"
        a kind of "veil."
    That is how Mary lived for many years
    in intimacy with the mystery of her Son,
    going forward in her pilgrimage of faith.
        When found in the temple,
        the twelve-year-old Jesus, answered her question,
        "Son, why have you treated us so?"
        saying: "Did you not know
        that I must be in my Father's House?"
        And the evangelist adds:
            "And they [Joseph and Mary]
            did not understand" (Lk 2:48–50).
    Mary lived through faith and continued doing so
    day by day even during Jesus' public life,
    faithful to Elizabeth's words: "Blessed is she who believed."

18. This blessing reached its full meaning
    when Mary stands under the cross of her Son,
    "faithfully preserving her union with her Son
    even to the cross" (LG 58).
        It is at the foot of that cross
        that Mary shares through faith
        in the mystery of Jesus' self-emptying.
        Through faith Mary shares in the death of her Son,
        while Simeon's words were confirmed:
        that her son would be a "sign of contradiction"
        and that a sword would
        "pierce through your own soul also."

19. "Blessed is she who believed."
    Elizabeth's words reecho at the cross.
        "The knot of Eve's disobedience
        was untied by Mary's obedience;
        what the virgin Eve bound through unbelief,
        Mary loosened by her faith" (LG 56).
    In those words "Blessed is she who believed"
    we find a "key" to unlock Mary's innermost reality,
    hailed by the angel as "full of grace."
        Through faith she became — on her earthly journey —
        a sharer in the mystery of Christ.

Advancing on her pilgrimage of faith,
she made the mystery of Christ present
to the whole of humanity.
She still continues to do so.
Through the mystery of Christ
she, too, is present within humankind.

3. Behold Your Mother

20. Fleshing out the Gospel of Jesus' infancy,
a woman raised her voice in the midst of the crowd,
praising Mary as Jesus' mother in the flesh:
"Blessed the womb that bore you,
and the breasts that you sucked" (Lk 11:27).
Jesus replies in a significant way,
"Blessed rather are those
who hear the word of God
and keep it" (Lk 11:28),
diverting the attention from motherhood in the flesh
to those bonds that develop from hearing and keeping God's word.
This shift is seen even more clearly in another response of Jesus
reported in all the Gospels, when he is told
that his mother and brothers are outside wishing to see him:
"My mother and my brothers
are those who hear the Word of God
and do it" (Lk 8:20–21).
Such statements seem to fit
with the reply the twelve-year-old Jesus gave
when he said that he was "concerned with
his Father's business" (Lk 2:49).
Within this new dimension
"brother/sisterhood" and "motherhood"
mean something different
from brother/sisterhood and motherhood
according to the flesh.
Does this mean that Jesus is distancing himself
from his mother according to the flesh?
The new motherhood Jesus speaks of
refers precisely to Mary in a very special way.
Is Mary not the first among those
"who hear the word of God and do it"?
Mary is worthy of blessing
as the mother of Jesus in the flesh,
but also and especially because she believed
and was obedient to God, because she "kept" the word
and "pondered it in her heart" (Lk 1:38).

That is why "all generations will call her blessed" (Lk 1:48),
and the unnamed woman praising her
confirmed unwittingly that prophecy,
beginning the Magnificat of the ages.
    Mary discovered and accepted
      this new and other motherhood,
        from the beginning being the one who believed.
She became in a sense the first "disciple" of her Son,
the first to whom he said:
    "Follow me,"
    before he addressed this call to anyone else (Jn 1:43).

21. At Cana Jesus seems to have been invited because of his mother.
She is there as the mother of Jesus,
    contributing to the beginning of the signs given by him.
      When Mary tells Jesus, "They have no wine" (Jn 2:3–4),
      her motherhood gets a new meaning.
      A motherhood not just according to the flesh,
        but according to the spirit:
      a motherhood manifested in Mary's solicitude for human beings.
The human need ("They have no wine")
has symbolic value.
There is a mediation.
Mary places herself between her Son and humankind,
she puts herself in the "middle,"
she acts as a mediatrix, not as an outsider,
but in her position as mother.
    In her words to the servants:
    "Do whatever he tells you" (Jn 2:5)
    she presents herself as the spokeswoman
    of her Son's will,
      pointing out the things that must be done
      so that the saving power of the Messiah
      may be manifested.
At Cana Jesus begins "his hour";
Mary's faith evokes his first sign
and helps to kindle the faith of the disciples.

22. In this episode at Cana we find a first manifestation
of Mary's maternal care —
    a role that does not obscure
    or diminish the unique meditation of Christ;
    it rather shows its efficacy (LG 60).
Cana offers a first announcement of Mary's mediation,
wholly oriented toward Christ, and revealing his saving power,
a meditation that is maternal,

a "maternity in the order of grace
that will last until the eternal fulfillment of all the elect" (LG 62).

23. It is when Mary is standing under the cross
that this motherhood is confirmed,
when Jesus, seeing his mother and his beloved disciple John,
said to Mary: "Woman, behold your son";
and to John: "Behold your mother" (Jn 19:25–27).
    Jesus expresses here his care for his mother,
    and at the same time
    gives her as mother to every single individual
    and to all humankind.
The Second Vatican Council does not hesitate to call her
"the mother of Christ and mother of humankind" (LG 54).

24. When Jesus calls Mary "Woman" from the cross
— as he had already done at Cana —
the word he uses goes to the very center
of the old promise:
the "seed of the woman…
will crush the head of the serpent" (Gn 3:15).
    The motherhood of her who bore Christ
    is continued in and through the church
    symbolized and represented by John.
At the moment
of the birth and manifestation of the church,
at Pentecost,
we see the apostles in prayer
with Mary the mother of Jesus (Acts 1:14),
who is imploring the gift of the Spirit,
that had overshadowed her in the Annunciation (LG 59).
    The one who links those two moments
    — the annunciation at Nazareth and Pentecost in Jerusalem —
    is Mary.
In both cases her presence indicates the path
"of the birth of the Holy Spirit."

Part II
THE MOTHER OF GOD AT THE CENTER
OF THE PILGRIM CHURCH

1. The Church, the People of God Present in All Nations of the Earth

25. Journeying through the desert
like the Israel of the old covenant,

the church of Christ presses forward
"like a pilgrim in a foreign land
amid the persecutions of the world
and the consolations of God,
announcing the resurrection of the Lord
until he comes" (LG 8).
    Mary is present in this pilgrimage
    through space and time,
    and even more in this interior
    pilgrimage through faith in the Holy Spirit.
She is like a mirror
in which the mighty works of God are reflected (Acts 2:11).

26. For those gathered at Pentecost in the Upper Room,
the church's pilgrimage
through the history of individuals and peoples
started there and then.
    Mary's journey of faith began before,
    at the Annunciation.
    Mary "goes before them,
    leading the way for them" (LG 63).
The mission of the apostles began
the moment they left the Upper Room,
as Jesus had foretold them:
"When the Holy Spirit has come upon you,
you shall be my witnesses, to the end of earth" (Acts 1:8).
    Mary did not directly receive this apostolic mission;
    she was not among those whom Jesus sent
    "to the whole world to teach all nations,"
    when he conferred his mission on them.
But in the church of that time,
and of every time,
Mary was the first to believe.
From the moment of the Annunciation
she followed Jesus in her maternal pilgrimage of faith;
she remained the one who, like Abraham,
"in hope believed against hope" (Rom 4:18).
    It was only after the resurrection
    that the promise began to be transformed into reality.

27. Mary's heroic faith
"precedes" the apostolic witness of the church.
It remains in the church's heart.
    All those who accept the church's witness
    share in a sense Mary's faith,
    fulfilling the prophecy of the Magnificat

— "All generations will call me blessed" (Lk 1:48) —
and seeking in her faith support for their own.

28. Mary's faith continues to become the faith
of the pilgrim people of God,
passed on through both the mind and the heart,
gained and regained in prayer.
    Approaching the year 2000
    the church reminds us to be
        "the one people of God,
        among all the nations of the earth"
        and of the truth
        that all faithful
        "scattered throughout the world,
        are in communion with each other
        in the Holy Spirit.
        devoting themselves to prayer,
        together with Mary, the mother of Jesus" (LG 13).
This presence of Mary means a wide field of action
    for individuals, families, parishes,
    missionary communities, religious institutes
    and dioceses.
It explains the radiation and attraction of the great shrines,
like those of Guadalupe, Lourdes, Fatima, and Jasna Góra,
where not only individuals or local groups,
but sometimes whole continents
seek to meet the mother of God,
who as "the handmaid of the Lord"
precedes the church, striving
    "to bring all humanity back to Christ its head
    in the unity of his Spirit" (LG 13).

2. The Church's Journey and the Unity of All Christians

29. Christians are seeking ways to restore unity,
deepening in themselves that "obedience of faith"
of which Mary is the first and brightest example.

30. By a more profound study of both Mary and the church,
clarifying each other, Christians will be able
to go forward together on this pilgrimage of faith.
    It is a hopeful sign that churches are finding agreement
    on fundamental points of Christian belief,
    including matters relating to Mary.
Why should we not all together look to her
as our common mother, who prays for our unity?

31. I wish to emphasize how profoundly the Orthodox Church,
    the ancient churches of the East,
    and the Coptic and Ethiopian traditions
    feel united with the Catholic Church
    by love and praise for the "Theotókos,"
    the mother of God.

32. In the Byzantine liturgy,
    praise of the mother is linked with praise of her Son
    and with the praise that, through the Son,
    is offered to the Father in the Holy Spirit.

33. Since the Second Council of Nicaea (787)
    — twelve hundred years ago this year —
    images of the Virgin have a place of honor
        in churches and houses.
        The icon of Our Lady of Vladimir
        continually accompanied the pilgrimage
        of the people of ancient Russia,
        just as her icons
        did that in the Ukraine and Byelorussia.

34. Such a wealth of praise for her
    could help us to hasten the day
    that the church can begin once more to breathe fully
    with its "two lungs," the East and the West,
    more than ever necessary today.

35. The Virgin Mother is constantly present
    on this journey of the people of God toward the light,
    reechoing the Magnificat
    that welled up from the depths of Mary's faith.

36. Singing her song, Mary confesses
    that she finds herself in the very heart of the fullness of Christ.
    She is conscious that the promise made
    "first of all to Abraham and to his posterity forever"
    is being fulfilled in herself.

37. The church keeps repeating Mary's Magnificat,
    boldly proclaiming — in contrast to Eve's disbelief —
    God as the source of all gifts,
    the one who "has done great things" in her,
    as well as in the whole of the universe.
        Repeating Mary's words
        near the end of the second millennium
        also involves a recommitment to preaching
        "the good news to the poor" (Lk 4:18).

The church's love of preference for the poor
is wonderfully inscribed in Mary's Magnificat.
Mary proclaims the coming
of the "Messiah of the poor" (cf. Is 11:4, 61:1),
casting down the mighty, filling the hungry with good things,
sending the rich away, scattering the proud-hearted,
and merciful on those who fear God.
These two messages contained in the Magnificat
cannot be separated;
they are intimately connected
with the Christian meaning
of freedom and liberation.
Mary is the most perfect image of freedom
and of the liberation of humanity and the universe.
She stands as mother and model of the church.

Part III
MATERNAL MEDIATION

1. Mary, the Handmaid of the Lord

38. "There is only one mediator, Jesus Christ" (1 Tim 2:5–6).
Mary's role neither obscures nor diminishes
this unique mediation.
It shows its power;
it is mediation in Christ (cf. LG 60).
    Mary's mediation is linked to her motherhood.
    Mary plays a unique subordinate role,
    which is special and extraordinary,
    being "a mother to us in the order of grace" (LG 61).

39. Mary's response
"Behold, I am the handmaid of the Lord" (Lk 1:38)
is the first submission to the mediation of Jesus Christ—
    a response in which she made a total gift of self
    to the saving plans of the Most High.
    God, the Eternal Father, entrusted God's very self
    to the Virgin of Nazareth.
Mary not only became the "nursing mother,"
but also the "associate of unique nobility" (LG 61)
of the Messiah and Redeemer
in maternal cooperation with the Savior's mission
through her actions and suffering.
    In a way all her own Mary entered
    into the one mediation of Christ Jesus.

And such cooperation is precisely
this mediation subordinated
to the mediation of Christ.

40. After the resurrection and Ascension
"the Handmaid of the Lord"
with the apostles awaited Pentecost,
left by her Son in the midst of the infant church.
    There began the special bond
    between his mother and the church,
    a bond that "will last without interruption
    until the eternal fulfillment of all the elect" (LG 62).

41. Assumed into heaven Mary contributes in a special way
to the union of the pilgrim church on earth
with the heavenly reality of the Communion of Saints.
    Mary is — as it were — clothed by the whole reality
    of the Communion of Saints.
        She is in union with and subordinated to him
        who is the one mediator
        until the final realization of "the fullness of time"
        when "all things are united in Christ" (Eph 1:10)
        and God will be "all in all."

2. Mary in the Life of the Church and of Every Christian

42. As virgin and mother, Mary remains for the church
a "permanent model," for the church too is called
"mother and virgin," names that have a profound justification.

43. The church "becomes a mother
by accepting God's word with fidelity" (LG 64);
she generates sons and daughters of the human race
to a new life in Christ.
    Following the example of Mary, the church remains the virgin
    faithful to her spouse (LG 64),
        for the church is the spouse of Christ (Eph 5:21–33),
        the "bride of the Lamb" (Rev 21:9).
Although this imagery
has become an image of marriage (cf. Eph 5:23–33),
it has value as the model
of total self-giving in celibacy,
in virginity consecrated to God (cf. Mt 19:11–12, 2 Cor 11:2),
the source of motherhood in the Holy Spirit.

44. Mary is much more than the model and figure of the church;
she cooperates in the birth and development
of the sons and daughters of Mother Church.

Her motherhood is particularly experienced
at the Eucharist
when the body born of the Virgin Mary becomes present.
Mary guides the faithful to the Eucharist.

45. Motherhood concerns the *person;*
the relation between child and mother is personal,
even when there are many children,
and this is true both for mother and child.
    That is why Jesus expressed
    Mary's new motherhood in the singular:
    "Behold your son."
The Redeemer entrusts Mary to John
because he entrusts John to Mary.
    This is true not only of John,
    but of every Christian.
Christ makes a gift
personally to every individual.
    "And from that hour the disciple
    took her to his home" (Jn 19:27).
    Entrusting themselves to Mary in a filial manner,
    Christians "welcome" the mother of Christ
    "into their own home" and bring her into everything
    that makes up the human and Christian *"I."*

46. This filial relationship has its beginning in Christ,
but is also directed toward him.
    Mary continues to say to each individual:
    "Do whatever he tells you."
The figure of Mary sheds light on womanhood as such
by the fact that God entrusted his Son to the ministry,
the free and active ministry of a woman:
    self-offering of total love,
    strength capable of bearing the greatest sorrows,
    limitless fidelity, tireless devotion to work,
    ability to combine penetrating intuition
    with words of support and encouragement.

47. Paul VI proclaimed Mary "the Mother of the Church."
Mary embraces each and every one *in* the church
and *through* the church.
    Mary is the woman who from the book of Genesis
    until the book of Revelation
    accompanies the revelation of God's salvific plan for humanity,
    taking part in that "monumental struggle
    against the powers of darkness" (GS 37).

Mary helps all her children, wherever they may be,
"to find in Christ the path to the Father's House."

3. The Meaning of the Marian Year

48. The special bond between humanity and this mother
led me to proclaim a Marian Year in the church,
in this period before the year 2000,
    a year meant to promote
    what the Second Vatican Council
    said about the Blessed Virgin Mary.
This is not only a question of doctrine,
but a question of the life of faith,
and thus of an authentic Marian spirituality
and its corresponding devotion.
    In this regard I would like to recall
    Saint Louis Marie Grignion de Montfort.

49. Mary constantly precedes
the church in its journey through human history.
    By means of this Marian Year — beginning June 7, 1987 —
    the church is called not only to remember
    everything in its past that testifies
    to the special maternal cooperation
    of the mother of God
    in the work of salvation in Christ the Lord,
        but also, on its own part,
        to prepare for the future
        the paths of this cooperation.

50. During the Marian Year
we will commemorate the millennium
of the baptism of Saint Vladimir,
Grand Duke of Kiev (988),
the beginning of Christianity in Eastern Europe.
    Notwithstanding our separation in 1054
    we can say that in the presence of the mother of Christ,
    we feel that we are real brothers and sisters,
    within the Messianic people
    called to be the one family of God.
Let all the faithful pray to the mother of God
and the mother of humankind
to intercede with her Son
until all the peoples of the human family
are happily gathered together in peace and harmony
into the one people of God,
for the glory of the Most Holy and Undivided Trinity (LG 69).

CONCLUSION

51. Loving Mother of the Redeemer,
    to the wonderment of nature
    you bore your Creator.
       God matched the divinization of humanity
       to humanity's historical conditions,
       ready — even after sin — to restore at a great price
       this eternal plan of love by the "humanization" of his Son,
       who is of the same being as God.

52. The Advent liturgy
    is at the heart of this transformation
    when it prays:
       "Assist your people
       who have fallen
       yet strive to rise again."
    This is the invocation addressed to Mary,
    the invocation addressed to Christ,
    asking in a world that has made wonderful discoveries
    in the fields of science and technology
    for the fundamental and "original" transformation
    from "falling" to "rising."
       The transformation from death to life
       is a constant challenge to people's consciences
       and to humanity's historical awareness.
    This is the challenge to follow the path of "not falling"
    and of "rising again," if a fall has occurred.
       The church in union with all men and women of good will
       addresses both the Redeemer and his mother
       with this plea:
          "Assist us!
          Assist your people
          who have fallen
          yet strive to rise again."

7

On Social Concern
Sollicitudo Rei Socialis

December 30, 1987

Updating and extending Pope Paul VI's On the Development of Peoples *(1967) this encyclical stresses that the inequalities between the rich and the poor in the North and the South are growing, though the goods in this world are created and meant for everybody. Greed, power, and the consequent "structures of sin" in the East and the West have to be replaced by solidarity and by respect not only for each human person, but also for our environment. The church's aim is a commitment to justice and a preferential love for the poor on a national as well as international scale.*

I. INTRODUCTION

1. The constant concern of the church
   for the development of humanity and earthly society
   has expressed itself in different ways.
   Recent popes have written letters about these issues,
   starting with the statement by Pope Leo XIII
   On the Condition of Workers in 1891.
      Since then the church has continued
      to read and interpret current events
      in the light of the Gospel of Jesus Christ, guided by the Holy Spirit.
      A whole body of social teaching developed in this way.

2. This present letter to you
   is written to mark the twentieth anniversary
   of a great and lasting contribution to this teaching,
   the letter of Pope Paul VI *On the Development of Peoples,*
   published March 26, 1967.

3.   We write this letter to you
      not only to commemorate and honor
      Paul VI and his insights,
      but also to update and extend them.

4. Today time passes more quickly
    because of the developments all around us.
    During the last twenty years,
    the structure of the world
    has been changing notably,
    presenting totally new features.
        So much so that on the eve of the year 2000
        a widespread expectancy has been growing,
        like a new "Advent."

II. ON THE DEVELOPMENT OF PEOPLES

5. The letter of Pope Paul VI
    On the Development of Peoples
    struck many as original.

6.   Yet it should be seen
      as a response to the declarations
      of the Second Vatican Council,
      which had ended on December 8, 1965.
      That Council stated in a document,
      The Church in the Modern World,
      that the joys and the hopes,
      the griefs and anxieties,
      the poverty and underdevelopment
      in which millions of human beings live,
      are the joys and hopes,
      the griefs and anxieties
      of the followers of Christ.

7. In his letter *On the Development of Peoples*
    Paul VI stressed that we in the church should be aware
    of what is happening around us;
    that we should interpret those signs of the times
    in the light of the Gospel;
    that we should be aware
    of the service we are supposed to render to humanity,
    and especially to the poor;
    that we should be conscious
    of the terrible inequalities
    between the different peoples in the world;

that we should not forget
that the goods in this world
were created and meant for everybody;
that we should cherish the culture and technology
that contribute to human liberation,
recognizing their limits;
and that we should insist
that the more developed nations
should help the developing countries.

8. This approach was new for three reasons.
   First: the term "development"
   comes from the vocabulary
   of the social and economic sciences.
   Pope Paul VI, however, emphasized
   the ethical and cultural character
   of the problems connected with development
   and the need of the church's intervention
   offering principles, norms, and directives,
   applying the Gospel.

9. A second newness is the wider outlook.
   It is the first time that the "social question"
   is seen in a worldwide, global dimension.
   Those problems did not lose their national or local importance,
   but they should no longer be seen
   as isolated and disconnected cases.
     The developing nations are more numerous
     than the developed nations.
     There is an unequal distribution of goods,
     neither through the fault of the poor,
     nor through a sort of inevitability.
   Christians, especially political leaders
   and citizens of rich countries,
   must be conscious of this fact
   and take it into consideration
   in their personal decisions
   and governmental decisions.
     This moral obligation
     is the duty of solidarity.
   Development should be defined
   taking into account our universal interdependence.
   Development cannot consist
   in the simple accumulation of wealth
   and the greater availability of goods and services
   at the expense of the development of the masses.

10. Third, we see the originality of
    On the Development of Peoples
    best in its best-remembered sentence
    — its summary and its historic label:
    "Development is the new name for peace."
    All over the world victims of injustice
    are tempted to respond with violence
    at those who first treated them with violence,
    as happens at the beginning
    of so many wars and conflicts.
       How can one justify the fact
       that huge sums of money,
       which could and should be spent
       on the development of the destitute,
       are used for the enrichment of some
       or to stockpile weapons?
    If development is the new name for peace,
    war and preparations for war
    are the major enemy
    of the healthy development of peoples.
       If we take the common good of all humanity
       as our norm,
       — their "spiritual and human development" —
       instead of individual greed,
       peace would be possible.

III. SURVEY OF THE CONTEMPORARY WORLD

11. Though the publication
    of the *Development of Peoples*
    was acclaimed for its novelty twenty years ago,
    the social conditions in which we live
    are no longer the same.
       So let us have a look
       at the world as it is now.

12. The first fact to note is
    that the optimistic hopes of development at that time
    appear far from realized.
    This in spite of some real individual
    and combined national efforts
    promoted by the United Nations Organization.

13. Certain results were achieved,
       but no one can deny
       that the present situation is negative.

Though it would suffice to face squarely
the hundreds of millions of people
whose situation got worse,
let us give some indicators
of the sad state of our world.

14. First, there is the persistent and widening gap
between the more developed North
and the developing South —
    though there are some pockets
    of appalling poverty in the North
    and a good number
    who are scandalously rich in the South.
The major part of humanity, living in the South,
lag far behind in food, availability of drinking water,
hygiene, health, and housing,
working conditions (especially for women),
and life expectancy.
    As the rate of progress in the North
    is more rapid than that in the South
    the underdeveloped nations find themselves
    falling behind faster and faster.
No wonder that we speak about different worlds
in our one world:
    the First World, the Second World,
    the Third World, and sometimes even the Fourth World.
These names are a sign
that things do not go well,
that our unity is compromised.
    We in the church
    — believing in the unity of the human race —
    cannot remain indifferent to this situation.

15. There are other,
even more disturbing evils
due to underdevelopment:
lack of education, illiteracy,
the impossibility of a higher education,
inability to share in the building of one's nation,
various forms of exploitation,
economic, social, political, and even religious oppression
of the individual's rights,
and discrimination, of which the meanest is racism.
    Another form of oppression
    is the denial of the right
    to economic initiative.

Experience shows
that the denial of this right
diminishes and destroys
the spirit of resourcefulness.
Everyone is leveled down
to a false and unwholesome equality,
leading to passivity, dependence,
and submission to an all-embracing bureaucracy
that is bad for all.
Not only Third World individuals
but even Third World nations
are sometimes deprived of the right
to determine their own economic,
political, social, and cultural life.
 Something else should be noted here.
 No one political party in a nation
 has the right to become the sole leader,
 a situation that always leads to a dictatorship
 where persons do not count,
 in spite of all that is said to the contrary.
Poverty is not only
a question of having no material goods.
Is the lack of human rights
not also a form of poverty?
 Maybe we have been thinking too much
 of poverty only as something economic.

16. Responsibility for the deterioration
 from bad to worse in so many underdeveloped regions
 rests on both the developing nations,
 especially on those holding economic and political power,
 and on the more developed nations,
 which have not made a sufficiently great effort.
  One must denounce
  the economic, financial, and social
  mechanisms and structures
  that are manipulated
  by the rich and powerful
  for their own benefit at the expense of the poor.

17. The world is now so interdependent
 that either all the nations of the world
 participate in a just way,
 or it will not be true development.
  One of the indicators of this lack of development
  is homelessness.

The housing crisis afflicts developing nations
but also developed nations.

18. Another common indicator
    of this lack of development
    is unemployment.
    The number of unemployed in the developed world
    in 1987 was 8 percent, or 29 million men and women.
    Unemployment in the developing nations
    is much greater.

19. A third indicator is the international debt.
    The hope had been to invest loans in development,
    but now the debtor nations find themselves in a position
    of exporting their capital to service their loans,
    thus crunching their own people's meager standard of living.
    The borrowed money became counterproductive.

20. One of the reasons for the delay
    in the process of development
    is the division of the world into two blocs,
    the East and the West—
    the capitalistic West and the communist East.
    Each bloc has its own ideology,
    its own propaganda and indoctrination.
    The opposition between the two
    is also a military one.
    This tension, which sometimes has taken
    the form of "cold war"
    and at other times has led to wars "by proxy,"
    has dominated the period after the Second World War.
    And though recently some progress has been made
    —agreeing on the destruction of one type of nuclear arms—
    the threat remains.

21. Neither the East's nor the West's
    ideas of development are perfect.
    Both systems need the correction
    of the church's social teaching.
    Many countries that recently have become independent
    are aware that they are involved
    in the struggle between those two blocs.
    This danger made some of them organize themselves
    into the International Movement for Non-Aligned Nations.

22. They were becoming mere cogs
    on the gigantic wheel of one of the two blocs.

Besides, both blocs got so concerned about their security
that astronomical amounts of money were spent on weapons,
instead of on development of the poorer nations.

23. It is urgent that the opposition
between the East and the West
be overcome and that their leadership
be willing to contribute to the common good.

24. The arms race, the production of arms,
the stockpiling of nuclear weapons, and the arms trade
are moral distortions in a world crying for justice.
They lead us more quickly to death
than to life and development.
The results of all this are millions of refugees
and many acts of terrorism.

25. Something must be said
about the population growth.
In the South there is the problem of very high birth rates,
while in the North the birth rate has dropped.
Attempts to solve these population problems
must respect the freedom of choice
and the difference in cultures.
It is wrong for richer nations
to economically force the poorer nations
to restrict their birth rate.

26. This survey of the world in which we live
would be incomplete if we did not mention
its positive points.
An ever increasing number of people are aware
of their human dignity and rights.
The Declaration of Human Rights
played a great role in this growing concern
not only for the rights of individuals
but also of nations and peoples,
each with its own culture and identity.
The conviction is growing that being radically interdependent
we have a common destiny and are in need of solidarity.
The desire for peace is intensifying.
We understand better
that peace is for all or for none.
We are more aware of the limits of our resources,
and of the need to respect nature.
More and more leaders are committed
to try to heal the world's ills.

Our great international and regional organizations
are a great help in all this.
    Some Third World countries
    have succeeded in reaching
    a certain self-sufficiency and development.

IV. AUTHENTIC HUMAN DEVELOPMENT

27. Development is not an easy, automatic,
    and limitless process.
    The old and optimistic dream
    of a spontaneous and continuous progress
    was shattered by what happened to us during this century.

28.   Getting richer
        or technologically better equipped
        does not make for happiness.
    Unless these developments are guided
    by moral understanding
    and the true good of the human race,
    they easily become oppressive.
        Next to the *underdevelopment* of the many,
        there is a *superdevelopment* for the few.
        Superdevelopment leads to a throwaway society
        and to enormous waste.
        Excessive access to all kinds of things,
        —sometimes called consumerism—
        enslaves people and does not make them happy.
    The more one possesses,
    the more one wants,
    while the deeper human hopes
    remain unsatisfied and even stifled.
        "Having" more things
        does not necessarily mean "being" more
        or being better.
    "Having" only helps us
    when it contributes
    to a more complete "being."
        The present picture is
        that there are *the few* who possess much
        but who are stunted in "being"
        because they want more and more;
        and there are *the many* who having little or nothing
        and who do not succeed in realizing
        their basic human vocation.

29. Material goods
    and the way we are developing the use of them
    should be seen as God's gifts to us.
    They are meant to bring out in each one of us
    the image of God.
    We must never lose sight of how we have been created:
    from the *earth* and from the *breath* of God.
        In this way we are related to the rest of creation,
        and we are asked to use creation
        according to the will of God,
        to whom we are related too.
    Human beings having a divine likeness
    and created from the beginning as a couple
    — and therefore social —
    are called to immortality.
        Our use of creation
        and human development in general
        should be related to that vocation.

30. Development and growth
    belong to humanity's vocation.
    The story of humankind in Sacred Scripture
    is one of constant achievements.
    In his turn Jesus asked us to use our talents
    and make them fruitful.
        All should work together
        for the full development of others:
        "development of the whole human being
        and of all people."

31. Faith in Christ should guide us
    in this task of working together.
    Part of God's plan in Christ includes precisely
    our personal and common effort
    to upraise the human condition
    and to overcome all the difficulties
    along our way.
        Humanity's dream of "unlimited progress"
        is validated as we are called
        to share in Christ's glory.
        Struggling against underdevelopment
        and superdevelopment,
        our corruptible bodies
        will one day put on incorruptibility,
        when all valuable human works and actions
        will be conserved and redeemed.

No wonder that in the early church
some had an optimistic vision
of human history and human effort.
They believed in the lasting value
of true human accomplishments,
and their contribution to God's kingdom
in Jesus Christ.
   From of old the church understood and felt
   that it is our task to relieve
   the misery of the suffering,
   both far and near.
The needs of the poor even outweigh
the "need" for costly decorations, vestments,
and utensils in worship.
   It could be obligatory to sell those goods
   in order to provide food, drink, clothing, and shelter
   for those who lack these things.

32. To commit oneself
    to the development of the whole person
    and every human being
    is an obligation not only for the individual,
    but also for societies and nations,
    and especially for the Catholic community
    and the other Christian churches.
    The Catholic Church is eager to collaborate
    with those other churches
    and other religions.
       Collaboration in this development
       is a duty for all and toward all,
       East, West, North, South.
    If people try to achieve it in only one part of the world,
    they can do it only at the expense of others,
    and their own development will be jeopardized.
       This need for development
       may not be used to impose on others
       one's own way of life or own religious belief.

33. True development must respect and promote
    personal, social, economic, and political human rights,
    including the rights of nations and of peoples.
    Mere economic development
    makes the human person prisoner
    of economic planning and selfish profit.
       If there is no respect
       for the moral, cultural, and spiritual dimensions

of the human person,
material gains, goods, and technical resources
will prove unsatisfactory and even debasing.
"What, then, will anyone gain
by winning the whole world
and forfeiting his life?" (Mt 16:26).
In every nation and society
this implies and presupposes a lively awareness
of the rights of each and every person,
the right to life at every stage of its existence,
the rights of the family as the basic social community,
justice in labor relations, political rights,
and religious freedom.
  On the international level
  there must be respect
  for the identity of each people,
  with its own culture and history.
  All have an equal right
  to be seated at the common table,
  instead of lying outside the door like Lazarus.
True development
must be based on love of God and neighbor.
  In the words of Pope Paul VI:
  it will be a "civilization of love."

34. We even have to respect
the natural world around us.
We cannot use the different kinds of beings
— animals, plants, minerals —
simply as we wish.
We have to take their nature into account.
  We should realize
  that our natural resources are limited.
We should be aware of the consequences
of the use of those resources, the pollution of our world,
with its serious consequences for our health.
  All these considerations show us again
  the moral dimension of these matters.

V. A THEOLOGICAL READING OF MODERN PROBLEMS

35. The reasons that development does not proceed
are not only economic.
Political motives play their role.
An effective political will is needed.

Sadly, that will has been lacking.
  Why was this?
  What are the reasons
  that people hinder development?
  Why are decisions not made to use
  the available scientific and technical resources
  to help people to develop?

36. A world divided into blocs,
    in which instead of solidarity
    imperialism and exploitation hold sway,
    can only be a world *structured in sin.*
      Those structures of sin
      are rooted in sins committed by individual persons,
      who introduced these structures
      and reenforced them again and again.
    One can blame selfishness,
    shortsightedness, mistaken political decisions,
    and imprudent economic decisions;
    at the root of the evils that afflict the world
    there is — in one way or another — sin.
      God's will, God's plan for humanity,
      God's mercy and justice
      — expressed in the ten commandments —
      are not respected.

37. Among the actions and attitudes opposed to God's will
    two are very typical:
    greed and the thirst for power.
      Not only individuals sin in that way;
      so do nations and world-blocs.
      That is why we spoke of
      "structures of sin."
    Hidden behind all kinds of so-called
    economic or political considerations,
    are real forms of idolatry:
    the worship of money, ideology,
    class, and technology.
      The evil that afflicts the world
      is a moral evil.
      That it is sin
      also indicates what we should do about it,
      what path to follow.

38. It is a long and difficult path,
    but we have to set out on it.

We have to be converted.
We have to change our spiritual relationship
with self, with neighbor,
with even the remotest human communities,
and with nature itself,
in view of the common good
of the whole individual and of all people.
To use the language of the Bible, we have to be converted.
The growing awareness of our interdependence
among individuals and nations,
the growing concern
for the injustices and violations of human rights
even in far-off countries,
can help in that conversion.
    This felt interdependence is a new moral category,
      and the response to it is the "virtue" of *solidarity*.
Solidarity is not a feeling of vague compassion
or a shallow sadness
but a firm and persevering determination
to commit oneself to the common good.
    It is an attitude squarely opposed
    to greed and the thirst for power.

39. The exercise of solidarity is valid
when members of each society
recognize others as persons —
the more influential feeling responsible for the weaker,
the weaker doing what they can for the good of all,
and the intermediate groups respecting the interests of the others.
    Positive signs in our world
    are the growing awareness of the solidarity
    of the poor among themselves
    and their efforts to support each other,
    even to the point of nonviolent demonstrations
    to present their needs and rights
    to oftentimes corrupt and inefficient authorities.
The same yardstick can be used in international relations.
Interdependence must be transformed into solidarity,
grounded on the principle that
the goods of creation are meant for all.
    Avoiding every type of imperialism,
    the stronger nations must
    feel responsible for the other nations,
    based on the equality of all peoples
    and with respect for the differences.

Solidarity helps us to see the "other"
as our neighbor, as a helper,
to be made a sharer in the banquet of life
to which all are equally invited by God.
  Solidarity is the path to peace
  and at the same time to development.
  Interdependence demands
  the abandonment of blocs,
  the sacrifice of all forms of economic,
  military, or political imperialism
  and the conversion of distrust into collaboration.
  The fruit of solidarity is peace.

40. Solidarity is a Christian virtue.
  It seeks to go beyond itself
  to total gratuity, forgiveness, and reconciliation.
  It leads to a new vision of the unity of humankind,
  a reflection of God's triune intimate life;
  it leads to *communion*.

VI. GUIDELINES

41. The church has no technical solutions to offer,
  but being an "expert in humanity"
  the church has something to say
  about the nature, conditions, requirements, and aims
  of authentic development
  and the obstacles that stand in its way.
    The church's social teaching
    is not a third way between capitalism and communism.
    It is not an ideology.
    Its aim is to guide Christians.
    It asks for a "commitment to justice."

42. A consistent theme of Catholic social teaching is
  the option or love of preference for the poor.
  Today, this preference has to be expressed
  in worldwide dimensions,
  embracing the immense numbers of the hungry,
  the needy, the homeless, those without medical care,
  and those without hope.
    Another characteristic principle of this teaching is
      that the goods of the world
      are originally meant for all.
    The right to private property is valid,
    but all private property is under a "social mortgage."

43. Concern for the poor must be translated at all levels
into concrete actions:
— reform of the international trade system
— reform of the world's monetary and financial system
— a more just use of technology exchanges
— a review and updating of the existing international organizations.

44. Above all, development demands
that the needy countries have a spirit of initiative,
favoring the self-affirmation of each citizen
and helping themselves in such areas
as literacy, basic education,
adequate food production,
and reformation of political institutions.

45. The less affluent nations of the same area
should establish forms of cooperation
that will make them less dependent
on more powerful producers.
They should come together in partnership
to be able to accomplish together
what they cannot do on their own.

VII. CONCLUSION

46. Peoples and individuals aspire to be free,
a noble and legitimate desire.
Human beings are totally free
only when they are completely themselves
in the fullness of their rights and duties.
    The main obstacle to that freedom
    is sin and the structures produced by sin.
    The freedom Jesus gave us
    encourages us to become
    the servants of all.

47. Even though the world situation looks grim,
there is no reason for despair.
In human beings there exists
a fundamental goodness,
and the history of today
is open to the future of the kingdom of God.
We are all called, indeed obliged,
to face the challenge of the last ten years
of the second millennium.

One may sin by greed and the desire for power,
but one may also sin in these matters
through fear, indecision, and cowardice!
Every individual is called to play his or her part
in this peaceful campaign to secure *development in peace*.
I appeal to all
to be convinced of the seriousness of the moment,
to fulfill your commitment by the way you live,
by the use of your resources,
by your civic activity,
by contributing to economic and political decisions,
and by personal involvement
in national and international undertakings.
I address all those baptized,
but likewise the Jewish people,
as well as the Muslims,
and the followers of the world's religions.

48. However imperfect and temporary are all things
that can and ought to be done
in order to make people's lives "more human,"
nothing will be lost or will have been done in vain.
It will all serve for the coming
of the definitive kingdom of God.

49. In these difficult moments in our world,
I entrust to Mary and to her intercession
all that I have written in this letter
and all the efforts being made to contribute
to the true development of peoples.
Her maternal concern
extends to all the personal and social aspects
of people's life on earth.

Father, you have given all peoples one common origin,
and your will is to gather them as one family in yourself.
Fill the hearts of all with the fire of your love
and the desire to ensure justice for all our brothers and sisters.
By sharing the good things you give us
may we secure justice and equality for every human being,
an end to all division,
and a human society built on love and peace.

8

The Mission of the Redeemer
Redemptoris Missio

December 7, 1990

Jesus prayed: "That they all may be one," that they may realize that they form the one family of God. Announcing this "good news" of forming the one family of God is the church's mission. Jesus lived this Kin(g)dom of God among us, and equipped with his Spirit we share his mission of "gathering together the scattered children of God." It is a mission we have hardly begun in our urbanized, networking, and pluralistic world, where proclamation by deeds often counts more than words. It asks for a renewed effort as regards Christian unity and continuous interreligious dialogue. Everyone in the church should be engaged in this work as individuals and as members of their Christian communities.

INTRODUCTION

1. The mission of Christ the Redeemer
   entrusted to the church
   is far from being completed.
   As the second millennium after Christ's birth
   draws to an end, this mission is only beginning.
   It is the Spirit who impels us:
   "Woe to me if I do not preach the Gospel" (1 Cor 9:16).
   I sense an urgent need
   to repeat this cry of Saint Paul.
   I have traveled to the ends of the earth
   to show this mission concern,
   and these travels convinced me
   of the urgency of mission activity.

The Second Vatican Council stressed
the church's missionary nature,
so "that they all may be one" (Jn 17:21).

2. There has been an increase of local churches,
   Christian communities are more evident,
   the communion of churches has enriched us,
   the commitment of the laity is changing the church's life,
   ecumenical dialogue and cooperation are growing,
   and there is a new awareness that mission
   is a matter for all Christians.
        However, there is also
        an undeniable negative tendency.
        The mission "to the nations" is waning.
        Internal and external difficulties
        have weakened the missionary thrust.
   This fact causes concern,
   for the missionary drive has always been
   a sign of vitality.
        Missionary activity renews the church,
        but even more important
        it is the primary service
        that the church can render individuals
        and humanity alike in the modern world,
        giving meaning to its life.
   There are many other reasons for this document:
        — to respond to the many demands to write it,
        — to clear up existing doubts about mission,
        — to confirm missionaries in their dedication,
        — to foster mission vocations,
        — to encourage systematic mission studies,
        — to give a fresh impulse to missionary work
          especially in young churches,
        — and finally to convince everyone
          that mission is meant to serve humankind
          by unveiling God's love as revealed in Jesus Christ.

3. *Open the doors to Christ, people everywhere!*
   You do not lose your freedom
   by opening yourself up to the Word of God.
        The number of those who do not know about Christ
        is constantly on the increase.
        It has doubled since the end of the Second Vatican Council.
   There are new opportunities:
        — oppressive political systems have collapsed,
        — closed frontiers have opened up,

— communications have increased,

— Gospel values like justice, fellowship,
   and concern for the needy are affirmed,

— and a soulless economy and technology
   stimulate the search for God and meaning in life.

The moment has come to commit all the church's energies
to a new evangelization and mission to all.

Chapter One:
JESUS CHRIST, THE ONLY SAVIOR

4. As I have written before:
the church's function is to direct the whole of humanity
toward the mystery of Christ (cf. RH 10).

   "For each one is included in the mystery of the redemption,
   and with each one Christ has united himself
   forever throughout history" (RH 13).

Some wonder whether in our days
mission has not been replaced
by interreligious dialogue,
or whether human development
is not its adequate goal.

   Does our respect for conscience and freedom
   not exclude all effort at conversion?

   Is it not possible to attain salvation in any religion?

   Why then should there be missionary activity?

"No One Comes to the Father but by Me" (Jn 14:6)

5. Peter's statement before the Sanhedrin,
that there is salvation in no one else
but Jesus Christ (cf. Acts 4:12),
has a universal value.

   The universality of this salvation
   is asserted throughout the New Testament:
   Paul acknowledges Christ as the Lord,
   and according to John Christ is the Word
   that enlightens every human being (Jn 1:9).
   It is in Christ that God reveals to humanity
   who God is in the fullest way.
   This definitive self-revelation of God
   is the reason why the church is missionary.

No one can enter into communion with God
except through Christ by the working of the Holy Spirit.
Christ's mediation, far from being an obstacle
on the journey toward God,

is the way established by God,
though it does not exclude
participated forms of mediation.

6. One cannot separate the "Jesus of history"
   from the "Christ of faith."
   Christ is none other than Jesus of Nazareth.
   In him "the whole fullness of deity dwells bodily" (Col 2:9).
   It is this uniqueness of Christ
   that makes him history's center and goal,
   "the Alpha and Omega" (Rev 22:13).
   God's plan is "to unite all things in Christ" (Eph 1:10).

Faith in Christ Is Directed to Humanity's Freedom

7. Missionary activity derives its urgency
   from the radical newness of life brought by Christ,
   granting "participation in the very life of God:
   Father, Son, and Holy Spirit" (DM 7).
   But the human being is free;
   we can say no to God.
   "Is it legitimate to do this?"

8. In the modern world one tends
   to reduce the human being
   to the horizontal dimension only.
   What men and women become in this way
   is experienced by each individual,
   and it also written in the history of humanity
   with the blood shed in the name of ideologies
   that hoped to build a "new humanity" without God.
   Each human being
   has the right to religious freedom;
   and proclaiming Christ respects consciences
   and does not violate freedom.
   The "multitudes have the right to know
   the riches of the mystery of Christ....
   This is why the church keeps its missionary spirit alive
   and even wants to intensify it in the moment of history
   in which we are living" (EN 53).
   All human beings are impelled
   and bound — by their own nature —
   to seek religious truth.

The Church as Sign and Instrument of Salvation

9. The church is Christ's co-worker
   in the salvation of the world.

Christ dwells in the church.
She is his bride.
He causes her to grow,
carrying out his mission through her.
    These two truths should be kept together:
    the possibility of salvation for all in Christ
    and the necessity of the church for salvation.
In this way we come to know God's mercy
and our own responsibility.
The church is sent on a mission to the whole world,
to be its light and its salt.

Salvation in Christ Is Offered to All

10. Since salvation is offered to all,
it must be made available to all.
Many do not have the opportunity
to come to know the Gospel
or to enter the church.
    For such people salvation in Christ
    is accessible by virtue of a grace,
    of a mysterious relationship to the church,
    that does not make them formal members,
    but that enlightens them in a way
    accommodated to their situation.
This grace comes from Christ;
it is the result of his sacrifice,
and it is communicated by the Holy Spirit.
It enables each person to attain salvation
through his or her free cooperation.

We Cannot but Speak

11. The church cannot fail to proclaim
that Jesus came to reveal the face of God
and to merit salvation for all humankind
by his cross and resurrection.
    To the question "Why mission?"
    we reply that true liberation consists
    in opening oneself to the love of Christ.
We are tempted these days to secularize salvation and
to reduce Christianity to a pseudo-science of well-being
of a merely horizontal dimension.
Jesus came to bring *integral* salvation
to the whole person and the whole of humanity
opening up the prospect of divine filiation.

Why mission?
Because the newness of life in Christ
is the good news all are searching for,
albeit at times in a confused way.
Everyone has the right to know it,
and we are not allowed to keep it hidden from them
or to monopolize it.
    The church's mission does not derive only
    from the Lord's mandate,
    but also from the demands of God's life in us.

Chapter Two:
THE KINGDOM OF GOD

12. Jesus reveals to us God the Father's mercy.
    God chose Israel to witness to that mercy
    and to realize in the course of its history
    how its election had a universal meaning (cf. Is 2:2–5).

Christ Makes the Kingdom Present

13. Jesus of Nazareth brings God's plan to fulfillment.
    After his baptism he goes about Galilee preaching that
        "the time is fulfilled,
        the kingdom of God is at hand;
        repent and believe in the good news" (Mk 1:14–15).
    Jesus himself is the "good news";
    there is an identity between the message and the messenger,
    between saying, doing, and being.
    Jesus proclaims the "good news" by what he is.
        Before Easter the scope of his mission
        was focused on Israel,
        but his encounter with gentiles
        makes it clear that entry into the kingdom
        comes through faith and conversion
        and not by reason of ethnic background.
    The kingdom he preaches is not something
    to come at "the end of the world."
    It should be prayed for,
    and it is already at work in Jesus' miracles and exorcisms,
    in the choosing of the Twelve,
    and the proclamation to the poor.
        Jesus inaugurates the kingdom of God,
        whom he addresses as "Abba" (cf. Mk 14:36),
        a Father who is sensitive to the needs and sufferings
        of each and every human being,

granting forgiveness and bestowing gifts.
As John tells us, "God is love" (1 Jn 4:8).

Characteristics of the Kingdom and Its Demands

14. Jesus shows that the kingdom is for all
by reaching out to those on the margins of society.
He comes close to them, eating in their homes,
treating them as equals and friends.
He makes them feel loved by God.
    Two of Jesus' gestures are characteristic:
    healing and *forgiving.*
    His healing leads to salvation;
    it is a sign that "the kingdom of God has come" (Mt 12:28).

15. Before leaving, Jesus gives a new commandment:
"Love one another,
even as I have loved you" (Jn 13:34) —
a love that found its highest expression
in the gift of his life.
    God's kingdom is the concern of everyone.
    Working for it means promoting God's activity,
    present in human history and transforming it.
    It means working at liberation from evil in all its forms
    and at the realization of God's plan.

In the Risen Christ God's Kingdom Is Fulfilled and Proclaimed

16. In the risen Jesus God inaugurated God's kingdom.
Jesus was its prophet, it was already present in him,
and it is established in humanity and the world
in connection with him.
    After the resurrection his disciples proclaimed Jesus Christ
    with whom the kingdom was identified.
    The need to unite the two in our proclamation remains.
    The two are complementary; each throws light on the other.

The Kingdom in Relation to Christ and the Church

17. Nowadays the kingdom is not always spoken of
in a way consonant with the thinking of the church.
It is sometimes done in an anthropocentric way,
reducing it to earthly needs,
expressed in socioeconomic, political, and even cultural ways,
closed to the transcendent.
    There are values to be promoted at that level;
    the kingdom of God is, however,
    not one of purely earthly progress.

Others think that the church should be "kingdom-centered"
promoting values such as peace, justice, freedom, and dialogue,
without concern about itself.
    Together with positive aspects in all this,
    there are some negative aspects as well.
    The kingdom they speak of is "God-centered,"
    and they maintain that one cannot speak about *"Christ"*
    to those who lack a Christian faith,
    while one can find common ground in the one divine reality.
    For the same reason they stress creation,
    keeping silent about redemption,
    and leaving little room for the church.

18. This is not the kingdom of God
    as we know it from revelation.
    It is in Christ that the kingdom itself
    became present and was fulfilled.
    The kingdom is not a doctrine;
    it is before all else a person
    with the face and name of Jesus of Nazareth,
    the image of the invisible God.
    If the kingdom is separated from Jesus,
    it is no longer the kingdom of God.
        One may not separate the kingdom from the church either.
        Though not an end unto itself,
        the church is ordered toward the kingdom of God,
        being its seed, sign, and instrument.
        The Holy Spirit dwells in it
        and, while not restricted to its confines,
        gives it a special role announcing and inaugurating
        the kingdom of God.

19. The promotion of human and evangelical values
    is at the heart of the church,
    but it should not be detached from tasks such as
    proclaiming Christ and his Gospel
    and establishing communities
    that present the living image of the kingdom of God.

The Church at the Service of the Kingdom

20. The church serves the kingdom
        — in preaching the call to conversion,
        — by establishing and guiding new communities,
        — by spreading "Gospel values" throughout the world,
        — by being a dynamic force in humanity's journey
            toward the eschatological kingdom,

— by its prayer and intercession asking for the kingdom,
until the time Christ "delivers the kingdom to the Father"
and "God will be everything to everyone" (cf. 1 Cor. 15:24, 28).

Chapter Three:
THE HOLY SPIRIT, PRINCIPAL AGENT OF MISSION

21. Jesus entrusts his mission to human beings,
but in and through them the Holy Spirit remains the principal agent
for the accomplishment of this work.
From the early church onward (cf. Acts 10, 15, 16:6ff.),
the Spirit's action is especially at work in the mission *ad gentes*,"
working not only in the apostles but also in those who heard them.

Sent Forth "to the End of the Earth" (Acts 1:8)

22. All the evangelists end their Gospels
with the "missionary mandate"
(cf. Mt 28:18–20, Mk 16:15–18, Lk 24:46–49, Jn 20:21–23).
Christ sends his own into the world
as the Father has sent him,
and to this end he gives them the Spirit.

23. The different "missionary" mandates in the Gospels
have things in common and things that are proper to each.
The two elements they all have in common are:
— they are sent to "all nations"
— they will not be alone in their task:
"the Lord worked with them" (Mk 16:20).
As for the differences:
— Mark stresses the "preaching"
— Matthew emphasizes the "foundation of the church"
— Luke centers on the "resurrection and conversion"
— John speaks explicitly of a "mandate":
we are sent as Christ was sent,
we share in the communion that exists
between the Father and the Son
living in unity with one another,
so that the world may believe (cf. Jn 17:21–23).

The four Gospels bear witness to a pluralism
within a unity of the same mission,
a pluralism that reflects differences
within the first communities.

It makes us pay attention to the variety of missionary charisms
and to the diversity of circumstances and peoples.

The Spirit Directs the Church

24. The mission of the church
    is the work of the Spirit.
    The Spirit told the first evangelizers where to go
    and that it was not necessary for a gentile
    to submit to the Jewish law (cf. Acts 15:5–11),
    opening the door to all and making them feel at home
    while keeping their own culture and traditions,
    provided these are not contrary to the Gospel.

25. Along this path Paul dialogues
    on cosmic religion with the Lyaconians
    and on philosophy with the Greeks,
    showing them that the God Paul wants to preach
    is already to be found in their lives.
    His speeches are an example of inculturation.

The Holy Spirit Makes the Whole Church Missionary

26. The Spirit makes the believers form a community,
    to be the church.
    They live being "one in heart and soul"
    in "communion," in prayer, and in the Eucharist,
    all receiving "as they need" (cf. Acts 2:45, 4:35).
    They enjoyed "favor with all the people" (Acts 2:47).
    Even before activity, mission means witness,
    a way of life that shines out to others.

27. From the beginning "mission" developed at different levels.
    While the early church had missionaries,
    dedicated for life by a special vocation to it
    — like the Twelve and special envoys —
    the mission "ad gentes"
    was the normal outcome of Christian living
    to which every believer was committed.

The Spirit Is Present and Active in Every Time and Place

28. Though in a special way present in believers,
    the Spirit is at work in the heart of every person,
    in all times and in all places,
    stirring and affecting not only individuals,
    but also society and history,
    sowing the seeds of the word,
    preparing them for full maturity in Christ.

29. The Holy Spirit was already at work
    before Christ was glorified (AG 4),
    filling the world and holding all things together (cf. Wis 1:7).
       This fact guided me in meetings,
       like the one in Assisi,
       confirming my conviction that
       "every authentic prayer is prompted by the Holy Spirit,
       who is mysteriously present in every human heart."*
    This is the same Spirit who was at work
    in the incarnation
    in the life, death, and resurrection of Jesus Christ,
    and who is at work in the church.
       The universal activity of the Spirit
       is not to be separated from the Spirit
       at work in the church,
       in those who have the responsibility of discerning it.

Missionary Activity Is Only Beginning

30. Our own time asks for the resurgence
    of the church's missionary activity.
    We have been celebrating recently
    all kinds of mission millenniums and centenaries;
    we must now face the new challenges.

Chapter Four:
THE VAST HORIZONS OF THE MISSION
AD GENTES

31. "The church was sent by Christ
    to reveal and communicate the love of God
    to all people and nations" (AG 10).
    The church cannot withdraw from its mission
    of bringing the Gospel to the multitudes.

A Complex and Ever Changing Religious Picture

32. The contemporary religious situation is complex.
    Urbanization, mass migration, refugees,
    de-Christianization of Christian countries,
    Christian influences in non-Christian ones,
    messianic cults, and religious sects
    have done away with religious realities
    that were once clear and well defined.

---

*Address to Cardinals and the Roman Curia, December 22, 1986, 11.

Christian cities and regions
became mission territories.
    Traditionally non-Christian areas
    are sending missionaries,
    and traditionally Christian areas
    are in need of them.
Some ask whether it is still proper
to speak of "missions" and "missionaries."
Some prefer to speak about "mission" in the singular
and to use "missionary" as an adjective
to describe *all* the church's activities.
    This uneasiness shows a real change.
    In this way mission is not considered
    as a marginal task of the church,
    but it risks putting different activities
    at the same level and reducing or even eliminating
    a specific mission *ad gentes*.

Mission Ad Gentes *Retains Its Value*

33. We can distinguish three situations:
    — the church addressing peoples and contexts
      in which Christ and his Gospel are not known
      or are not yet sufficiently incarnated
      to proclaim it to other groups:
      this is mission *ad gentes* in the proper sense.
    — Christian communities with adequate ecclesial structures,
      fervent in their faith and committed to mission:
      in these communities the church
      carries out its pastoral mission.
    — An intermediate situation, where groups of the baptized,
      no longer consider themselves members of the church:
      this is a situation that is in need of "reevangelization."

34. Missionary activity in the proper sense
    (the mission *ad gentes*)
    is directed to those
    who do not yet believe in Christ,
    in whom the church has not yet taken root,
    and whose culture
    has not yet been influenced by the Gospel.
It is different from any other church activity,
though the boundaries between pastoral care and missionary activity
are not clearly definable.
    But this should not lessen the urge
    to bring the Gospel *ad gentes*.

Besides, the three above-mentioned different ministries
definitely influence, stimulate, and support each other.

To All Peoples, in Spite of Difficulties

35. The mission *ad gentes* faces an enormous task.
    Its horizon is ever wider,
    demographically and socio-culturally.
        If it were a merely human enterprise
        the difficulties would seem insurmountable.

36. The internal difficulties within the people of God
    are the most painful of all:
        — the lack of fervor,
        — the division among Christians,
        — the de-Christianization in Christian countries,
        — the decrease of vocations,
        — the counterwitness of believers,
        — and most serious of all the widespread indifferentism,
            characterized by a religious relativism,
            believing that "one religion is as good as another."
    These difficulties should not make us pessimistic,
    since we are certain
    that the principal agents of the church's mission
    are Jesus Christ and his Spirit.

Parameters of the Church's Mission Ad Gentes

37. Certain parameters can help us gain
    a real grasp of the mission situation.

(a) *Territorial Limits*
    The criterion of geography,
    though imprecise and provisional,
    is still a valid indicator of the frontiers
    toward which missionary activity must be directed.
    There are countries and cultural areas
    without any Christian communities,
    or where those communities are too small
    to be a clear sign of a Christian presence.
    This is particularly true in Asia,
    toward which the church's mission *ad gentes*
    ought to be chiefly directed.

(b) *New Worlds and New Social Phenomena*
    In some countries in the southern hemisphere
    over half the population lives in a few "megalopolises."
    Efforts should be concentrated on these big cities.

We should not overlook
the most abandoned and isolated human groups,
but we should not neglect the centers
where a new humanity is arising.
The future is being shaped in the cities.
   We cannot forget the young,
     who in many countries form half of the population.
     Ordinary pastoral work will not suffice;
     we need modern ecclesial movements.
Migrations have brought numerous non-Christians
to traditionally Christian countries.
Among them refugees deserve special attention;
the church must make them part of its overall pastoral concern.
     Finally, we mention the poor;
     mission must become the means of restoring
     the human dignity of these people.

(c) *Cultural Sectors*
The first Areopagus in the modern age
is the world of communications,
turning humankind into a "global village."
We neglected the mass media.
We should not only use them
but integrate our message
into that new culture,
though this will be a complex issue.
   There are other forms of the "Areopagus"
   toward which we should direct our mission:
      — the commitment to peace,
      — the development of the nations,
      — human rights,
      — the rights of minorities,
      — the advancement of women and children,
      — safeguarding the created world,
      — the whole area of scientific research,
      — and the world of international relations.

38. The modern phenomenon of "religious revival,"
though not without ambiguity,
represents an opportunity for the church's mission.

Fidelity to Christ and the Promotion of Human Freedom

39. By proclaiming Jesus Christ
one furthers human freedom.
The church has the obligation
and the right to carry out its mission.

Religious freedom remains the premise
and the guarantee of all other freedoms.
It should be granted everywhere
as an inalienable right of everyone.
  Open the doors to Christ!
  The Gospel spirit should overcome
  all national and cultural barriers.

Directing Attention toward the South and the East

40. Missionary activity
    is the greatest challenge for the church.
    Toward the end of the second millennium
    the majority of humankind
    has not yet heard about Jesus Christ.
      The church is established on every continent;
      the majority of believers and churches
      are no longer found in Europe.
      Yet "the ends of the earth"
      are growing ever more distant.
      New peoples appear on the world scene;
      the population in the non-Christian South and East
      is constantly increasing the number of people
      unaware of Christ's redemption.
      They need our attention.

Chapter Five:
THE PATHS OF MISSION

41. Missionary activity is nothing other
    and nothing else than the manifestation of God's plan.
    What paths does the church follow
    to achieve this "epiphany"?

The First Form of Evangelization Is Witness

42. People put more trust in witnesses
    than in teachers (cf. EN 41).
    The witness of a Christian life is the first
    and irreplaceable form of mission:
    Christ is the "witness" par excellence (Rev 1:5, 3:14)
    and the model of all Christian witness.
    Everyone in the church must bear this kind of witness;
    in many cases it is the only way of being a missionary.
      The most appealing witness
      is that of charity toward the poor,
      the weak, and those who suffer

and the commitment to peace, justice,
human rights, human promotion,
and integral human development.

43. Christians and Christian communities
are part of their nations,
to which they should be faithful
while preserving the universal community
and freedom Jesus brought.
    They are called to bear witness to Christ
    by their prophetic stand in the face of corruption.

The Initial Proclamation of Christ the Savior

44. Proclamation is the priority in mission,
a clear proclamation that in Jesus Christ
salvation is offered to all as God's gift.
Proclamation has a central and irreplaceable role.
Faith is born of preaching;
all missionary activity is directed
to the proclamation of Christ,
who was crucified, died, and is risen,
bringing freedom from sin and evil.
This is the "good news" that should be announced to all
in a language that is adapted and practical.

45. Missionaries, even when alone,
bring the good news in union with the whole church
by virtue of the mandate they have received.
    Their proclamation is inspired by faith
    that makes them speak frankly and with courage,
    in the conviction that through the work
    of the Holy Spirit in them,
    their listeners are expecting
    to know the truth about God,
    about themselves, and about redemption.
The missionaries' enthusiasm comes from their conviction
that they are responding to this expectation
and that the Spirit of the Father is speaking through them.
Their supreme test has often been to give their lives
to bear witness to their faith in Jesus Christ.

Conversion and Baptism

46. The aim of proclamation is conversion.
Conversion is a gift from God:
"No one can come to me
unless drawn by the Father" (Jn 6:44).

Conversion means accepting Christ,
becoming his disciple in a dynamic and life-giving process.
The church calls all people to conversion.
It is not sufficient to help people to become more human,
to be more faithful to their own religion,
or to build communities working for justice and solidarity.
Every person has the right to hear the "good news"
so that all can live life to the full.

47. From the beginning the apostles asked people
to be converted and to be baptized.
Peter did this at Pentecost,
and that very day three thousand were baptized.
Jesus asked his apostles to go out and baptize,
and Jesus told Nicodemus:
"Unless one is born of water and the Spirit,
one cannot enter the kingdom of God" (Jn 3:5).
   In baptism we are born into a new life,
   the life of God's children, united to Christ
   and anointed in the Holy Spirit.
   Baptism is a sacrament
   that signifies and effects
   rebirth from the Spirit.
This needs to be said,
as some regard baptism as unnecessary.
Many profess an interior commitment to Jesus Christ
but do not wish to be committed sacramentally,
owing to prejudice or because of the failings of Christians.
   Yet the church is the "place" where
   in fact they would find Jesus Christ.
   And I invite the Christian faithful
   not to disappoint the newly baptized.
   We ourselves are to be converted anew every day.

Forming Local Churches

48. Mission is not completed until it succeeds in building
a new and particular church,
functioning normally in its local setting.
The whole mystery of the church
is contained in each particular church
that remains in communion with the universal church,
becoming missionary in its own turn.

49. The first phase in this process,
that of the "planting" of the church,
has not yet reached its end;

in fact for much of the human race
it still has to begin.
    The universal church, every particular church,
    and the whole people of God in fact
    are responsible for this.
    Evangelizing activity is the clearest sign
    of a mature faith;
    it is the best measure of its effectiveness.
Mission personnel coming from other churches
must work together with their local partners
under the directives of the local bishops.
In this way Christian communities will be able to overcome
internal divisions and tensions,
rediscovering their unity and strength.
    Every church should be mindful of its own flock,
    but at the same time also of "the other sheep
    that are not of this fold" (Jn 10:16).

50. This concern will stimulate
our commitment to ecumenism,
necessary for two reasons:
    — the division among Christians damages
      the preaching of the Gospel;
    — some kind of communion already exists
      among all those baptized in Jesus Christ.
Catholics should collaborate in a spirit of fellowship
with their separated brothers and sisters,
especially in this time that Christian and para-Christian sects
represent a real threat to the Catholic Church
and all the ecclesial communities
with which it is engaged in dialogue.

"Basic Ecclesial Communities" as a Force for Evangelization

51. Basic ecclesial communities
[or small Christian communities]
are groups of Christians who, at the level of the family
or in a similar restricted setting,
come together to pray,
to read Holy Scripture,
and to discuss their common commitment.
They are a starting point for a new society
based on a "civilization of love."
    Taking root in less privileged and rural areas,
    decentralizing and reorganizing the parish community,
    they become a leaven of Christian life,

caring for the poor and the transformation of society.
They become a means of evangelization,
the initial proclamation of the Gospel,
and a source of new ministries,
showing how divisions,
racism, and tribalism can be overcome.

Incarnating the Gospel in People's Cultures

52. Carrying out its missionary activity,
the church encounters different cultures
and gets involved in the process of inculturation.
    This process is a lengthy one.
    It means
        "the intimate transformation of authentic cultural values
        through their integration into Christianity
        and their insertion of Christianity
        into the various human cultures."*
    Through it the universal church is enriched,
    coming to know better the mystery of Christ
    and motivated to renew itself.
It is a slow process that accompanies
the whole missionary life,
involving the missionaries, the communities,
and their bishops, discerning and encouraging.

53. Missionaries for other countries must immerse themselves
in the culture of those to whom they are sent,
moving beyond their own cultural limitations,
learning the language,
and becoming familiar with the local culture,
not renouncing their own, but appreciating the one new to them.
    Finding their own expression of Christianity,
    the new communities should work
    in communion with each other and with the universal church,
    "translating" the treasure of faith into a variety of expressions.

54. Two basic guidelines have to be taken into account:
    "compatibility with the Gospel,
    and communion with the universal church."
Bishops will have to ensure fidelity
and provide balanced discernment.
    There is the danger of overestimating a culture;
    cultures are human creations, marked by sin,
    that need to be "healed, ennobled, and perfected" (LG 17).

---

*Extraordinary Assembly of 1985, *Final Report*, II, D, 4.

Inculturation is an "incubation" of the Christian mystery
in the genius of a people
so that its voice may be raised in the chorus of other voices
in the universal church.
 Inculturation must be the expression
 of the community's life,
 and not only the research of some experts.

Dialogue with Our Brothers and Sisters of Other Religions

55. One of the expressions of mission is interreligious dialogue.
God calls all peoples.
God is present in many ways,
not only in individuals but in peoples
through spiritual riches,
of which their religions are the main expression,
even when they contain "gaps, insufficiencies, and errors" (LG 16).
 There is no conflict between proclaiming Jesus Christ
 and interreligious dialogue.
 The two are distinct and intimately connected;
 they should not be confused or regarded as identical.
Followers of other religions can receive God's grace
and be saved by Christ apart from the ordinary means of salvation.
Dialogue should be done in the conviction
that the ordinary way of salvation,
as willed by Jesus Christ, is the church.

56. Dialogue is not a question of tactics or of self-interest;
it is demanded by a deep respect for everything
that has been brought about in human beings by the Spirit,
who blows where the Spirit wills.
Through dialogue the church seeks to uncover
"the seeds of the word," a "ray of that truth that enlightens all."
Other religions are a positive challenge to the church,
asking it to discover the signs of Christ's presence
by examining its own identity
and bearing witness to the fullness of revelation.
 Dialogue must be done with truth, humility, and frankness;
 there must be no false irenicism or abandonment of principles,
 but witness leading to eliminating prejudices,
 to inner purification, and to conversion.

57. Dialogue can assume many forms:
 — exchanges between experts,
 — cooperation for integral development,
 — sharing spiritual experiences, or the "dialogue of life,"
 — helping each other to build a more just society.

Each Christian is called to practice dialogue,
though not to the same degree and to the same extent.
The contribution of the laity is indispensable in this area.

Promoting Development by Forming Consciences

58. For the most part the church carries out
its mission *ad gentes* in the South of the world,
where integral development and liberation are most urgent.
Today even more than in the past missionaries
are seen as promoters of development.
    It is not the church's mission to work directly
    on the economic, technical, or political levels,
    or to contribute to material development.
    Its mission is not to offer people "to *have* more"
    but "to *be* more" through its evangelization.
Church and missionaries also offer development
through schools, hospitals, printing presses,
universities, and experimental farms.
The church considers the human being,
created in God's image, as the principal agent of development—
and not money or technology.

59. The church promotes development through the Gospel message,
which leads to conversion of heart and ways of thinking,
the recognition of each person's dignity,
solidarity, commitment and service of one's neighbor,
building the kingdom of peace and justice,
as the beginning of the "new heavens and new earth" (cf. Is 65:17).
    It struggles not only against the material poverty
    of the people in the South
    but also against the moral and spiritual poverty
    caused by "overdevelopment" in the North.
    A soulless society can be as harmful
    as an excessively poor one.
We need to turn to a more austere way of life,
favoring a new model of development
in which we become true brothers and sisters
through the conversion of all to an "integral development"
open to the Absolute.

Charity: Source and Criterion of Mission

60. The church wishes to be the church of the poor.
The poor deserve preferential attention,
because in them the image of God is obscured and violated.
For this reason God becomes their defender, loving them.

Their evangelization is the sign and proof of the mission of Jesus.
The church is called to be on the side of the poor.
I therefore ask all Christian communities
to carry out a sincere review of their lives
regarding their solidarity with the poor.
And I thank all those who live that solidarity;
their works of charity reveal the soul
of all missionary activity.

Chapter Six:
LEADERS AND WORKERS
IN THE MISSIONARY APOSTOLATE

61. Without witnesses there can be no witness.
Jesus chose the College of Apostles.
This collegiality does not prevent
some having prominence over others,
such as James, John, and above all Peter.
That is why we say: "Peter and the apostles."
There are lesser figures who should not be overlooked,
individuals, groups, and communities.
The early church saw mission as a community task,
acknowledging special "missionaries"
devoted to the gentiles, like Paul and Barnabas.

62. What was done from the beginning remains valid.
The church is missionary by its very nature,
and the young churches should share as soon as possible
in the universal mission of the church.
Young and old churches need each other,
drawing on each other's riches.

Those Primarily Responsible for Missionary Activity

63. Jesus gave the College of Apostles, with Peter as its head,
the responsibility for mission.
In the same way my brother bishops, together with me,
are responsible for it.
Bishops are consecrated not only for a particular diocese,
but for the salvation of the entire world.
Each bishop has a wide-ranging missionary duty,
it falls to him
to promote, direct, and coordinate missionary activity,
devoting a fair share of personnel and funds
to the evangelization of non-Christians.

64. Each particular church must be generous and open
to the needs of other churches.
As the bishops in Latin America declared:
"We have need of missionaries ourselves;
nevertheless we must give from our own poverty."

Missionaries and Religious Institutes Ad Gentes

65. Of fundamental importance in the missionary apostolate
are persons and institutes with a "special vocation"
patterned on that of the apostles,
manifested in a total commitment to evangelization
with one's whole person and life.

66. The missionary institutes, remaining faithful to their charism,
should prepare their candidates,
and renew their members spiritually, morally, and physically.
They are a vital part of the church.
It is praiseworthy that they receive
more and more candidates
from the young churches they have founded.
They remain "absolutely necessary,"
not only for the mission *ad gentes,*
but also for stirring up mission fervor
both in the older and younger churches.
The missionary vocation "for life" retains its validity.
Those missionaries should not be daunted by doubts,
but revive their charism and courageously press on,
preferring the most demanding places.

Diocesan Priests for the Universal Church

67. Every priestly ministry shares in the universal scope
of the mission that Christ entrusted to his apostles.
Their formation should aim at the Catholic spirit,
transcending their diocese, country, or rite,
ready to preach the Gospel anywhere.
Priests must have the mind and heart of missionaries,
with the concern of the church for all humankind,
and ready to be sent anywhere.

68. Pope Pius XII in his encyclical *Fidei Donum*
encouraged bishops to offer some of their priests
for temporary service in the churches of Africa.
They make a valuable contribution,
and I hope that this spirit of service
will increase among the priests
of the old and new churches.

The Missionary Fruitfulness of Consecrated Life

69. Because of their dedication to the service of the church,
    the institutes of consecrated life
    have been rendering an outstanding service
    in the spread of the faith and the formation of new churches.
    a) I invite the institutes of contemplative life,
       to establish communities in the new churches
       to bear witness to the love of God;
    b) I recommend to the institutes of active life
       the opportunities for works of charity,
       the proclamation of the Gospel,
       and solidarity with the poor.
       No one witnesses more effectively
       than those who profess the consecrated life
       of chastity, poverty, and obedience
       in their total gift of self to God
       and the service of humankind
       after the example of Jesus Christ.

70. This is especially true of those missionary religious sisters,
    whose virginity for the sake of the kingdom
    is transformed into a motherhood in the spirit
    that is rich and fruitful.

All the Laity Are Missionaries by Baptism

71. The mission *ad gentes* rests on the shoulders
    of the entire people of God.
    Whereas the foundation of a new church
    requires the Eucharist,
    and hence the priestly ministry,
    the missionary activity is the task of
    all Christian faithful.
    From the beginning the laity
    shared in spreading the faith.
    Some churches owe their origins
    to the activity of lay men and women.
    This sharing is a right and a duty
    based on the baptismal dignity,
    whereby the baptized share in the threefold mission of Christ
    as priest, prophet, and king.
    It is a general obligation,
    all the more important in circumstances
    in which only through them people
    are able to hear the Gospel and to know Christ.

72. The lay people's own field is the vast and complicated world
of politics, society, and economics
on the local, national, and international levels.
There are various ways of promoting the Christian life,
"ecclesial movements"
filled with missionary dynamism.
I recommend that they be spread,
especially among young people,
in view of the pluralistic ways
in which Christians can express themselves.
The laity form an essential and undeniable element
in the planting of the church.

The Work of Catechists and the Variety of Ministries

73. Among the laity who become evangelizers
the catechists have a place of honor.
Old and young churches flourishing today
would not have been built up without them.
There will always be a need for their ministry.
They are specialists recognized as such
by the new Code of Canon Law.
    Their work is more and more difficult,
    because of all the changes taking place.
    They need a careful training,
    a decent standard of living, and social security.

74. Other leaders need to be mentioned, too,
those in charge of prayer, song, and liturgy,
the leaders of basic communities, administrators, and teachers.
All the laity ought to devote part of their time to the church.

The Congregation for the Evangelization of Peoples and Other Structures for Missionary Activity

75. The church's mission requires organization.
The Congregation for the Evangelization of Peoples
is responsible for missionary activity and cooperation.
Its task is to recruit and distribute missionaries,
draw up a plan of action, issue norms, directives, and principles,
and assist in the initial stages.
Episcopal conferences, major superiors, and all others
should faithfully cooperate with this congregation.
    The congregation itself should keep in close contact
    with all the other congregations,
    with local churches and the various missionary forces.

76. Episcopal conferences
are asked to look into the directing and coordinating
of missionary activity
and to consider the complex issue of inculturation,
so that the missionary concern will be shared by all.
Missionary institutions should join their forces and initiatives,
and cooperate in formation, study, and the actual apostolate.

Chapter Seven:
COOPERATION IN MISSIONARY ACTIVITY

77. All Christians share responsibility for missionary activity,
rooted and lived in personal union with Christ.
All should renew their awareness of this responsibility.
It is the way to show one's charity
and one's concern for others.

Prayer and Sacrifice for Missionaries

78. In this sharing the first place goes to prayer.
Prayer should accompany the missionaries' journey.
Prayer needs to be accompanied by sacrifice.
I urge pastors to teach the sick to become missionaries
by offering their sufferings for missionaries.

Here I Am, Lord! I Am Ready! Send Me!

79. The vocation to a lifelong commitment to mission
in missionary institutions and congregations should be promoted.
Promoting such vocations is at the heart of missionary cooperation.
How is it that in some countries the money given is on the increase,
while missionary vocations are in danger of disappearing?

80. Parents should foster missionary vocations,
and young people should listen to Christ's invitation:
"Follow me!" replying: "Here I am, Lord!"
They will have a wonderful life ahead of them,
knowing the joy of proclaiming the "good news."

"It Is More Blessed to Give Than to Receive" (Acts 20:35)

81. The material and financial needs of the missions are many.
The missionary church gives to the poor what it receives.
I wish to thank all those who make this possible.
World Mission Day is an important day;
it teaches how to give for all the missions in the world.

New Forms of Missionary Cooperation

82. Today cooperation includes new forms,
    not only of economic assistance,
    but also of direct participation.
    Tourism can be an enriching experience,
    and visiting the missions is commendable,
    especially on the part of the young
    who go there to serve and gain experience.
        Reasons of work can bring Christians to areas
        where Christianity is unknown, forbidden, or even persecuted.
        They offer opportunities to live the faith
        and bear witness to it.
    People from mission countries
    settling in traditionally Christian countries
    challenge hospitality, dialogue, service, sharing, witness,
    and direct proclamation.
        The increasing interdependence between peoples
        offers a new stimulus for witness and evangelization.

Missionary Promotion and Formation among the People of God

83. Missionary formation is central to the Christian life.
    Churches should make it a key element in their pastoral activity.
        It is necessary that
        missionary publications and audiovisual aids
        spread information.
        It is important that missionary institutes
        devote personnel and resources to them,
        especially in the younger churches.
    The church's universal mission, ecumenism,
    the great religions, and missiology
    should be studied in seminaries
    and houses of formation for men and women religious,
    ensuring that some specialize
    in the different fields of missiology.
        Mission promotion must always give the full picture.
        It is not right to present missionary activity
        as if it was only helping the poor,
        contributing to human development,
        or defending human rights.
        The missionary church is certainly engaged in all this,
        but its primary task is to bear witness to and proclaim
        salvation in Christ and to establish local churches,
        which then become means of liberation in every sense.

The Primary Responsibility of the Pontifical Mission Societies

84. The four Pontifical Mission Societies:
    — Propagation of the Faith,
    — Saint Peter the Apostle,
    — Holy Childhood,
    — and the Missionary Union,
    have as a common purpose the promotion
    of missionary consciousness and formation
    and the fostering of lifelong vocations *ad gentes*.
      Under the leadership of the pope and the College of Bishops,
      and depending on
      the Congregation for the Evangelization of Peoples,
      they unite the churches for the conversion of the whole world.

Not Only Giving to the Missions but Receiving from Them as Well

85. Cooperating in missionary activity
    means not only giving, but also receiving.
    By virtue of catholicity,
    the individual parts bring their own gifts
    to other parts and the whole church.
      I urge all to be open to this universality
      and to avoid provincialism or feelings of self-sufficiency.
      The temptation to become isolated can be strong.
      The older churches may think that their mission is now at home,
      and they may slacken their drive
      toward the non-Christian world.
      But it is by giving that we will receive.
    The young churches, concerned about their own identity,
    might be tempted to close their doors to missionaries.
    To these churches, I say, "Do not isolate yourselves;
    you need to be in contact with your brothers and sisters in the faith."

God Is Preparing a New Springtime for the Gospel

86. A look at today's world can lead to pessimism.
    Yet there are signs that God is preparing
    a great springtime for Christianity,
    while the third millennium of the redemption draws near.
      People are gradually drawing closer to Gospel values:
          — the rejection of violence and war,
          — respect for the human person and human rights,
          — the desire for freedom, justice, and brother/sisterhood,
          — the surmounting of racism and nationalism,
          — the affirmation of the dignity and the role of women.

The number of those awaiting Christ is immense,
requiring us to unite all the church's resources.
The missionary task must remain foremost
for it concerns the destiny of humanity.

Chapter Eight:
MISSIONARY SPIRITUALITY

Being Led by the Spirit

87. Missionary activity demands a specific spirituality
applying to all those whom God has called as missionaries:
a docility to the Spirit that molds them ever more like Christ,
committing them to fortitude and discernment,
essential elements of a missionary spirituality.
   The Spirit transformed the apostles
   into courageous witnesses to Christ
   and enlightened heralds of his word.

Living the Mystery of Christ, "the One Who Was Sent"

88. An essential characteristic
of missionary spirituality is intimate communion with Christ,
who became obedient unto death,
even death on a cross (cf. Phil 2:5–8).
   Missionaries are required
   to renounce themselves
   and to make themselves
   everything to everyone (AG 24).

Loving the Church and Humanity as Jesus Did

89. Missionary spirituality is marked by apostolic charity,
the charity of Christ, who came "to gather into one,
the children of God who are scattered abroad" (Jn 11:52).
Missionaries are the "universal brothers/sisters"
proclaiming that God loves all
by showing their love to all,
overcoming barriers of race, caste, and ideology.
   Missionaries love the church;
   this love is a focal point for them.

The True Missionary Is the Saint

90. The call to mission derives from the call to holiness.
The renewed impulse to mission *ad gentes*
demands holy missionaries.

> Underlying the missionary enthusiasm
> of the first Christian communities
> was the holiness of those first Christians.

91. That is why I appeal especially
to the Christians in the young churches.
They are the hope of this two-thousand-year-old church.
You must be like the first Christians
and radiate enthusiasm and courage,
setting yourselves on the path to holiness.
> Missionaries should be "contemplatives in action."
> My contacts with Asia have confirmed me in the view
> that the future of mission depends to a great extent
> on contemplation:
>> "that which we looked upon...,
>> we proclaim also to you" (1 Jn 1:1–3).
Missionaries are people of the Beatitudes
because they live them out;
missionaries show concretely
that the kingdom of God has already come
and that they have accepted it.
> Joy is the characteristic of authentic missionary life;
> in a tormented world missionaries
> are the ones proclaiming hope.

CONCLUSION

92. Today the church has the opportunity
to bring the Gospel to the world as never before.
We must gather in the Upper Room as the apostles did,
"together with Mary, the mother of Jesus" (Acts 1:14),
to be guided by the Holy Spirit.
> On the eve of the third millennium
> the whole church is invited
> to cooperate in Christ's work of salvation.
I entrust the church and in particular
those who commit themselves to the missionary mandate
to Mary's mediation.

9

The Hundredth Year

"New Things" One Hundred Years Later

Centesimus Annus

May 1, 1991

Commemorating and praising Leo XIII's Of New Things *(1891), this
encyclical repeats its main point: human persons should be respected, for
they are created in God's image and charged with God's life. Overlooking this fact led to the brutalization of the work force in Pope Leo's
time, the horrors of the two world wars, the holocaust, the recent dictatorships in the East, and the gap between the rich and the poor. The
break-up of atheistic communism was due to its disrespect for the dignity
and the consequent rights of the human being. The encyclical calls for
a revolution that offers the hope of a new, alternative world in which
God's gifts are shared in a just way and where all human rights are
respected.*

1. The church remains grateful to Pope Leo XIII
   for the encyclical *Rerum Novarum* ("Of New Things"),
   which he wrote a century ago.
      The energy it gave is not yet spent.

2. This encyclical is meant to honor that letter
   and the "church's social teaching" that flowed from it.

3. Besides rereading it
   we should look at our own "new things,"
   to bring forth — in the tradition of the church —
   "new and old" from the Lord's treasure.
      "Old" is the defense of the human person,
      the building of a more just society,
      and the curbing of injustice.

"New" is an analysis of recent history,
in view of continuing
the "good news."

I. THE "NEW THINGS" A HUNDRED YEARS AGO

4. At the end of the last century,
      the church was facing a new world.
         A new type of ownership had appeared
         and a new form of labor.
      Human work was bought and sold,
      according to the law of supply and demand,
      leaving the workers
      continually threatened by unemployment,
      which — without any social security —
      meant starvation.
         Society had divided into two classes,
         separated by a deep gulf.
      When people began to realize
      the injustice of this situation
      and a revolution threatened,
      Pope Leo XIII wrote his letter
      on "the condition of the workers."

5. Society was torn by the conflict
      between capital and labor,
      "the worker question."
         The two sides faced each other as "wolves"
         with mere physical survival on one side,
         and opulence on the other.
      Because the pope wanted peace
      he condemned class struggle;
      but aware that peace is built on justice
      he set out some of its conditions.
         Not everyone accepted
         the church's right and duty to do this.
         Many believed that the church
         should restrict itself
         to heavenly salvation.
      The pope's letter put the church
      in the midst of public life.
         The church's social teaching
         is an essential part
         of the Christian message.

There can be no solution
to the "social question"
apart from the Gospel.

6. Pope Leo XIII wrote
of the dignity of work
and of the rights and the dignity of workers,
who "exert themselves for the sake
of procuring what is necessary
for the various purposes of life,
and first of all for self-preservation."
The energy they use while working
is part of their person
and belongs to them.
Work is humanity's vocation
through which we realize ourselves.
Pope Leo XIII stressed
the "right to private property."
Everyone has the right
to the things necessary
for oneself and for one's family.

7. Pope Leo XIII stressed the right
to form associations and trade unions
— a right no state can take away
without betraying
"the very principle of its own existence."
He addressed the right
to a limit on working hours
and the right to rest,
albeit different for women, men, and children.
"It is neither just nor human
so to grind women and men down
with excessive labor
as to stupefy their minds,
and wear out their bodies."

8. He wrote of the right to a just wage:
"A worker's wage should be sufficient
to support himself, his wife,
and his children."
This right is so essential, he stated,
that it cannot be left
to the free consent of the partners.
It is the strict duty
of the public authority

to provide properly
for the welfare of the workers.
   "Every individual has a natural right
   to procure what is required to live
   And the poor can procure that in no other way
   than by what they earn."
   "If a worker accepts harder conditions
   he is made the victim of force and injustice."

9. All have the right
   to fulfill their religious duties,
   Leo XIII affirms, stressing the right to,
   and the need of, Sunday rest.
      We might ask ourselves whether
      industrialized societies
      ensure this basic right to Sunday rest.

10. Pope Leo XIII criticizes
    "socialism" and "liberalism."
       Against "socialism" he affirms
       the right to private property.
    As for liberalism
    he states that the state may not favor
    the rich while neglecting the poor.
       It is the poor who have a claim
       to special consideration.
    The richer class can help itself;
    the poor have no resources of their own to do so.
    They chiefly depend on the help of the state.
       This remains valid today,
       considering the poverty in the world.
    It does not depend
    on any ideology or political theory,
    but on the principle of solidarity,
    valid in the national and international order.
       Leo XIII uses the term "friendship" for it;
       Pius XI calls it "social charity";
       Paul VI, extending it even further,
       speaks of a "civilization of love."

11. Expressing Jesus' and the church's
    "preferential option for the poor,"
    Pope Leo XIII calls upon the state
    to do something about the condition of the poor,
    though he does not expect the state
    to solve every social problem.

He insists on limits
to the state's intervention.
The individual, the family, and society
should be protected by it
and not stifled.
The main point made in Leo XIII's encyclical
and in the church's social doctrine
is a correct view of the human person.
  Human persons are willed by God;
  they are imprinted with God's image.
  Their dignity does not come
  from the work they do,
  but from the persons they are.

II. TOWARD THE "NEW THINGS" OF TODAY

12. The events of 1989 and 1990
    proved Leo XIII to be right about
    the consequences of "real socialism":
      that the worker would be the first to suffer,
      that it would distort the role of the state
      and create utter confusion in the community.

13. "Real socialism" considers the human person
    as a mere element or molecule
    in a social organism
    to which he or she is completely subordinated.
    There is no free choice,
    nothing of one's own
    or done on one's own initiative.
    One depends totally on the social machine
    and on those who control it.
      This is a situation in which it is difficult
      to realize one's personal dignity
      and to build a human community.
    The Christian vision is different.
    The social nature of a person
    is not totally fulfilled by the state,
    but is realized in various other groups,
    beginning with the family.
      The denial of God is at the root
      of this total lack of respect for human dignity.

14. It is the denial of God
    that explains the choice of class struggle
    as a means of action.

Condemning class struggle
does not mean condemning
every possible form of social conflict.
Such conflicts inevitably arise
and Christians must often take a position
in the "struggle for social justice."
What is condemned is "total war,"
which has no respect
for the dignity of others
(and consequently of oneself).
It excludes reasonable compromise,
does not pursue the common good
but the good of a group,
and sets out to destroy
whatever stands in its way.
In a word, it does in relation to
conflict between social groups
what militarism and imperialism do
internationally,
replacing the search for a proper balance
with the destruction
of the other side's capacity to resist.
Class struggle in the Marxist sense
and militarism
have atheism
and the consequent contempt
for the human being
as their common root.

15. *Rerum Novarum* is against
any form of state control
that makes the citizen
a mere "cog" in the state machine.
It is also opposed to a state
that is not interested
in the economic sector.
The state has to determine
the legal framework
to conduct economic affairs,
so that the interests of one group
do not overrule another.
Society and state need to afford protection
against the nightmare of unemployment
through economic policies
that ensure balanced growth and full employment

or through unemployment insurance
and retraining programs.
    Wages must be sufficient
    to maintain a worker's family
    and allow a certain amount for some saving.
The exploitation of the most vulnerable workers
—immigrants and those marginalized—
must be prevented.
    "Humane" working hours and adequate leisure
    need to be guaranteed
    as well as the right to express one's own personality.
The role of trade unions is decisive
in these deliberations.
    The state must contribute to all this
    according to the principles of
    subsidiarity and solidarity,
    defending the weakest
    and ensuring the necessary minimum support
    for the unemployed.
The encyclical
and the subsequent social teaching of the church
influenced numerous reforms in the years
bridging the nineteenth and twentieth centuries.

16. Reforms were carried out by states
and were achieved by workers' movements,
often including Christians
    who started producers', consumers',
    and credit cooperatives
    and promoted general education, professional training,
    and new forms of participation and sharing.

17. Lack of respect for human dignity
led to the wars that ravaged Europe
between 1914 and 1945.
    The holocaust, in particular of the Jewish people,
    has become a symbol of what happens
    when human beings turn against God.

18. Though weapons
have remained silent in Europe since 1945,
there has been no peace.
    Half of Europe fell under
    a communist dictatorship,
    and the other half
    organized itself in self-defense.

Cultures have been threatened,
and masses of peoples displaced.
>An insane arms race swallowed up
>resources needed for development.
Power blocs formed and fought,
causing enormous bloodshed
in various parts of the world.
>Extremists were armed;
>those in favor of peaceful solutions
>remained isolated or fell as victims.
Third World countries were armed,
terrorism spread,
and the whole world was oppressed
by the threat of a nuclear war.
>Such a war would be without winners
>calling in question
>the issues of "total war"
>and "class struggle."

19. Though these new ideas about peace and war
    started to stir people's consciences,
    the threat of communism distracted people's attention
    and provoked different responses.
    >Some countries made a positive effort
    >to build a democratic society
    >inspired by the ideal of social justice.
    Others set up systems of "national security"
    against the threat of Marxism,
    but risked destroying the very freedom
    they wanted to defend.
    >A third response was the consumer society,
    >which showed that it could defeat Marxism
    >by the production of material goods,
    >while equally overlooking spiritual values.

20. "Decolonization" meant that many countries
    gained or regained their independence.
    >But they often remained
    >in the hands of foreign companies
    >and controlled by foreign powers.
    >Lacking competent leadership,
    >they did not always integrate all ethnic groups
    >into genuine national communities.

21. In reaction to the horrors
    of the Second World War

a lively sense of human rights
led to a number of international documents
and to the United Nations Organization.
   There was more awareness of the rights of individuals,
   but also of the rights of nations,
   shifting the center of the social question
   from the national
   to the international level.
Notwithstanding the progress made,
not all efforts were positive,
and no effective alternative to war was found
to solve international conflicts.

III. THE YEAR 1989

22. In the 1980s oppressive regimes fell
in Latin America, Africa, and Asia.
Progress was made
toward more just political structures.
   The church committed itself
   to defending and promoting human rights.
Heroic witness to this was given
by pastors, Christian communities, and individuals,
showing that problems can be resolved
through dialogue and solidarity
rather than by war and destruction.

23. The decisive factor
in the fall of oppressive regimes
was the violation
of the rights of workers.
   It all began in Poland
   in the name of solidarity.
   The oppressed working people
   recovered and discovered
   the church's social teaching.
The Europe left over after the Second World War,
and its resulting Marxist bloc, has been overcome
by the nonviolent commitment of people
witnessing to the truth.
   May their example teach others.

24. A second factor in this crisis
was the failure of an economic system
that was not only technically inefficient,
but violated the human right

to private initiative,
to ownership of property,
and to freedom in the economic sector.
To this must be added the violation
of cultural and national rights.
Cultures express in different ways
the meaning of life and person.
When these differences are overlooked,
society and life deteriorate.
The main cause of this collapse
was the reaction of the younger generations
to the spiritual void brought by atheism.
Youth did not find
any sense of direction
until they rediscovered
the roots of their national culture
and the person of Jesus Christ.
Marxism promised to uproot
the need for God from the human heart;
it actually showed that the heart
cannot be left empty in this way.

25. The events of 1989 were born from prayer.
They would have been unthinkable
without trust in God,
and union with the sufferings
of Christ on the cross.
It is in this way
that we are able to accomplish
the miracle of peace and freedom.
This freedom, however,
bears the wound of original sin,
which draws us to evil
and puts us in constant
need of redemption.
This belief is not only
part of Christian revelation;
it also helps us to understand
our human reality.
The social order will be all the more stable
if it takes this fact into consideration.
When people think that,
possessing the secret of a perfect social organization,
they can make evil impossible,
they also think

they can use any means,
even violence and deceit,
to realize it.
No political society
should be confused with the kingdom of God.
It is only God who — at the end of time —
will finally separate
the weeds from the wheat.
The struggle between good and evil will continue
as long as time lasts.
The kingdom of God,
being "in" the world,
without being "of" the world,
throws a critical light on society,
calling everyone, especially the laity,
to infuse human reality
with the spirit of the Gospel.

26. The events of 1989
are of worldwide importance.
The church met a workers' movement
that for almost a century
had been partly under the influence of Marxism.
Workers found their consciences,
in their demand for justice and dignity
as offered in the church's social teaching.
The crisis of Marxism
does not rid the world
of the injustices
on which it thrived.
To those looking for a new way,
the church offers its teaching,
as well as its concrete commitment
and material assistance
in the struggle against
marginalization and suffering.
Beyond an impossible compromise
between Marxism and Christianity,
the church reaffirms
integral human liberation —
with consequences important
for the countries of the Third World,
searching for their own path to development.

27. As regards Europe,
so much ill will

has accumulated during the communist regimes
that there is a danger
of a serious explosion of hatred.
   We need some concrete steps of arbitration
   to intervene in the conflicts
   that will arise between nations.
   A patient material
   and moral reconstruction
   is needed.
The fall of Marxism
and the end of the world's division
highlight our interdependence.
   Peace and prosperity
   belong to the whole of the human race.
   They cannot be achieved in isolation
   at the cost of other peoples and nations.

28. Some countries in Europe
     at the moment need
     the kind of help given to others
     after the Second World War.
        They find themselves in this predicament
        as a result of the tragic situation
        imposed on them.
     The countries
     that were partly responsible for that situation
     owe them a debt
     as a matter of justice.
        This need should not diminish
        the willingness to sustain and assist
        the countries of the Third World,
        which often suffer even more.
     Priorities have to be redefined.
     Enormous resources could become available
     by disarming the huge military machines
     built by East and West for conflict.
        These resources
        could become even more abundant
        if we found a way of resolving conflicts
        without war.
     A change of mentality is needed,
     no longer seeing the poor as a burden,
     or as intruders
     trying to profit from others,
     but as people seeking to share

the goods of the world
so that we can create
a just and prosperous world for all.

29. Development must be understood
as something fully human,
not as something merely material;
its real aim is the enhancement
of everyone's capacity
to respond to God's call.
The rights of the human conscience
must be fully recognized.
It is important to reaffirm these rights:
a) because some dictatorships
have not yet been overcome;
b) because, in the developed countries,
the promotion of and demand for instant gratification
devalue respect for human rights and values; and
c) because, in some countries
new forms of religious fundamentalism
deny minority groups their rights.

IV. PRIVATE PROPERTY AND THE UNIVERSAL DESTINATION OF MATERIAL GOODS

30. The church has always defended
the right to private property,
teaching at the same time
that this right is not absolute.
Pope Leo XIII wrote:
"How must one's possessions be used?
The human being should not consider
material possessions as his or her own,
but as common to all."
The Second Vatican Council stated:
"Of its nature private property
also has a social function,
based on the law of
the common purpose of goods."

31. God gave the earth to the whole human race
for the sustenance of its members,
without excluding or favoring anyone.
The earth does not yield its fruits
without human work.

Through work, a human being
makes part of the earth his or her own,
which is the origin of individual property.
We obviously must not prevent others
from having their own part of God's gift.
Access to work and land are to be found
at the basis of every human society.
Work and land
change their relationship continuously.
At one time the natural fruitfulness of the earth
was the primary factor of wealth;
in our time the role of human work
is more important.
Work "with" and "for" others
depends more and more on insight
into the productivity of the earth
and knowledge of our human needs.

32. In our time, know-how,
technology, and skill
are no less important than land.
The wealth of industrialized nations
is based more on the ownership of technology
than on possession of natural resources.
Another important source of wealth
is the ability to know the needs of others
and how to satisfy those needs.
Because all of this often requires
the co-operation of many people,
organizational skills, planning, timing, and management
are also sources of wealth.
The role of discipline, creativity,
initiative, and entrepreneurial ability,
is evident and decisive.
It affirms what Christianity
has constantly affirmed:
next to the earth,
humanity's principal resource
is the human being itself.
Once the decisive factor of production was land;
then it was capital;
now it is the human being.

33. Many are faced with the impossibility
of acquiring the needed knowledge
to take their place in the working world.

They are exploited or marginalized,
development takes place over their heads,
and they cannot keep up
with new forms
of production and organization.
In their quest for wealth
they are attracted
to the cities of the Third World,
where there is no room for them.
     Sometimes there are even attempts
     to eliminate them
     through population control.
Many others struggle to earn a bare minimum,
in conditions that are as bad
as those at the beginning of industrialization.
     Those cultivating land
     are excluded from land ownership
     and often are practically no more than slaves.
With no land, no material goods,
no knowledge, no training,
they cannot escape their humiliation.
     Some development programs
     have been set up,
     and the countries that managed
     to gain access
     to the international market in this way
     have suffered less from stagnation and recession
     than those who isolated themselves.
Some aspects typical of the Third World
also appear in developed countries,
where the elderly, the young, and women
can easily be marginalized
in a so-called Fourth World.

34. The free market
appears to be the most efficient tool
for utilizing resources
and responding to needs.
     But this is true
     only if you are able to buy and sell.
Justice and truth demand
that basic human needs should be met
and that none should be left to perish.
     The possibility of surviving
     and of making a contribution to the common good

is something that simply belongs to the human person
as a human person.
In the Third World
Pope Leo XIII's objectives
are still goals to be reached.

35. Trade Unions and other workers' organizations
find here a wide range of opportunities
for commitment and effort for the sake of justice.
    It is right to struggle
    against an unjust economic system
    that does not uphold
    the priority of the human being
    over capital and land.
The alternative to it is not a socialist system
that leads to state capitalism,
but a society with free work,
enterprise, and participation —
    an alternative that is in favor of a market
    that guarantees
    the basic needs
    of the whole of society.
Profit, though it plays a legitimate role,
is not the only indicator
of a firm's condition.
    The people in it
    might be humiliated and offended.
The aim of a business
is not simply profit,
but to form a particular group
at the service of the whole of society.
    After the fall of "real socialism"
    capitalism is not
    the only economic alternative left.
Individuals and nations
need the basic things
to enable them to share in development.
    The stronger ones
    must assist the weaker ones,
    and the weaker ones must use
    the opportunities offered.
Foreign debts affect these efforts.
The principle
that debts should be paid remains,
but this should not be asked for

at the cost of the hunger and despair
of entire peoples.
    There is the need
    to lighten, defer, or even cancel the debts,
    and indeed, this does sometimes happen,
    to let people subsist and progress.

36. In advanced economies
    the demand
    is no longer for quantity,
    but for quality.
        Hence the issue
        of consumerism arises.
    The new material, physical, and instinctive needs
    should remain subordinate
    to humanity's interior and spiritual needs.
        Appealing to instinct only
        may create lifestyles and consumer attitudes
        that are damaging
        to spiritual and physical health.
    The education and cultural formation
    of consumers and producers and of the mass media
    are urgently needed,
    as well as the intervention of public authority.
        A striking example
        of false consumerism
        is the use of drugs.
            Drug abuse is a sign
            of the malfunction of a society,
            destructive reading of human needs,
            and the idle filling of a spiritual void.
        The same could be said of pornography
        and other forms of exploitative consumerism.
    It is not wrong to want to improve our lives.
    It is wrong to seek improvement
    in what one "has," and not in what one "is."
        Even the decision to invest
        in one way rather than another
        is always a moral and cultural choice,
        that should be determined
        by human sympathy
        and trust in divine providence.

37. Consumerism also raises
    the ecological issue.
    Humanity is consuming

the resources of the earth and life
in an excessive and disordered way,
    forgetting the earth's own needs
    and God-given purpose,
    provoking a rebellion
    on the part of nature,
    and overlooking
    our duties and obligations
    toward future generations.

38. While there is much concern, and rightly so,
    about the natural environment
    and the various animal species
    threatened with extinction,
    little effort is made
    to safeguard our "human ecology."
        Urbanization and work
        can give rise to "structures of sin"
        that need to be destroyed
        and replaced by authentic forms
        of community life.

39. The first and fundamental structure
    for a "human ecology"
    is the family, founded on marriage,
    in which the mutual gift of self
    as husband and wife
    creates an environment
    in which children can be born
    and grow up.
        Too often life is considered
        to be a series of sensations
        rather than as something to be accomplished.
    The result is a lack of freedom
    to commit oneself to another person
    and to bring children into this world.
        The family is sacred;
        it is the sanctuary of life.
    It is life's heart and culture.
    It is the opposite of the culture of death,
    the destruction of life by abortion,
    and the systematic anti-child-bearing campaigns.

40. There are needs and common goods
    that cannot be satisfied
    by the market system.

It is the task of the state
and of all society
to defend them.
An idolatry of the market alone
cannot do all that should be done.

41. Marxism blamed capitalist society
because it alienated the human being.
    Its idea of alienation was mistaken,
    and its remedy of a collectivized society
    also proved to be a mistake.
Yet alienation is still a reality
in Western societies,
because of consumerism,
that does not help one appreciate
one's authentic personhood,
and because of work,
which shows interest only in profit,
and none in the workers,
considering them to be mere means.
    The way out of this impasse
    is to reconsider
    the Christian vision of the human person
    and its "capacity for transcendence."
A human society is both alienated and alienating
if its organization, production, and consumption
make transcendence more difficult.
    Exploitation, in the Marxist sense,
    has been overcome in the West;
    alienation has not.
It exists when people use one another,
ignoring their own and each other's authentic needs
    and when the mass media
    hinder authentic human growth
    by imposing fashions and opinions
    through carefully orchestrated
    promotion campaigns.

42. After the failure of communism,
should capitalism be the goal
for Eastern Europe and the Third World?
    The answer is complex.
    If capitalism means
    a "market" or "free" economy
    that recognizes the role of business,
    the market, and private property,

as well as free human creativity,
     then the answer is "yes."
If it means a system
in which economic, religious,
and ethical freedom are denied,
then the answer is "no."
     Marxism failed,
     but marginalization and exploitation remain,
     especially in the Third World,
     just as alienation does
     in the more advanced countries.
The collapse of communism
is not enough to change these conditions.
     A radically capitalist system
     might not even try to solve them.

43. The church has no models to offer.
Models develop out of concrete situations.
     Instead, the church offers its social teaching
     as an indispensable and ideal orientation.
It insists on the right of workers
to be respected and to be involved
in the life of industrial enterprises
so that, in a certain sense,
they "work for themselves."
     This might weaken power structures,
     but it will promote
     a greater productivity and efficiency.
A business is not only
a "society of capital goods,"
it is also a "society of persons."
     A broad associated workers' movement
     is still needed to achieve these goals.
The relationship between
private property
and the universal destination
of material wealth
has to be reestablished.
     By their work workers commit themselves
     "with" others and "for" others.
They work in order to provide
for their families, communities, nations,
and ultimately for all humanity.
     They collaborate in this
     with others, suppliers and customers,

in an ever expanding chain
of solidarity.
Ownership is just
if it serves a useful work.
    It is unjust when it is not used
    or when it is used to hinder others,
    or to break the solidarity among workers
    to gain profit.
The obligation to earn one's bread
presumes the right to do so.
    A society that denies this right
    cannot be justified,
    nor can it attain social peace.

V. STATE AND CULTURE

44. Pope Leo XIII speaks of a society
where the three powers —
legislative, executive, and judicial —
keep each other in balance.
In this way law is sovereign,
and not the will of some individuals.
    Marxist-Leninism contradicted this.
    It holds that some people
    have more knowledge than others
    and that they should rule
    others in an absolute way.
It denies the inborn dignity
of each and every human being,
created in the image of God.

45. This totalitarianism
rejected the authority of the church.
    By defending its own freedom,
    the church also stood up
    for the freedom of the human person.

46. The church values democracy
and cannot encourage narrow ruling groups
to use the power of the state
for their own interests.
    Real democracy requires a state,
ruled by law, true education and formation,
    participation and shared responsibility.
Democracy does not mean
that there is no ultimate truth.

If that were true,
ideas and convictions
could easily be manipulated
for reasons of power.
The church is aware of the danger
of fanaticism and fundamentalism.
   Christian truth is not an ideology;
   it knows that human life
   is realized in history,
   and it always respects human freedom.
Freedom attains its full development
when accepting the truth.
   Christians will listen to every fragment of truth
   they meet in their contact with others.

47. The democratic ideal prevails these days;
so does attention to human rights.
   That is why mention should be made
   of the most important of these rights:
   the right
      to life,
      to develop from the moment of conception,
      to live in a united family,
      to education,
      to work,
      to support oneself and one's dependents,
      to establish a family freely,
      to have and rear children,
      to live in the truth of one's faith.
Even in democracies
these rights are not always respected.
Sometimes certain demands are not met
for narrow opportunistic, electoral,
or financial reasons.
   This leads to distrust and apathy
   and in the end to the inability to see any issue
   within the framework of a coherent vision
   of the common good.

48. The economy cannot be run
in an institutional,
juridical, or political vacuum:
the state has its role to play,
   guaranteeing personal freedom,
   a stable currency,
   and efficient public services.

Lack of stability, corruption,
improper ways of growing rich, and speculation
hinder development and social order.
    The state has to intervene
    when monopolies hinder development;
    in certain cases it can substitute its own services
    when certain sectors of business
    are too weak to render the services
    needed for the common good.
    Those interventions should be
    as brief as possible
    in order to avoid
    removing from society and business
    tasks that belong to them.
The range of these interventions
has expanded to the point
of creating the so-called welfare state
as a response to poverty and deprivation.
    Recent excesses and abuses —
    to the point that the welfare state has been dubbed
    the "social assistance state" —
    are the result
    of an inadequate understanding
    of the role of the state.
The "principle of subsidiarity"
must be respected:
    "A community of a higher order
    should not interfere with the life
    of a community of a lower order,
    taking over its functions."
In case of need it should, rather, support
the smaller community and help
to coordinate its activity with activities
in the rest of society
for the sake of the common good.
    Not doing this
    leads to a loss of human energy,
    an increase of bureaucratic agencies,
    and an increase in costs.
Needs are best understood
by the real neighbor
of those who are in need,
and such needs often demand
more than just material support,
a deeper, personal support.

Help is most effective when given
in genuine fraternal support.

49. Active charity has never ceased
to be practiced in the church —
witness the amount of voluntary work being done.
    To overcome
    today's individualistic mentality,
    a concrete commitment
    to solidarity and charity is needed,
    beginning in the family.
The state should develop family policies
that help families to bring up their children
and to look after the elderly,
strengthening the relations between the generations.
    Other intermediate communities play a role
    in personalizing society
    and deepening our understanding
    of who we are.

50. It is in this way
that the culture of a nation is born,
generation after generation,
always challenged by the young,
not in order to destroy or reject it,
but to make it more real, relevant, and personal.
    When a culture becomes inward-looking
    rejecting any dialogue,
    it is heading for its end.

51. The first and most important things
happen within a person's heart.
It is at this level that the church
contributes to true culture,
    promoting peace,
    preaching how creation
    is placed in human hands
    to make it fruitful and more perfect,
    preaching how the Son of God
    saved and united us,
    making us responsible for each other.
These duties are not restricted to
one's family or one's nation,
but extend to all humankind.
They are made all the more urgent
by both the new means of communication

that have brought us closer together
and by the terrifying power for destruction now available
that makes it practically impossible
to limit the consequences of a violent conflict.

52. "War, never again!"
Just as personal revenge has given way
to the rule of law within states,
so the time has come for
a similar step to be taken at an international level,
    not forgetting that at the root of war and conflict
    there are usually real grievances.
As Pope Paul VI once said,
"Another name for peace is development."
Together we are responsible
for avoiding war;
together we are responsible
for promoting development.
    It should be possible to organize
    at an international level
    the kind of solid economy
    that is possible in an individual society.
The poor — whether individuals or nations —
need realistic opportunities.
    This calls for a concerted worldwide effort
    to promote development.
This may mean important changes
in established lifestyles,
limiting waste of environmental
and human resources.
    It also means utilizing
    the new and spiritual responses
    of peoples who today are at the margin
    of the international community,
    thus enriching the family of nations.

VI. THE HUMAN BEING IS THE WAY OF THE CHURCH

53. The church is not interested in
recovering former privileges
or imposing its vision.
    Its interest is the human being,
    the "concrete" human being,
    the individual person to whom Christ
    united himself.

The human being is the primary route
that the church must travel
to fulfill its mission.

54. The human and social sciences are helpful
    in explaining
    how this concrete person
    is involved in a complex network
    of relationships.
    Faith reveals our real identity.
        That is why the church concerns itself
        with the rights of the individual,
        the working class, the family,
        the state, national and international society,
        with economic life, culture, war and peace,
        and respect for human life from conception.

55. The social teaching of the church
    belongs to moral theology,
        "a sign and safeguard
        of the transcendence
        of the human person."

56. I thank all those devoted
    to the church's social teaching.
    I wish it to be known and applied
        in the countries
        where "real socialism" has collapsed;
    in the Western countries
    that need to correct their system;
        in the Third World countries
        with their underdevelopment.
    As Pope Leo XIII stated:
        "All should put their hands to the work
        which falls to their share,
        and that at once and straightway,
        lest the evil which is already so great
        become through delay absolutely beyond remedy."

57. The social message of the Gospel
    is and always has been a basis for action:
        the first Christian communities
        redistributed their goods to the poor;
        in the early Middle Ages
        monks engaged in rural development;
        later, religious women and men founded hospitals.
    We, too, need the witness of actions.

58. Love for others, and especially for the poor,
    is made concrete by promoting justice.
        It is not a matter of giving some surplus,
        but of helping entire peoples.
    It requires a change of lifestyles,
    a reorientation of ourselves
    and our organizations
    toward the whole of the human family.
        It asks for effective international agencies
        to coordinate the powerful nations
        and take into account the weaker ones —
        which even the most powerful state on earth
        would not be able to do on its own.

59. The gift of grace is needed,
    a newness in the following of Jesus.
        The church's social teaching
        should begin a practical and scientific dialogue
        at the crossroads
        where it meets the world as it is.

60. Pope Leo XIII wrote:
    "This most serious question
    demands the attention
    and the efforts of others."
        John XXIII addressed his letter on peace
        to "all people of good will."
    Now, even more than in those days,
    we are aware that all —
    even those who profess no religion —
    can contribute to a solution.
        I already invited all Christian churches
        and all the great world religions
        to offer their witness
        to the dignity of the human being
        created by God.
    I am convinced that they will play
    a role in preserving peace
    and building a society worthy of
    the human being.

61. A hundred years ago
    industrialized society was:
    "a yoke little better than that of slavery itself."
        That is why the church spoke
        in defense of humanity.

The church did so
after the First and Second World Wars
for exactly the same reason.
And now it does so
with regard to the developing countries
living in conditions that are still
"a yoke little better than that of slavery itself."

62. This encyclical, looking at the past,
is directed to the future.
   As in the years of *Rerum Novarum*
   we live on the threshold of a new century.
The intention is — with God's help —
to prepare for that moment.
God's promise is:
"Behold I make all things new."
   This newness has been present since creation,
   and especially since Jesus became one of us.
I thank God
for enlightening humanity
on its earthly journey,
   and I pray that Mary,
   the mother of Jesus,
   may accompany the church
   on its journey,
   as she accompanied Jesus, her son.

10

The Splendor of Truth
Veritatis Splendor

August 6, 1993

This encyclical, addressed to the bishops of the Catholic Church, reaffirms the fundamentals of the church's moral teaching, fundamentals that can be found only in God. God determines what is good and what is evil, as God does in the ten commandments, protecting human life, marriage, private property, and people's good name. The commandments are the "natural law" we know with our natural reason. They transcend us. They are objective and cannot be manipulated. They are in no way negotiable. Those ten negative "words" are the bottom line in moral human behavior, to which Jesus adds the positive ideals presented in the Sermon on the Mount.

Introduction:
JESUS CHRIST, THE TRUE LIGHT THAT ENLIGHTENS EVERYONE

1. Called to salvation through faith in Jesus Christ
   people are made holy by "obedience to the truth" (1 Pet 1:22).
   This obedience is not always easy.
   People are constantly tempted by Satan
   to exchange "the truth about God for a lie" (Rom 1:25),
   giving themselves over to relativism and skepticism.
   > But no darkness of error or sin
   > can extinguish the light of God the Creator.
   > In the depth of the human heart there will always remain
   > the yearning for truth.
   This is proved by our tireless search for knowledge,
   and even more by our search for the meaning of life—

searches that do not free us from the obligation
to ask the ultimate religious questions.

2. "What must I do?"
"How do I distinguish good from evil?"
The answer is possible thanks to the splendor of the truth
that shines forth deep within the human spirit.
     God's face shines in all its beauty
     on the countenance of Jesus Christ,
     "the reflection of God's glory" (Heb 1:3),
     "the way, the truth, and the life" (Jn 14:6).
     The decisive answer to our questions
     is given by Jesus Christ,
     or rather *is* Jesus Christ himself.
Jesus Christ, the light of the nations,
shines upon the face of the church
sent forth to proclaim the Gospel
to every creature (Mk 16:15),
offering everyone the answer
that comes from Jesus Christ and his Gospel
while attentive to the new challenges of history,
and examining the signs of the times.

3. The church's pastors are close
to the faithful in this effort.
Knowing that morality touches every person,
the church involves all people,
even those who do not know Christ, the Gospel, or even God.
     The church knows that it is on the path of a moral life
     that the way of salvation is open to all.

Purpose of the Present Encyclical

4. Especially in the last two centuries,
popes have been proposing moral teaching
on sexuality, the family, on social, political, and economic life.
     Today it seems necessary
     to recall certain fundamental truths
     of Catholic doctrine
     because of the spread of doubts and objections
     to the church's moral teaching.
It is no longer a question of some occasional dissent,
but of an overall calling into question
of the traditional moral doctrine.
     The traditional doctrine regarding natural law
     and the validity of its precepts are rejected;

certain teachings are simply found unacceptable
even in certain seminaries and theological faculties.
The question is asked whether
the commandments of God written in the human heart
really have the capacity to clarify
the daily decisions of individuals and societies.
Is it possible to love God without listening to them?
  One also hears frequently the opinion
  that questions the link between faith and morality,
  as if one could remain a member of the church
  based on one's faith alone, while in the sphere of morality
  all kinds of behavior and opinions could be tolerated.

5. That is why I decided to write an encyclical
on the very foundations of moral theology,
based on Sacred Scripture and the living apostolic tradition,
shedding at the same time light on the presuppositions
and the consequences of the dissent.
  I address this encyclical to you, my brother bishops,
  after the publication of the Catechism of the Catholic Church.
  That is why I can limit myself here
  to some fundamental questions
  as regards the church's moral teaching.

Chapter One
"TEACHER, WHAT GOOD MUST I DO?" (Mt 19:16)

Christ and the Answer to the Question about Morality

• *"Someone came to him" (Mt 19:16)*

6. The dialogue of Jesus with the rich young man
can serve as a useful guide.

7. This young man stands in for anyone approaching Christ
to ask him about morality and about the full meaning of human life,
  a question that is the echo of a call from God,
  an appeal to the absolute good.
God willed the church to make this encounter with Christ
possible for each person,
"in order that Christ may walk with each person
the path of life" (RH 13).

• *"Teacher, what good must I do to have eternal life?" (Mt 19:16)*

8. The question is an unavoidable one;
the young man senses that there is a connection between
the answer and his destiny.

He asks Jesus the question
not because he is ignorant of the law,
but because he is attracted by the newness
Jesus had begun to live and preach.
People need today to turn to the risen Christ,
whose life sheds light on humanity's condition and vocation.
Jesus, as a patient and sensitive teacher,
answers the young man by leading him step by step
to the full truth.

- *"There is only one who is good" (Mt 19:17)*

9. Jesus makes this remark to make the young man understand
   that the answer to his question can only be found in God.
   The young man's question is really
   a religious question.

10. The church believes
    that humanity, made in the image of God,
    redeemed by the blood of Christ,
    and made holy by the presence of the Holy Spirit,
    has as ultimate purpose:
    to live "for the praise of God's glory" (cf. Eph 1:12),
    striving to make each of one's actions
    reflect the splendor of that glory.
    Who human beings are and what they must do
    become clear as soon as God reveals himself.
    In the ten words of the covenant with Israel
    God is revealed as the one "who alone is good":
    "I am the Lord, your God,
    who brought you out of the land of Egypt" (Ex 20:2–3).
    God is the "model"
    for moral action:
    "You shall be holy,
    for I, the Lord your God, am holy" (Lev 19:2).
    The moral life is humanity's response
    to God's love, reflecting God's glory.

11. The good is to belong to God,
    obeying and walking humbly with God,
    in doing justice and in loving kindness (cf. Mic 6:8).
    Acknowledging the Lord as God is the heart of the law.
    But no human effort succeeds in "fulfilling" this law.
    This "fulfillment" can come only as a gift from God,
    the offer of a share in the divine goodness
    given to us in Jesus, the "good" teacher.

- *"If you wish to enter into life, keep the commandments"*
  (Mt 19:17)

12. God answered the question
    with the law that is written in our human hearts,
    the "natural law" (cf. Rom 2:15),
    whereby we know what to do
    and what not to do.
      God gave that answer in the history of Israel
      when he gave the "ten words,"
      bringing into existence "a holy nation,"
      that would radiate God's holiness
      to all peoples (cf. Wis 18:4, Ez 20:41).
    That is why Jesus tells the young man,
    after saying "there is only one who is good,"
      "If you wish to enter into life,
      keep the commandments."
    Those commandments are linked to a promise.
    In the old covenant the promise was the possession of a land;
    in the new covenant the promise is the "kingdom of heaven" —
      or as Jesus would tell his disciples
      after speaking to the young man:
      "eternal life," sharing in the very life of God.

13. The young man asks: "Which commandments?"
    and Jesus answers:
          "You shall not murder; you shall not commit adultery;
          you shall not bear false witness;
          honor your father and your mother;
          also you shall love your neighbor as yourself" (Mt 19:18–19).
    It is clear that Jesus does not intend
    to list each and every commandment "to enter into life";
    he wants to draw the attention
    to what the word "I am the Lord your God"
    means to a human being,
    the summary and foundation of which
    is the commandment of love of neighbor:
    "You shall love your neighbor as yourself" (Mt 19:19).
      The many commandments are really
      only so many reflections of the one commandment
      about the good and the dignity of the person.
    The negative precepts Jesus mentions
    express forcefully the ever urgent need
    to protect human life,
    the communion of persons in marriage,
    private property, truthfulness, and people's good name.

They represent the basic condition for the love of neighbor,
and they are at the same time the proof of that love.
They are the first step toward freedom.

14. Christ does not put the love of neighbor above
or even apart from the love of God.
These two commandments
— on which depend all the law and prophets (Mt 22:40) —
are connected and mutually related
in both the Old and the New Testaments.
    Saint John makes the point
    with extraordinary forcefulness:
    "Anyone who says, 'I love God,'
    and hates his neighbor is a liar" (1 Jn 4:20).

15. In the Sermon on the Mount Jesus said:
    "Do not think that I have come to abolish the law and the prophets;
    I have not come to abolish them but to fulfill them" (Mt 5:17).
Jesus shows that the commandments
must not be understood as a limit
but rather as a path involving a moral and spiritual journey
toward perfection, at the heart of which is love.
    Thus the commandment "You shall not kill"
    becomes a call to attentive love
    that protects and promotes
    the life of one's neighbor.
Jesus becomes himself a living and personal law,
inviting people to follow him.
    Through the Spirit he gives us the grace
    to share his life and love.

  • *"If you wish to be perfect"*

16. Though the young man is able to make the reply,
"I have kept all these commandments,"
he knows — encountering the person of Jesus —
that he is still far from the goal, and he adds:
"What do I still lack?" (Mt 19:20).
    That is why Jesus invites him
    to enter the path to perfection:
        "If you wish to be perfect,
        go, sell your possessions, and give the money to the poor,
        and you will have treasure in heaven;
            then, come follow me" (Mt 19:21).
This answer must be read
in the context of the whole of the Gospel
and in the context of the Beatitudes.

The Beatitudes do not coincide with the commandments;
they are open to the perfection proper to the Beatitudes.
The Beatitudes are a sort of self-portrait of Christ,
inviting us to discipleship
and to communion with him (CCC 1717).

17. The young man, having observed all the commandments,
shows that he is incapable of taking the next step by himself alone.
   To do so requires mature human freedom
   ("If you wish to be perfect")
   and God's gift of grace
   ("Come, follow me").
      Jesus points out to the young man
      that the commandments are the first
      and indispensable condition
      for having eternal life,
      while to give up all he possesses
      and to follow the Lord is presented as an invitation:
      "if you wish."
These words of Jesus reveal the particular dynamic
of freedom's growth toward maturity,
and at the same time they bear witness
to the relationship between freedom and divine law.
   Human freedom and law are not in opposition;
   they appeal to one another.
   The followers of Christ know
   that their vocation is freedom,
   allowing them through love
   to be servants of one another (Gal 5:13).

18. Those who "live by the flesh"
experience God's law as a burden;
those "who walk by the Spirit" (Gal 5:16)
find in God's law the way to practice love
as something freely chosen and lived out.
They feel an interior urge
not to stop at the minimum demands of the law,
but to live them in their fullness.
   This invitation to go and sell your possessions
   is not restricted to a small group of individuals.
   Made possible by grace
   it is meant for everyone.
The invitation "come, follow me,"
is the new, specific form of the commandment of the love of God.
   "Be merciful
   as your heavenly Father is merciful" (Lk 6:36).

- *"Come, follow me" (Mt 19:21)*

19. Jesus calls people to follow him.
Every believer is called to be a follower of Christ.
It involves holding fast to the very person of Christ,
sharing his loving obedience to the will of the Father.
    To imitate the Son
    means to imitate the Father.

20. Jesus asks us to love one another
"as I have loved you" (Jn 15:12).
Jesus' way of acting, his words, his deeds, and his precepts
constitute the moral rule of Christian life.
His passion and death on the cross
reveal his love for the Father and for others.
    The word "as" indicates the degree of love
    his disciples are called to:
        "Greater love has no one than this,
        to lay down one's life for one's friends" (Jn 13:34–35).

21. Being a follower of Christ means
becoming conformed to him,
which is the effect of the active presence of the Holy Spirit.
    One with Christ, the believer
    becomes a member of his body,
    "clothed in Christ" (cf. Gal 3:27),
    as Saint Augustine rejoiced:
    "We have become Christ!"*
Sharing in the Eucharist
is the culmination of our assimilation to Christ.

- *"With God all things are possible" (Mt 19:26)*

22. Not only the rich man,
but also his disciples are taken aback
by Jesus' condition for discipleship,
which transcend human aspirations and abilities.
    But Jesus tells them:
    "With God all things are possible" (Mt 19:26).
The human person becomes capable of this love
by virtue of a gift received,
    "the love of God poured in our hearts
    through the Holy Spirit given to us" (Jn 15:9).

23. The apostle Paul explains
how the law enables sinners to take stock

---

*In Ioannis Evangelium Tractactus, 21, 8.

of their own powerlessness,
stripping them of their self-sufficiency,
and leading them to ask for and to receive
"life in the Spirit."
    Or in the words of Saint Augustine:
    "The law was given that grace might be sought;
    and grace was given that the law might be fulfilled."*

24. We are speaking here of a possibility
opened to the human person by the gift of grace,
by the gift of God, by God's love —
a gift that generates and sustains
the free response of a full love for God
and for our brothers and sisters.
    The new law is the grace of the Holy Spirit
    given through faith in Christ,
    giving us also the power to "do what is true" (cf. Jn 3:21).

• *"Lo, I am with you always to the close of the age" (Mt 28:20)*

25. The young man's question arises in every individual's heart;
the teacher is always present and at work in our midst
in his body, which is the church "to the close of the age."
    The moral prescriptions in the old covenant,
    which reached their perfection in the new covenant
    in the very person of the Son of God,
    must be kept and put into practice
    in the various cultures
    throughout the whole of human history.
Jesus entrusted the task of interpreting them
to the apostles and their successors,
with the special assistance of the Holy Spirit:
"He who hears you, hears me" (Lk 10:16).

26. From the very beginning
the apostles were vigilant
over the right conduct of Christians.
    The first Christians differed from others
    not only in their faith and liturgy,
    but also in their moral conduct.
    Their rule of life was "faith working through love" (Gal 5:6).
No damage should be done
to the harmony between faith and life.
    The unity of the church is damaged
    not only by Christians who reject or distort the truths of faith

---

*De Spiritu et Littera, 19, 34.

but also by those who disregard
the moral obligations to which they are called by the Gospel.

27. Preserving the unity of the church,
    promoting and preserving the faith and moral life,
    is the task entrusted by Jesus to the apostles,
    and their successors.
    "The task of authentically interpreting the word of God,
    whether in its written form or in that of tradition,
    has been entrusted only to those charged
    with the church's living magisterium,
    whose authority is exercised
    in the name of Jesus Christ" (Vatican II, *Dei Verbum*, 8).
    Being in this way "the pillar and bulwark of truth" (1 Tim 3:15)
    the church senses the duty
    to offer its own discernment and teaching
    with regard to new tendencies and theories
    frequently debated in moral theology today.

Chapter Two
"DO NOT BE CONFORMED TO THIS WORLD"
(Rom 12:2)

*The Church and the Discernment of Certain Tendencies
in Present-day Moral Theology*

• *Teaching What Befits Sound Doctrine (cf. Tit 2:1)*

28. Our meditation on the dialogue
    between Jesus and the rich young man
    taught us the essentials as regards moral action:
      — the subordination of the human being and human activity to God,
         the one who "alone is good";
      — the relation between the moral good and eternal life;
      — Christian discipleship, opening the perspective of perfect love;
      — the gift of the Holy Spirit,
         source and means of the moral life of the "new creation."
    The church has always kept in mind Jesus' words,
    developing these truths on moral action
    — assisted by the Holy Spirit
    who is leading it into all the truth —
    just as it developed the truths of faith.

29. This is how the church developed
    the science of moral theology.

The Second Vatican Council invited scholars
to take "special care for the renewal of moral theology"
and to look for better ways to communicate it
to the people of their time and in their culture (cf. GS 62).
The church, and particularly the bishops,
are deeply appreciative of the work done,
and they encourage theologians to continue their efforts.
   But there have been certain interpretations
   of Christian morality
   that are not consistent with "sound teaching" (2 Tim 4:3).
Certainly the church's magisterium does not intend
to impose on the faithful any particular theological system,
still less a philosophical one.
Nevertheless, it has the duty to state
that some trends in theological thinking
and certain philosophical affirmations
are incompatible with revealed truth.

30. It is my intention to state what is contrary to "sound doctrine"
     and to put forward once more the master's reply to the question:
     "Teacher, what good must I do to have eternal life?"
     We do this living out Saint Paul's admonition to Timothy:
        "Be urgent in season and out of season...
        for the time will come when people
        will suit their own likings
        and turn away from listening to the truth
        and wander into myths" (2 Tim 4:1–5).

   • *"You will know the truth and the truth will make you free"*
      (Jn 8:32)

31. In contemporary moral thinking
     all discussions are closely related
     to one crucial issue: "human freedom."
        Today people have a strong sense of freedom,
        due to a heightened sense of the dignity
        of the human person and of his or her uniqueness.
     This is definitely a positive achievement of modern culture,
     but it is expressed sometimes in ways
     that diverge from the truth about the human person
     as a creature and the image of God,
     ways that need to be corrected and purified
     in the light of faith.

32. Certain currents in modern thought
     made of freedom something absolute,
     which then becomes the source of values.

In this way the sense of the transcendent is lost,
    or one is explicitly atheistic.
In this case it is the individual conscience
that decides categorically and infallibly
what is good and what is evil.
    To the affirmation that one has to follow one's conscience
    is added the affirmation that a moral judgment is true
    because it has its origin in conscience.
The inescapable claims of truth disappear,
yielding their place to a criterion
of sincerity, authenticity, and of "being at peace with oneself."
    Once the idea of a universal truth about the good,
    knowable by human reason, is lost,
    the notion of conscience inevitably also changes.
One's conscience is then no longer
an act of a person's intelligence
applying the universal knowledge of good to a particular situation
in a judgment about the right conduct
to be chosen here and now.
    Instead there is the tendency
    to grant to the conscience of the individual the prerogative
    to determine on its own and independently
    what is good and evil and to act accordingly.
In the latter way each individual
is faced with his or her own truth
different from the truth of others.
In the final instance it can lead to a denial
of the very idea of human nature.

33. Side by side with its exaltation of human freedom
    modern culture questions — oddly enough —
    its very existence.
        The "behavioral sciences" rightly drew
        attention to the many kinds
        of psychological and social conditioning
        that influence the exercise of human freedom,
        insights that found applications in various areas
        like pedagogy or the administration of justice.
But some, going beyond the conclusions
that can be legitimately drawn from these observations,
question or even deny the reality of human freedom.
        Others, misusing scientific research
        about the human person
        and arguing from the great variety of customs,
        behavior patterns, and institutions,

end up with the denial of universal human values
or a relativistic conception of morality.

34. The questions about freedom and morality
cannot be separated.
Though each individual has the right to be respected
in his or her own journey,
there remains a prior moral obligation
to seek the truth.
   As Cardinal J. H. Newman put it:
   "Conscience has rights because it has duties"*
Under the influence of the subjectivism and individualism
just mentioned,
certain tendencies in contemporary moral theology
developed novel interpretations
of the relationship of freedom to moral law,
of human nature to conscience,
and of the norms
for the moral evaluation of human acts.
   To evaluate these tendencies critically
   we must examine them in the light of Christ's words:
      "You will know the truth
      and the truth will set you free" (Jn 8:32).

I. *Freedom and Law*

   • *"Of the tree of the knowledge of good and evil you shall
      not eat" (Gn 2:17)*

35. The prohibition to eat from the tree of knowledge
is the imagery revelation uses to teach that the power to decide
what is good and what is evil does not belong to humanity,
but to God alone.
   Human persons are free;
   they can even eat from the tree of knowledge.
   But their freedom is not unlimited;
   it must halt before the moral law given by God.
Human freedom finds its fulfillment
precisely in the acceptance of that law.
God's law does not reduce or do away
with human freedom;
instead it protects and promotes that freedom.
   Some present-day doctrines center upon
   the conflict between freedom and law,

---

*A Letter Addressed to His Grace the Duke of Norfolk: Certain Difficulties Felt by Anglicans
in Catholic Teaching* (London: Longman, Green and Company, 1868–1881), 2:250.

granting individuals the right to determine
what is good and what is evil.
Human freedom would then be able to "create values";
it would enjoy a primacy over truth,
so that truth would be its creation.
In this way freedom would claim
an absolute moral autonomy and sovereignty.

36. These modern concerns have influenced Catholic moral theology.
It has never attempted to set human freedom
against the divine law,
and it has never denied
the ultimate religious foundation of moral laws.
But it has been rethinking the role of reason and faith
in identifying moral norms
with reference to specific "inner-worldly" kinds of behavior,
involving oneself, others, and the world.
Dialoguing with modern culture
— in response to the Second Vatican Council —
some have emphasized the rational character
of the norms belonging to the natural moral law,
wishing to make them
universally understandable and communicable.
Some have attempted to affirm
the inner character of those norms,
obliging the will only after being acknowledged by human reason
and concretely by the human conscience.
These trends of thought have led
to the denial of the fact
that God is the author of the natural moral law,
and not the human person.

37. Some theologians have introduced a distinction
between an ethical order valid for this world
and an order of salvation for which
only certain intentions and interior attitudes
regarding God and neighbor would be significant.
The word of God would be limited in this way
to an exhortation, a general recommendation,
to be filled in and completed
by the autonomous human reason alone
in an objective way with normative directives,
adapted to the concrete historical situation.
An autonomy understood in this way
denies the church magisterium's competence
to deal with moral norms when dealing

with the so-called human good,
as those norms would be no part
of the proper content of revelation.
  This interpretation is incompatible
  with Catholic teaching.

- *"God left human beings in the power of their
  own counsel" (Sir 15:14)*

38. These words indicate that persons
  share in God's dominion even as regards themselves.
    This exercise of dominion over the world
    represents a great and responsible task.
    Consequently a rightful autonomy
    is due to every person as well as to the human community
    in obedience to the Creator:
      "Created things have their own laws and values,
      which are to be gradually discovered, utilized,
      and ordered by humanity" (GS 36).

39. In the words of the Second Vatican Council
  not only the world, but human persons themselves
  have been entrusted to their own care and responsibility
  to seek their Creator and attain perfection.
    The Council warns against the false concept that
    "created things are not dependent on God
    and that they can be used
    without reference to their Creator" (GS 36).

40. At the heart of morality we find
  the principle of humanity's "rightful autonomy" (GS 41),
  the possession in ourselves of our own law, received from the Creator.
    This autonomy cannot mean that our reason itself
    creates values and moral norms:
      "of the tree of the knowledge of good and evil,
      you shall not eat" (Gn 2:17).

41. Human freedom and God's law are called to meet.
    God's will does not alienate us from ourselves;
    it is not foreign to us or intolerant of our freedom.
    We participate in God's wisdom and providence.
    We do not have our moral knowledge on our own,
    but by sharing in the eternal wisdom
    through the light of our natural reason
    and of divine revelation.
  Law is an expression of divine wisdom;
  submitting to the law is submitting to the truth of creation.

In the freedom of the person
we meet the image and the nearness of God
who is present in all (cf. Eph 4:6),
and yet greater than all.

• *"Blessed is the one who takes delight in the law of
the Lord" (cf. Ps 1:1–2)*

42. In our journey to God we must freely do good and avoid evil,
but in order to do this we must be able to distinguish
good from evil.
    And this takes place above all
    thanks to the light of natural reason,
    which is nothing else but
    "an imprint on us of the divine light" (ST, Ia–Iae, q. 93, a. 2).
    Natural law is precisely so called
    because the reason that promulgates it
    is proper to human nature (CCC 1955).

43. God cares for human beings not "from without,"
like for beings who are not persons,
but "from within," through reason,
which by its natural knowledge of God's eternal law
shows the person to take the right direction
in free actions.
    In this way we are called to share
    in God's providence.

44. The church included this doctrine of natural law
in its own teaching and frequently emphasized it.
    We are able to recognize good and evil by our reason,
    enlightened by divine revelation
    beginning with the commandments
    given on Mount Sinai and received
    with great joy and thankfulness by Moses and his people —
    sentiments that we find expressed
    numerous times in the psalms:
        "The commandment of the Lord is pure,
        enlightenment for the eyes" (Ps 18:8–9).

45. The church, preserving the entire deposit of revelation,
receives in addition the gift of the new law,
the fulfillment of God's law
in Jesus Christ and in his Spirit.
    It is an interior law
        "written not with ink
        but with the Spirit of the living God,

not on tables of stone
  but on tablets of human hearts" (2 Cor 3:3).
Though one usually distinguished
between the "old" and the "new" law,
the author is the one and same God.
The two support each other and intersect,
conforming us "to the image of his Son" (Rom 8:29).

• *"What the law requires is written on their hearts" (Rom 2:15)*

46. There always have been debates
on the alleged conflict between nature and freedom.
Our own time is marked by a similar tension.
    Empiricism and certain forms of liberalism
    set the two terms as opposed,
    if not in direct conflict with each other.
    To many the world of the senses
    within space and time,
    physiochemical constants, bodily processes,
    psychological impulses, and social conditioning
    seem the only human reality.
In this context even moral facts
are often treated as statistically verifiable data
and as patterns of behavior
that can be explained as psychosocial processes.
Some moralists can be tempted to take
concrete human behavior patterns
as the standard for their disciplines.
    Other moralists remain sensitive to the dignity of freedom,
    but they often conceive of freedom
    as in conflict with material and biological nature,
    over which it must progressively assert itself,
    thus overlooking the created dimension of nature
    and misunderstanding its integrity.
    "Nature" becomes a raw material
    in need of being transformed
    and overcome by human freedom.
    It is in this advancement of humankind's power
    that values, even moral ones, are established.
        In all this nature means in the first place
        the human body itself, its makeup and its processes.
Human nature could in this way be reduced and treated
as biological or social material.
The person would become humanity's own life-project.
    We would be nothing more
    than our own freedom.

47. In this context objections have been raised
    against the traditional concept of natural law,
    which is accused of presenting as moral laws
    what are only biological laws.
    In this way a permanent and unchanging character
    would have been attributed
    to certain kinds of human behavior.
        This kind of "biologistic" or "naturalistic" argumentation
        would be found even in some documents
        of the church's magisterium on sexual and conjugal behavior.
    It was on the basis of this understanding, they maintain,
    that contraception, sterilization, autoeroticism, premarital sex,
    homosexual relations, and artificial insemination
    were condemned as morally unacceptable.
        According to those moral theologians,
        a morally negative evaluation of these acts
        fails to take into adequate consideration
        the person who as a rational being
        not only can, but actually must
        determine the meaning of his or her behavior.
    This process of "determining the meaning"
    would have to take into account the human being
    as existing in a body and in history.
    It would have to take into account
    the behavioral models and the meanings
    in any given culture.
    It would have to respect the fundamental commandment
    of love of God and neighbor.
        Love of neighbor would mean above all
        — and even exclusively —
        respect for others' freedom to make their own decisions
        in determining their individual acts
        so complex from the viewpoint of situations.

48. In such a theory freedom becomes an absolute;
    the human body is treated as a raw given devoid of any meaning
    until freedom has shaped it with its design.
        Human nature and the human body
        would be foreign (extrinsic)
        to the person, the subject, and the human act,
        a way of thinking that would
        divide the human person.
    It contradicts the church's teaching
    on the unity of the human person
    whose rational, spiritual, and immortal soul

is the principle of the human being,
whereby it exists as a whole, as a person.
   The body, promised the resurrection,
   will share in glory.
   Reason and free will are linked
   with all the bodily and sense faculties.
The human being cannot be reduced
to a freedom that is self-designing;
rather it entails a spiritual and bodily structure,
demanding a respect without which
one would fall into relativism and arbitrariness.

49. This reduction of the human person
to a "spiritual" and formal freedom
misunderstands the moral meaning of the body.
Body and soul are inseparable; they stand or fall together.

50. Natural law refers
to a human person's proper nature,
which is the person's self in the unity of body and soul.
   "The natural moral law expresses and lays down
   the purposes, rights, and duties that are based upon
   the bodily and spiritual nature of the human person.
   Therefore this law cannot be thought of
   as simply a set of norms on the biological level;
   rather it must be defined as the rational order
   whereby a person is called by the Creator
   to direct and regulate his or her life and actions
   and in particular to make use of his or her own body."*
By rejecting all manipulation of corporeity
that alters its human meaning,
the church serves humanity showing the path to true love,
the only path to find God.

• *"From the beginning it was not so" (Mt 19:8)*

51. Because it is "truth" the natural law is universal.
It makes itself felt to all human beings.
Any separation between the freedom of individuals
and the nature we all have in common
obscures this universality,
which is the foundation for the fundamental rights and duties
extending to the whole of humankind.

---

*Congregation for the Doctrine of the Faith, Instruction on Respect for Human Life in Its Origin and on the Dignity of Procreation, *Donum Vitae*, 1987, Introduction, 3; cf. HV 10.

This universality embraces
the individuality and uniqueness
of the free acts of each human person.
By submitting to the common law
those acts build up the true community of persons.

52. Positive precepts ordering us
to perform certain actions and to cultivate certain dispositions,
such as serving God and honoring one's parents,
are universally binding and "unchanging" (GS 29).
    They unite in the same common good
    all people in history,
    created with the same divine calling and destiny.
The negative precepts of the natural law
oblige each and every individual,
always and in every circumstance regardless of the cost,
never to offend in anyone — beginning with oneself —
the personal dignity common to all.
    The fact that only negative commandments oblige
    always and under all circumstances
    does not mean that in the moral life
    prohibitions are more important
    than the obligation to do good,
    as indicated by the positive commandments.
The commandment to love God and neighbor
does not have any higher limit,
but it does have a lower limit
beneath which the commandment is broken.
    Besides it is always possible that people
    can be hindered from doing good,
    but they can never be hindered
    from not doing certain things,
    especially if they are prepared to die
    rather than to do evil.

53. Contemporaries have been asking
whether it is really possible
that the objective norms of human behavior
can be universally valid
because they were established in the past
when no one knew the progress humanity
would make in the future.
    True, the human person always exists in a particular culture,
    but no one is exhaustively defined by culture.
    There is something in the person
    that transcends every culture.

This "something" is precisely the human nature
Jesus spoke about when he said
in his own social and cultural context:
"from the beginning it was not so" (Mt 19:8).
　　But certainly there is the need to discover
　　the best formulation for those absolute moral norms
　　in the light of different cultural contexts.

II. Conscience and Truth

　• *The Human Sanctuary*

54. Human persons have in their hearts a law written by God.
　　Their conscience speaks to their hearts: "Do this, shun that."
　　Obeying this law is their very dignity,
　　and they will be judged accordingly (cf. Rom 2:14–16).
　　　　Setting freedom and law in opposition to each other
　　　　or exalting freedom to the point of idolatry
　　　　leads to a "creative" understanding of the moral conscience
　　　　that diverges from the church's tradition.

55. Some theologians hold
　　that general norms cannot be expected to foresee
　　and to respect all the individual concrete acts of the person
　　in their uniqueness and particularity,
　　as — according to their opinion — was sometimes done in the past.
　　　　Some others even state that those general norms offer only
　　　　a general perspective that helps to put order
　　　　into one's personal and social life.
　　　　They point to the complexity typical of conscience,
　　　　because of the numerous influences
　　　　a person is subjected to
　　　　psychologically, emotionally, and culturally.
　　　　The conscience they value
　　　　leads the person not so much
　　　　to a meticulous observance of general laws
　　　　— so they say —
　　　　as to a creative and responsible acceptance
　　　　of the personal tasks entrusted to the person in question.
　　Some authors,
　　emphasizing the "creative" character of conscience,
　　no longer speak of its "judgments," but of its "decisions,"
　　adding that this process is inhibited in many moral questions
　　by the intervention of the church's magisterium.

56. Those authors propose a kind of double moral truth.
　　Beyond the abstract and doctrinal level

one has to acknowledge the priority
of a more concrete, existential level.
   The latter, on account of circumstances and the situation,
   could be the basis of certain exceptions
   to the general rule and thus would permit
   one to do in good conscience
   what is qualified as evil by the moral law.
On this basis an attempt is made
to legitimize so-called pastoral solutions,
contrary to the teaching of the church.
   These approaches challenge
   the very identity of the moral conscience.

- *The Judgment of Conscience*

57. Speaking about the "gentiles" Paul wrote:
"What the law requires is written on their hearts,
while their conscience also bears witness
and their conflicting thoughts
accuse or perhaps excuse them" (Rom 2:14–15).
   Conscience confronts persons with the law
   and becomes a witness to them
   of their faithfulness or unfaithfulness,
   of their moral goodness or badness.

58. This interior dialogue in the person with self
is also a dialogue with God, the author of the law,
the image and final end of the person.
Saint Bonaventure teaches:
   "Conscience is like God's herald and messenger,
   ...when he proclaims the edict of the king.
   This is why conscience has binding force."*
Conscience is the witness of God's very self
calling the person to obedience.

59. The judgment of conscience is a practical judgment,
judging what a person should do or not do
and assessing what has already been done.
It applies to a concrete situation
the conviction that one must love and do good and avoid evil.
This first principle is like an imperishable spark
shining in the heart of each human being.
   Conscience is the application of the natural law
   to a particular case,
   an inner dictate for the individual,

---

*In *II Librum Sentent.* dist. 39, 1, 3, conclusion. Ed. Ad claras aquas, II, 907 b.

a summons to do what is good in a particular situation,
respecting the universality of the law.

60. The person must act in accordance
with the judgment of conscience.
If persons act against their judgment
or, in a case where they lack certainty
about the rightness and goodness of a certain act,
still perform the act,
they stand condemned by their own conscience.
   Conscience does not establish the law;
   it bears witness to the authority
   of the natural law (cf. *Dominum et Vivificantem*, 43).

61. If persons do evil, the just judgment of their conscience
remains with them, as a witness to the universal truth
and also as a pledge of hope and mercy,
bearing witness to the evil done
and reminding of the need
to ask — with the help of God's grace — for forgiveness
and to do good and cultivate virtue.
   Conscience expresses itself in "judgments"
   and not in arbitrary "decisions."
One's maturity and responsibility
are not measured by the liberation
of one's conscience from objective truth
and by one's alleged autonomy,
but by an insistent search for truth
and by allowing oneself to be guided by that truth.

   • *Seeking What Is True and Good*

62. Conscience can err because of invincible ignorance
but also because someone shows little concern to find out
what is good and what is evil,
and conscience becomes gradually almost blind
by becoming accustomed to sin.
   In order to have a "good conscience" (1 Tim 1:5)
   one must seek the truth
   and make one's judgments accordingly.
An ignorance of which one is not aware
and which one is unable to overcome by oneself
does not take away the dignity of one's conscience.
   Such a conscience, though erring,
   continues to speak in the name of that truth
   everyone is called to seek sincerely.

63. A "subjective" error about the moral good,
    should not be confused with
    the "objective" truth about the moral order.
    The moral value of an act performed
    with an erroneous conscience is not equivalent
    to the moral value of an act performed
    with a true and correct conscience.
    >   The evil committed
    >   — though not chargeable to the person in question —
    >   does not cease to be evil and disorder of the moral order.
    Nor does a good act not recognized as such not contribute
    to the moral growth of the person who performs it.
    >   Conscience compromises its dignity
    >   when it is culpably erroneous,
    >   showing no concern for seeking
    >   what is good and what is evil.
    >   As Jesus said:
    >   "If the light in you is darkness,
    >   how great is the darkness!" (Mt 6:23).

64. Jesus' words call us to "form" our conscience
    in a continuous conversion to what is true and good.
    Christians find in the church a great help
    in this formation of their consciences.
    >   The church's authority does not undermine
    >   their freedom of conscience,
    >   because that freedom is not "from" the truth
    >   but always "within" the truth.
    The magisterium does not bring to the conscience
    truths that are foreign to it,
    but truths that it ought already to possess.
    >   Especially in more difficult issues
    >   the church helps consciences to attain the truth
    >   and to abide in it.

III. Fundamental Choice and Specific Kinds of Behavior

- *"Only do not use your freedom as an opportunity for the flesh"*
  (Gal 5:13)

65. The heightened concern for freedom in our day
    has led to the insight that freedom
    is not only the choice for one or another action,
    but also the decision about oneself
    and about setting one's life for or against truth
    and ultimately for or against God,
    thus shaping one's entire moral life.

Some even speak of a "fundamental freedom"
deeper than and different from the freedom of choice.
According to them the key role in a person's life
is the "fundamental option,"
the overall self-determination one makes
in a "transcendental" way.
   The particular acts that flow from this option
   would never express it definitively;
   their object is not the absolute good,
   but only particular goods,
   which do not determine the freedom
   of a person as a totality.
In this way they introduce a distinction
— and sometimes a separation —
between this fundamental option
and the deliberate choices
of one's concrete behavior.
   This eventually leads to a position
   where the moral assessment of persons
   depends on their fundamental option,
   and not on their behavior in this world.

66. Christian moral teaching acknowledges
the importance of a fundamental choice for God
that through love (cf. Gal 5:6) comes from the "heart" (cf. Rom 10:10),
in the submission of oneself to God.
   The fundamental decision for Israel
   was to obey the first and basic command
   "I am the Lord, your God" (Ex 20:2).
Jesus calls the young rich man
to a fundamental choice when he says:
   "If you wish to be perfect...come and follow me" (Mt 19:21).
      This is a call to the greatest possible human freedom,
      as Paul notes: "You were called to freedom" (Gal 5:13).
      But Paul adds a warning:
      "Only do not use your freedom
      as an opportunity for the flesh."
And this is the case when concrete acts
are separated from an act of faith
in the sense of a fundamental option.

67. These tendencies are therefore
contrary to the teaching of Holy Scripture,
which links that option to how one acts.
   The fundamental option is worked out
   in one's free decisions in which one conforms to God's will.

It is revoked when a person decides
to go against that will in a morally grave matter.
To separate the fundamental option from one's concrete acts
denies the integrity of a person
and the unity between body and soul.

68. A person does not suffer perdition
only by being unfaithful to that fundamental option
by which that person made
"a free self-commitment to God" (*Dei Verbum* 5);
with every freely committed mortal sin
one offends God as the giver of the law
and as a result becomes guilty
with regard to the entire law (cf. Jas 2:8–11).
Even if one perseveres in faith,
one loses "sanctifying grace," "charity,"
and "eternal happiness."

• *Mortal and Venial Sin*

69. All this has led some theologians to revise the distinction
between mortal sins and venial sins.
They insist that losing sanctifying grace
could only be done by an act
that engages the whole of the person.
That is why they say that it is difficult to accept
— at least psychologically —
that a Christian wishing to remain united to Christ
could so easily and repeatedly commit mortal sins,
as the "matter" of those acts
sometimes seems to indicate.
It would also be hard to accept — so they say —
that one is able over a short period of time
to sever one's bond with God
and regain it afterward by sincere repentance.
The gravity of a sin, they maintain,
does not depend so much on the matter of the sin
but on the degree of engagement of the freedom
of the person who acts.

70. The 1983 Synod of Bishops reaffirmed the distinction
between venial and mortal sin,
and recalled that mortal sin is a sin in a grave matter
committed with full knowledge and deliberate consent.
"Care should be taken not to reduce mortal sin
to an act of fundamental option
— as it is commonly said today — against God" (RP 17).

One sins mortally in idolatry, apostasy, and atheism,
but also in any act of disobedience
to God's commandments in a grave matter.

IV. The Moral Act

- *Teleology and Teleologism*

71. Moral acts express and determine
the goodness or evil of the individual
who performs them.
> Saint Gregory of Nyssa put it well:
> "Human life is always subject to change;
> it needs to be born ever anew....
> But here birth is the result of a free choice....
> Thus we are in a certain sense our own parents,
> creating ourselves as we will, by our decisions."*

72. When the young man asked Jesus:
"What good must I do to have eternal life?" (Mt 19:6),
he made the connection between the moral value of an act
and a person's final end.
> Jesus answered by referring to the commandments,
> making it clear that the path to that end
> is marked by respect for the divine laws
> that safeguard the human good.
> Only acts in conformity with the good
> can be the path leading to life.
An activity is not morally good
only because one's intention is good;
it is good when it expresses a person's voluntary ordering
toward the human good
as it is acknowledged in its truth by reason.
> If a concrete action is not in harmony
> with the true good of the person,
> then the choice of such an act is morally evil
> and in conflict with our ultimate end,
> the supreme good, God's very self.

73. In Jesus Christ and in his Spirit
Christians are a "new" creation, showing by their actions
likeness or unlikeness to the image of the Son,
who is the firstborn among many (cf. Rom 8:29).
> "The beauty of [Christ's] image
> shines forth in us,

---

*De Vita Moysis, II, 2–3.

when we show ourselves to be good
in our works."*
The moral life leads us to the supreme good
and our ultimate end (*telos*),
not solely depending on our intention,
but on our acts that conform
to the moral good of the human being.
   Jesus says it himself:
   "If you wish to enter into life,
   keep the commandments" (Mt 19:17).

74. What is it that ensures
this ordering of the human acts to God?
   To answer this question
   some new theological trends emerged
   during recent decades that ask for a careful discernment.
Certain ethical "teleological" theories
draw their norms to evaluate the moral rightness of an action
from the weighing of the goods to be gained
and the consequent values to be respected.
   Right conduct would be the one
   capable of "maximizing" good
   and "minimizing" evil.
Their research into a rational foundation for moral life
is valid and needed
and helps us to dialogue and cooperate
with others in our pluralistic societies.

75. But trying to work out
such a rational (or autonomous) morality
some arrived at false solutions
called "consequentialism" and "proportionalism."
   Consequentialism claims to draw its evaluation
   of the rightness of a certain way of acting
   from a calculation of the foreseeable consequences of an act.
   Proportionalism focuses on the proportion
   between the good and bad effects of a choice
   in view of the "greater good" or "lesser evil"
   in a certain situation.
While acknowledging that moral values
are indicated by reason and by revelation,
both theories maintain that it is never possible to formulate

*Tractatus ad Tiberium Diaconum sociosque, II. Responsiones ad Tiberium Diaconum sociosque: Saint Cyril of Alexandria, *In Divi Johannis Evangelium*, vol. III, ed. Philip Edward Pusey (Brussels: Culture et Civilisation, 1965), 590.

an absolute prohibition of particular kinds of behavior
because they would be in conflict in every circumstance
and in every culture with those values.
    In this way the acting person would be responsible
    in two ways for the value pursued:
        the values or goods involved would be,
        from one point of view, of the *moral* order,
        and, from another point of view,
        of the *premoral, nonmoral, or physical* order.
In a world where goodness is always mixed with evil
and every good effect linked to other evil effects,
a moral act should — according to those theories —
be judged in two ways:
        its moral "goodness" on the basis of a person's intention
        in reference to goods
        such as love of God and neighbor, justice, etc.,
        and its "rightness" on the basis of a consideration
        of the foreseeable effects
        such as health or its endangerment,
        life, death, loss of material goods, etc.
Acts could be described as "right" or "wrong"
without our being able to judge
whether the person choosing them
is morally "good" or "bad."
    In such a case a person could be faithful
    to the highest values of charity and prudence,
    but this faithfulness
    would not necessarily be incompatible
    with choices against certain moral precepts.
Those precepts — even in grave matter —
would be considered as relative and open to exceptions.

- *The Object of the Deliberate Act*

76. These theories can gain some persuasive force
because they are in line with technical and economic activities
run on the basis of calculating resources and profits.
    They are, however, not in line with the church's teaching
    when they believe that they can justify
    the choice of a behavior that is against the commandments
    of the divine and natural law.
God and love of neighbor
cannot be separated from the observance
of the commandments of the covenant
renewed in the blood of Christ
and in the gift of the Holy Spirit.

Many even accepted martyrdom
as a consequence of their faithfulness.

77. One certainly has to take into consideration
both one's intention
— as Jesus told those who prescribed outward practices
without paying attention to the heart (Mt 15:19) —
as well as the goods obtained and the evils avoided.
   But neither the weighing of the intention
   nor the weighing of the goods
   is sufficient for judging
   the morality of an act.
Besides, everyone recognizes the difficulty,
or rather the impossibility,
of evaluating all the good and evil consequences
of one's own acts.
   If this is not possible,
   how would one go about finding the norms
   to find the proportion between the two?
How would one ever come to an absolute obligation
based on such debatable calculations?

78. The morality of a human act depends primarily
on the "object" chosen by the will of the acting person.
If this object is in conformity with reason,
it is the cause of the goodness of the will.
   As the *Catechism of the Catholic Church* teaches:
   "there are certain specific kinds of behavior
   that are always wrong to choose,
   because choosing them involves
   a disorder of the will, that is, a moral evil" (CCC 1761).
No evil done with a good intention can be excused.
Yet it is not enough to do good works;
they need to be done well
and for the sole purpose of pleasing God.

   • *"Intrinsic Evil": It is not licit to do evil that good
   may come of it (cf. Rom 3:8).*

79. One must therefore reject
the teleological theories of
"consequentialism" and "proportionalism,"
which hold that it is impossible to say
that certain acts are morally evil
because of their "object."
   The primary and decisive element
   for moral judgment is the object of the human act,

which establishes whether it is capable
of being ordered to the good
and to the ultimate end, which is God.
This capability is grasped by reason
in the very being of the person,
in a person's truth, inclinations, motivations, and finalities,
and has a spiritual dimension as well.

80. Reason attests that certain acts
cannot be ordered to God:
acts that are, and always will be,
intrinsically evil, by reason of their very object.
The Second Vatican Council gave a number of examples:
   "Whatever is hostile to life itself,
   such as any kind of homicide, genocide, abortion,
   euthanasia, and voluntary suicide;
   whatever violates the integrity of the human person,
   such as mutilation, physical and mental torture,
   and attempts to coerce the spirit;
   whatever is offensive to human dignity,
   such as subhuman living conditions, arbitrary imprisonment,
   deportation, slavery, prostitution,
   and trafficking in women and children;
   degrading conditions of work which treat laborers
   as mere instruments of profit,
   and not as free responsible persons" (GS 27).
In regard to contraceptive practices
Pope Paul VI added,
   "Though it is true that sometimes it is lawful
   to tolerate a lesser moral evil in order to avoid a greater one
   or in order to promote a greater good,
   it is never lawful even for the gravest reason
   to do evil that good may come out of it" (HV 14; cf. Rom 3:8).

81. Sacred Scripture teaches that intrinsically evil acts
remain "irremediably" evil acts,
incapable of being ordered to God
and the good of the person (cf. 1 Cor 6:9–10).

82. Consequently norms that prohibit such acts
oblige without any exception,
and it is an error to say that one has to take into account
the intention why such an act was chosen
or the foreseeable consequences of such an act.
   Saying something like that
   would make it impossible to affirm

"an objective moral order"
and would be to the detriment of the human community,
the truth about the good,
and the ecclesial community.

83. Consequently the church must reject
the theories set forth above,
which contradict the integral truth
about the human person.
    Dear Bishop Brothers, we must not only warn the faithful;
    we must show the truth that is in Jesus Christ himself.
    In him we are able to make the law our own
    by living it,
    "the perfect law, the law of liberty" (Jas 1:25).

Chapter Three
"LEST THE CROSS OF CHRIST BE EMPTIED
OF ITS POWER" (1 Cor 1:17)

Moral Good for the Life of the Church and the World

• *"For freedom Christ has set us free" (Gal 5:1)*

84. Only the freedom that submits to truth
leads human persons to their true good.
Surrounded by contempt for human life,
people are no longer convinced
that salvation can be found only in the truth.
    This leads to a lack of trust in the wisdom of God,
    which guides humanity with the moral law.

85. The church seeks to help all the faithful
to form a moral conscience leading to judgments
in accordance with the truth.
The church finds its support — the "secret" of its educative power —
in constantly looking to Jesus Christ.
    The crucified Christ reveals
    the authentic meaning of freedom;
    he lives it in the total gift of self.

86. Reason and daily experience affirm
the weakness of human freedom.
A person's freedom is in some mysterious way
inclined to betray the openness to the true and the good.
    Within these errors and wrong decisions
    one glimpses the source of a deep rebellion.

Consequently freedom itself has to be set free.
It is Christ who "has set us free for freedom" (cf. Gal 5:1).

87. Jesus told Pilate that he came
"to bear witness to the truth" (Jn 18:37).
Jesus reveals by his whole life and not only by his words
that freedom is acquired in love, that is, in the gift of self.
"Greater love has no one than this
to lay down one's life for one's friends" (Jn 15:13).
Contemplation of Jesus crucified
is the highway that the church must walk every day
if it wishes to understand freedom.
We are called to share in the grace and responsibility
of the Son of humankind, who came
"not to be served but to serve
and to give his life as a ransom for many" (Mt 20:28).

• *Walking in the Light (cf. 1 Jn 1:7)*

88. The separation of faith from moral life
is one of the most serious pastoral problems
in today's growing secularism.
Believers often make moral judgments
contrary to the Gospel.
It is urgent that believers rediscover
the authentic reality of the Christian faith,
which is a question not only of intellectual assent to Christ,
but a living remembrance of his commandments
to be lived out,
enabling us to live as he lived in profound love of God
and of our brothers and sisters.

89. Through the moral life,
faith becomes "confession" not only before God,
but also before the people we live with.
It becomes witness:
"You are the light of the world.
Let your light so shine before all,
that they may see your good works
and give glory to your Father
who is in heaven" (Mt 5:14–16).
Christ's witness is the source,
the model, and the means
for the witness of his disciples,
who are called to walk on the same road.
It can even lead to the supreme witness of martyrdom.

> • *Martyrdom, the Exaltation of the Inviolable Holiness*
> *of God's Law*

90. Martyrdom confirms in an eloquent way
    that moral norms are valid without exception
    and that ethical theories that deny this
    are unacceptable.

91. Already in the Old Testament we find
    admirable witnesses of fidelity to God's law
    to the point of accepting voluntary death.
      Susanna, refusing to sin with the two unjust judges,
      though they threatened to have her condemned to death,
      is a prime example of someone who
      bears witness to the absoluteness of the moral order,
      being willing to die as a martyr (cf. Dan 13:22–23).
    John the Baptizer gave his life in witness to truth and justice,
    like Saint Stephen and Saint James
    and so many followers of Jesus Christ
    who confirmed the truth of his message
    at the cost of their lives.
      The church has canonized numerous saints
      who preferred death to a single mortal sin,
      setting them as examples.

92. Martyrdom rejects as false
    whatever "human meaning" one might acclaim to attribute
    —even in "exceptional" circumstances—
    to an act that is morally evil in itself.
      It unmasks the true face of such an act;
      it is a violation of a person's "humanity."
      Hence martyrdom is also the exaltation
      of a person's perfect "humanity" and true "life."

93. Martyrdom is also a sign
    of the holiness of the church.
    Martyrs and in general all saints
    light up every period of human history
    by reawakening its moral sense.
      Martyrdom represents the high point of the witness
      all Christians must daily be ready to give.
      Faced with the many difficulties
      that fidelity to the moral order
      can demand even in the most ordinary circumstances,
      the Christian is called, with the grace of God invoked in prayer,
      to a sometimes heroic commitment.

94. Christians are not alone in this.
    They are supported by the moral sense in peoples
    and the great religious and sapiential traditions of East and West,
    from which the mysterious workings of the Holy Spirit
    are not absent.

    • *Universal and Unchanging Moral Norms at the Service*
      of the Person and of Society

95. Sometimes the church's inflexibility in these matters
    is seen as an intolerable intransigence
    in light of the actual complex and conflict-ridden situation
    in the moral life of individuals and society.
       The church, one hears, is lacking in
       understanding and compassion.
    But the church is in no way
    the author or arbiter of these norms.
    Out of love for the true good of the person
    the church can never renounce
    "the principle of truth and consistency,
    whereby it does not agree
    to call good evil and evil good" (RP 34)
       though it must always be careful
       not to break the bruised reed,
       or to quench the dimly burning wick (Is 42:3).

96. The church's firmness in defending
    the universal and unchanging norms
    is not demeaning at all.
    Its only purpose is to serve the person's freedom.
    It is a service directed to all humankind.
    This service is not only for the individual
    but also for the community, for society as such,
    offering a solid foundation
    for a just and peaceful coexistence.

97. Civil authorities and individuals,
    even though they might have good intentions,
    never have authority to violate
    the fundamental rights of the human person.

    • *Morality and the Renewal of Social and Political Life*

98. There is a growing reaction
    on the part of so many
    whose fundamental rights have been held in contempt
    and an ever more acute sense of the need
    for a radical personal and social renewal

capable of ensuring justice,
solidarity, honesty, and openness.
  It is not difficult to discover "cultural" causes
  at the bottom of these situations,
  but at the heart of them we find the moral sense,
  which in turn is rooted in the religious sense.

99. Only God constitutes the unshakable foundation
needed to reconstruct a renewed society
and especially to overcome
the various forms of totalitarianism.
  If there is no transcendent truth,
  then there is no sure principle for guaranteeing
  just relations between people.
Self-interests of class, group, or nation
would set them inevitably
in opposition to one another.

100. The *Catechism of the Catholic Church* affirms
that respect for human dignity requires
the practice of temperance,
moderation in our attachment to worldly goods,
and the virtues of justice and solidarity.
  It condemns theft,
  deliberate retention of goods lent or lost,
  business fraud, unjust wages,
  excessively high prices, private use of corporate property,
  work badly done, tax fraud,
  forgery of checks and invoices,
  excessive expenses, waste, etc.

101. In the political sphere openness in public administration,
impartiality, respect for the rights of political adversaries,
safeguarding the rights of the accused,
an honest use of public funds,
and the rejection of illicit means to gain power
are all principles rooted
in the transcendent value of the person
and the objective moral order.
  In every sphere of life
  morality renders a primordial service
  to the individual and society.

• *Grace and Obedience to God's Law*

102. As universal and daily experience shows,
the human being is tempted to break

the harmony between freedom and truth.
Humanity's history of sin began
the moment it wished to be independent
and to determine what is good and what is evil —
a temptation that echoes in all other temptations.
> But temptation can be overcome
> and sins can be avoided.
> Keeping God's commands can be difficult,
> but it is never impossible,
> for "God does not command the impossible" (cf. 1 Jn 5:3).

103. In the mystery of Christ's redemption
we discover the "concrete" possibilities of ourselves.
Christ has redeemed us!
This means that he has given us the possibility
of realizing the entire truth of our being.

104. It is quite human for sinners
to acknowledge their weakness
and to ask mercy for their failings.
It is unacceptable to make one's own weakness
the norm of the truth about the good.
It would corrupt the morality of society as a whole.
> Take to heart the parable of the repentant tax collector
> and the self-satisfied Pharisee (cf. Lk 18:9–14).

105. In our days the attitude of the self-justified Pharisee
is expressed in the attempt to adapt
the moral norm to one's own capacities and personal interests
and even in the rejection of a norm.
> Accepting the "disproportion"
> between the law and human ability
> kindles the desire for grace
> and prepares one to receive it.

• *Morality and New Evangelization*

106. Our time needs a "new evangelization,"
an evangelization that is new in its ardor, methods, and expression.
De-Christianization involves not only the loss of faith,
but also a decline of the moral sense.
> Today's widespread tendencies
> toward subjectivism, utilitarianism, and relativism
> appear not merely as pragmatic attitudes
> or patterns of behavior,
> but rather as approaches having a basis in theory
> and claiming full cultural and social legitimacy.

107. A "new evangelization" involves
the proclamation and presentation of morality.
Jesus proclaiming the kingdom of God
called people to faith and conversion.
    This new evangelization will show its authenticity
    not only in the word proclaimed,
    but also in the word lived.
    A life of holiness is the simplest
    and most attractive way to perceive
    the liberating force of God's love.
It is in the lives of the saints
and above all in the life of the Virgin Mother of God
that we find the full expression
of the task of "priest, prophet, and king,"
which all Christians receive as a gift at their rebirth in baptism.

108. At the heart of the new evangelization
is the Spirit of Christ.
The Spirit of Jesus received
by the humble and docile heart of the believer,
brings about the flourishing of the Christian moral life
and the witness of holiness
amid the great variety of vocations, gifts,
responsibilities, conditions, and life situations.
    We can now understand the place in the church
    of those who reflect theologically
    upon the moral life.

  • *The Service of Moral Theologians*

109. The whole church is called to evangelization
and to the witness of a life of faith.
In order to carry out that mission,
the church must constantly reawaken its own life.
The vocation of the theologian in the church
is at the service of the effort to understand the faith.
    Theology is an ecclesial science;
    it is a service in and for the church.

110. All that has been said about theology in general
can and must be said of moral theology.
The church's magisterium intervenes not only
in the sphere of faith, but also in the sphere of morals,
discerning and warning.
    Moral theologians in seminaries and faculties of theology
    have the grave duty to instruct the faithful
    — and especially future pastors —

about all the commandments and practical norms
authoritatively declared by the church.
They are called to develop a deeper understanding
of the reasons underlying these teachings,
expound their validity and obligation,
and show their interconnection
and their relation with humanity's ultimate end.
They should be examples of loyal assent,
deeply concerned to clarify more fully
the moral doctrine and vision set forth by the church.

111. The service that moral theologians
are called to provide at the present time
is of the utmost importance,
not only for the church's life and mission,
but also for human society and culture.
They have the task of highlighting
the dynamism that will trigger off
a person's response to the divine call
in the process of growth in love
within a community of salvation.
They will help to develop fully
the "image of God" in the human being.
This is a difficult task in our days,
which cannot be accomplished by working merely
with the data of the so-called behavioral sciences.
Their importance must always be measured
against the moral questions:
"What is good or evil"
and "What must be done to have eternal life?"

112. The behavioral sciences,
despite the great value of the information they provide,
cannot be considered decisive indications of moral norms.
The statistical "normality" they provide
bears the traces of a fall from humanity's original situation;
in other words, it is affected by sin.
It is the Gospel that reveals the full truth
about the human person and the moral journey.

113. Moral teaching can in no way
be established following the rules
and procedures of a democracy.
Dissent in the form of protests and polemics in the media
is opposed to ecclesial communion and to a correct understanding
of the hierarchical constitution of the people of God.

Opposition to the teaching of the church's pastors
cannot be seen as a legitimate expression of Christian freedom
or of the diversity of the Spirit's gifts.

• *Our Own Responsibility as Pastors*

114. It is the common duty of us, pastors of the church,
     and even before that our common grace,
     to teach the faithful the things that lead them to God,
     just as the Lord did with the young man in the Gospel.
         The answer to the question "What good must I do?"
         has been entrusted in a special way to us
         as prophets, but also as priests.

115. This is the first time that the magisterium
     has set forth the fundamental elements of this teaching,
     represented today with the authority of the successor of Peter.
     Each of us knows how important this teaching is
     and what is involved not only for individuals
     but also for the whole of society,
     when we reaffirm the universality and immutability
     of the moral commandments,
     especially those that prohibit intrinsically evil acts.

116. My brothers in the episcopate,
     it is part of our pastoral ministry to see to it
     that this moral teaching is faithfully handed down
     and to have recourse to appropriate measures to ensure
     that the faithful are guarded
     from every doctrine and theory contrary to it.
         In carrying out this task
         we are all assisted by theologians;
         even so theological opinions constitute
         neither the rule nor the norm of our teaching.
     Its authority comes from our fidelity
     to the Catholic faith that comes to us
     —with the assistance of the Holy Spirit—
     from the apostles.
         Bishops are responsible for Catholic institutions;
         it falls to them to grant the title "Catholic"
         or, if institutions fail to live up to that title,
         to take it away.

117. In the heart of every Christian,
     in the heart of each person lives this question:
         "Teacher what good must I do
         to have eternal life?" (Mt 19:16).

The church answers with the voice of Jesus,
the voice of the truth about good and evil.
The answer becomes light and fire
for the one who asked the question.
"All of us ... are being changed into his likeness. ...
For this comes from the Lord, the Spirit" (2 Cor 3:5–6, 17–18).

CONCLUSION

Mary, Mother of Mercy

118. At the end of these considerations
let us entrust ourselves to Mary,
Mother of God and Mother of Mercy.
    Mary is Mother of Mercy
    because her son, Jesus Christ,
    was sent by the Father
    as the revelation of God's mercy.
No human sin can erase the mercy of God,
if only we call upon God.
God's mercy toward us is redemption.
It reaches its fullness in the gift of the Holy Spirit,
who gives new life and asks that it be lived.

119. Such is the consoling certainty of the Christian faith.
It can seem that Christian morality is too demanding,
but this is untrue, for it consists in the simplicity of the Gospel,
in following Jesus Christ.
    By the light of the Holy Spirit
    it can be understood by everyone.
    Yet it faces reality in all its complexity
    and leads to a better understanding of that reality.

120. Mary is also the Mother of Mercy
because Jesus entrusted to her from the cross
the whole of humanity.
    Mary lived her freedom
    by giving herself to God
    and accepting God's gift within herself.
    She became the model of all those
    who hear the word of God and keep it (cf. Lk 11:28),
    earning the title "Seat of Wisdom."
        O Mary, Mother of Mercy,
        watch over all people.

11

The Gospel of Life
Evangelium Vitae

March 25, 1995

As explained in The Splendor of Truth, *the commandment "You shall not kill" is an absolute. This absoluteness is here applied to the issues of abortion and euthanasia. The Christian "culture of life" is explained as opposed to the "culture of death," which allows and sometimes legalizes abortion and euthanasia. The future of society depends on the rediscovery of our human dignity. The Gospel of Life must be celebrated in our love for each other. It is not only for Christians; it is for everyone.*

INTRODUCTION

1. The Gospel of Life is at the heart of Jesus' message.
   Presenting the heart of his mission,
   Jesus said:
   > "I came that they may have life,
   > life to the full" (Jn 10:10).

Incomparable Worth of the Human Person

2. The human person is called to a fullness of life
   that exceeds this earthly life,
   for it consists in sharing God's life
   even in its temporal phase.
   Life in time
   is the fundamental condition,
   the initial stage and an integral part
   of the entire unified process of human existence.
   This process is enlightened by the promise
   and renewed by the gift of divine life,
   which will reach its fullness in eternity.

Life on earth is not an ultimate,
but a penultimate reality,
a sacred reality entrusted to us
and to be brought to perfection
in the gift of ourselves to God
and to our sisters and brothers.
The Gospel of Life has a profound echo
in the heart of every person,
fulfilling all the heart's expectations
while even surpassing them.
 Every person open to truth and goodness
 and led by the light of reason and grace
 can come to recognize
 — in the natural law written in the heart (Rom 2:14–15) —
the sacred value of human life from its beginning to its end
and the right to have it respected.
It is upon this right
that every human community is founded.
Believers in Christ have a special duty
to defend and promote this right
because "by the incarnation,
the Son of God has united himself in some fashion
with every human being" (GS 22).
The church feels called to proclaim this "gospel"
to the peoples of all times.
The living human person is the way for the church.

New Threats to Human Life

3. Every threat to human dignity is felt in the church's heart.
It affects its faith and engages its mission
of proclaiming the Gospel of Life —
 a proclamation especially pressing
 because of the new threats
 to the life of individuals and peoples,
 especially where life is weak and defenseless.
 Next to the old scourges
 of poverty, hunger, disease, violence, and war,
 new threats are arising at an alarming scale.
I repeat the words of the Second Vatican Council
condemning crimes and attacks against human life:
 "— whatever is opposed to life itself
  such as any type of murder, genocide,
  abortion, euthanasia, or willful self-destruction;
 — whatever violates the integrity of the human person
  such as mutilation,

torments inflicted on body or mind,
attempts to coerce the will itself;
— whatever insults human dignity,
such as subhuman living conditions,
arbitrary imprisonment, deportation,
slavery, prostitution,
the selling of women and children;
— as well as disgraceful working conditions,
where people are treated
as mere tools for profit,
rather than as free and responsible persons . . .
all these things and others of their kind
are infamies indeed.
They poison human society,
but they do more harm to those who practice them
than to those who suffer from injury.
Moreover they are a supreme dishonor
to the Creator" (GS 27).

4. But this disturbing state of affairs is expanding.
Scientific and technological progress gave rise to new forms
of attacks on the dignity of the human being.
A new cultural climate is growing and taking hold,
giving crimes against life an even more sinister character.
   Broad sectors of public opinion
   justify crimes against life
   in the name of the rights of individual freedom,
   claiming not only exemption from punishment,
   but even authorization by the state,
   so that they can be done with total freedom
   and with the assistance of health-care systems.
The fact that many countries decided
— against their own constitutions —
not to punish these practices against life and even to legalize them
is a disturbing symptom and a grave cause of moral decline.
   Choices once considered criminal
   are gradually becoming socially acceptable.
   Certain sectors of the medical profession
   are increasingly willing to carry out these acts.
   Demographic, social, and family problems
   are left open to false and deceptive solutions.
The end result is tragic:
not only are human lives still to be born
or in their final stage destroyed,
but the distinction between good and evil is darkened.

In Communion with All the Bishops of the World

5. The Extraordinary Consistory of Cardinals in April 1991
   was devoted to the threats to human life today.
   The cardinals unanimously asked me to reaffirm
   with the authority of the successor of Peter
   the value of human life and its inviolability.
   That is why I wrote a letter to each of my brother bishops,
   a letter at Pentecost 1991,
   to help me to draw up a specific document.
   I am grateful for the answers I received.
   > Just as a century ago the church came to the defense
   > of the oppressed working classes,
   > the church feels now in duty bound
   > to speak out for those who have no voice.
   There is a multitude of weak and defenseless people,
   unborn children in particular,
   whose right to life is trampled upon.
   The church cannot remain silent today
   when the social justices of the past
   are being compounded in many regions of the world
   with even more serious forms of injustice and oppression,
   though these developments are being presented
   as elements of progress in view of a new world order.
   > This encyclical appeals in the name of God to everyone
   > to repent and to protect, love, and serve every human life.

6. Together with all my brothers and sisters in the faith,
   I wish to meditate once more and proclaim the Gospel of Life.
   I pray that a general commitment
   to support the family will reappear,
   as the family will always remain the "sanctuary of life."
   > Let us together offer this world new signs of hope,
   > affirming a new culture of life
   > and building a civilization of truth and love.

I. THE VOICE OF YOUR BROTHER'S BLOOD CRIES TO ME FROM THE GROUND: Present-Day Threats to Human Life

- *"Cain rose up against his brother Abel and killed him" (Gn 4:8): The Roots of Violence against Life*

7. God did not make death;
   God created humankind
   in the image of God's own eternity ... (Wis 1:13–14, 2:23–24).

Death came into the world
as a result of the devil's envy (cf. Gn 3:1, 4–5)
and the sin of our first parents (cf. Gn 2:17, 3:17–19).
And death entered it in a violent way
through the killing of Abel by his brother Cain (Gn 4:8).
This first page in the book of Genesis
is rewritten daily in the book of human history.

8. Cain was angry with Abel because
— for a reason not further explained —
God preferred Abel's sacrifice,
without interrupting the bond God had with Cain.
God admonishes him, reminding Cain of his freedom
in the face of sin:
"Its desire is for you,
but you must master it" (Gn 4:7).
Envy and anger have the upper hand,
and Cain kills his own brother.
Every murder is a violation
of the "spiritual" kinship
uniting humankind in one great family
in which all share the same fundamental good:
equal personal dignity.
Not infrequently the kinship "of flesh and blood"
is also violated, when threats to life
arise between parents and children
or in the wider context of the family or kinship,
as happens in abortion
or when euthanasia is encouraged or practiced.
At the root of every act of violence
is a concession to the "thinking" of the evil one,
"who was a murderer from the beginning" (Jn 8:44).
When God asks him about Abel's fate,
Cain arrogantly eludes the question:
"I do not know, am I my brother's keeper?" (Gn 4:9).
He tries to cover up his crime with a lie,
just like all kinds of ideologies try to justify and disguise
the most atrocious crimes against human beings,
refusing to accept responsibility for their brothers and sisters.
Symptoms include
the lack of solidarity toward society's weakest members,
such as the elderly, immigrants, and children,
and the indifference often found
in the relations between the world's peoples
even when basic values as survival, freedom, and peace are involved.

9. God cannot leave crime unpunished.
   Among the "sins that cry for justice"
   the church has included willful murder as the first.
   Life, especially human life, belongs to God;
   whoever attacks human life attacks God's very self.
       Cain is cursed by God and by the earth;
       he will live in the wilderness and desert.
       Murderous violence changes humanity's environment.
       From being the garden of Eden,
       a place of plenty, interpersonal harmony,
       and friendship with God,
       the earth becomes the "Land of Nod" (Gn 4:16),
       a place of scarcity, loneliness, and separation from God.
       Uncertainty and restlessness will follow Cain forever.
   Yet God, always merciful even when punishing,
   "puts a mark on Cain, lest anyone who came upon him
   should kill him" (Gn 4:15).
   Not even murderers lose their personal dignity,
   and God pledges to guarantee this,
   showing the paradoxical mystery
   of God's merciful justice.
       As Saint Ambrose writes:
           "God, who preferred the correction
           rather than the death of the sinner,
           did not desire that a homicide be punished
           by the exaction of another act of homicide."*

   • *"What have you done?" (Gn 4:10):
     The Eclipse of the Value of Life*

10. The Lord said to Cain:
    "What have you done?
    The voice of your brother's blood
    is crying to me from the ground" (Gn 4:10).
        The Lord's question
        is addressed to the people of today
        to make them realize the extent
        of the attacks against human life
        that continue to mark human history,
        to discover their causes,
        and to ponder their consequences.
    Some come from nature,
    made worse by the culpable indifference and negligence
    of those who could remedy them.

---

*De Cain et Abel, II, 10, 38.

Others are the results of violence,
hatred, and conflicting interests,
leading to war, slaughter, and genocide.
    How can we fail to consider
    the violence against life done to millions,
    especially against children
    forced into poverty, malnutrition, and hunger
    because of the unjust distribution of resources
    between peoples and social classes?
What of the violence not only in wars,
but in the scandalous arms trade?
What about death caused
by reckless tampering with the world's ecological balance,
the spread of drugs,
or the promotion of sexual activity—
morally unacceptable and involving grave risks to life?
    It is impossible to catalogue completely
    the threats to human life today.

11. Here we will pay particular attention
    to those attacks affecting life in its earliest and final stages,
    attacks that present new characteristics
    and that raise extraordinarily serious questions.
        It is not only that those attacks tend no longer
        to be considered as "crimes,"
        but that they paradoxically assume the nature of "rights,"
        to the point that states
        are called upon to give them legal recognition
        and provide the free services of health-care personnel.
    Such attacks strike human life
    at the time of its greatest frailty,
    when it lacks any means of self-defense;
    and even more seriously they strike
    at the very heart and with the complicity
    of the family, by its nature the "sanctuary of life."
        How did this happen?
        There are many factors to be taken into account:
            the profound crisis of culture that generates skepticism
            as regards ethics, rights, and duties;
            the interpersonal and existential problems
            that leave individuals, couples, and families alone;
            the situations of acute poverty, anxiety, frustration, pain,
            and especially violence against women.
    All this explains, at least in part,
    an "eclipse" of the value of life,

though conscience does not cease to point to it
as a sacred and inviolable value,
as is shown by the use of innocuous medical terms
to distract attention from what is involved.

12. This moral uncertainty can in some way be explained
by the gravity of today's social problems,
sometimes mitigating the responsibility of individuals,
but it is no less true that we are confronted
by a true structure of sin,
which takes the form of a "culture of death."
    This culture denies solidarity
    and is fostered by currents that encourage a society
    that is excessively concerned with efficiency.
It is in a certain sense
a war of the powerful against the poor.
A life that would require greater acceptance, love, and care
is considered useless and an intolerable burden
and is therefore rejected in one way or another.
    A disabled or ill person compromises
    the well-being of those more favored
    and is looked upon as an enemy to be resisted or eliminated.
This "conspiracy against life" damages not only individuals
in their personal, family, and group relations,
but also distorts the relations between peoples and states.

13. To facilitate the spread of abortion
enormous sums of money are invested in the production
of ever more simple and effective pharmaceuticals
to kill the fetus in the mother's womb
without recourse to medical assistance,
thus removing abortion
from any kind of control or social responsibility.
    It is often said that contraception
    is the most effective remedy against abortion.
    And the Catholic Church is then accused
    of actually promoting abortion
    because it obstinately continues to teach
    the moral unlawfulness of contraception.
This objection is unfounded.
It may be that many use contraception
to exclude the consequent temptation of abortion.
But the negative values inherent in the "contraceptive mentality"
— very different from responsible parenthood —
in fact strengthen this temptation
when an unwanted life is conceived.

The pro-abortion culture is especially strong
where the church's teaching on abortion is rejected.
Contraception and abortion are different evils,
    but they are closely connected as fruits of the same tree.
It is true that in many cases contraception and abortion
are practiced under the pressure of real-life situations,
which nevertheless can never exonerate people from striving
to obey God's law fully.
    Yet often such practices are rooted
    in a hedonistic mentality
    that is unwilling to accept responsibility
    in matters of sexuality;
    it implies a self-centered concept of freedom
    that regards procreation as an obstacle
    to personal self-fulfillment.
The close connection between contraception and abortion
is demonstrated in an alarming way
by the development of chemical products,
intra-uterine devices, and vaccines
— distributed with the same ease as contraceptives —
that really induce abortions in the very early stages
of the development of human life.

14. The various techniques of artificial reproduction,
which would seem to be at the service of life
and frequently used with that intention,
actually open the door to new threats against life.
    Apart from the fact that they are morally unacceptable
    because they separate procreation
    from the fully human context of the conjugal act,
    these techniques have a high rate of failure.
    The resulting embryo is exposed to the risk of death
    generally within a very short period of time.
The number of embryos produced is often greater
than that needed,
and the so-called spare embryos are destroyed
or used for research,
which reduces human life to simple "biological material."
    Prenatal diagnosis, which presents no moral objections
    if done in order to identify medical treatment
    needed by the child in the womb,
    all too often becomes a reason for a "eugenic" abortion,
    mistakenly held to be consistent
    with the demands of "therapeutic interventions,"
    which accept life only under certain conditions

and reject it when it is affected
by any limitation, disability, or illness.
The point has even been reached
that with the same logic basic care and nourishment are denied
to babies born with serious disability or illness.
The proposals advanced here and there to justify infanticide,
following the same arguments used to justify the right to abortion,
are even more alarming.

15. No less serious threats hang over the incurably ill and dying
as the attempt is made to eliminate suffering at the root
by hastening death so that it comes at a suitable moment.
    Various considerations usually contribute to such a decision:
the sense of anguish and frailty in the sick person
and the misplaced compassion
of those close to the sick person.
All this is aggravated by a culture
that considers suffering the epitome of evil,
failing to see any meaning or value in it,
especially in the absence of a religious outlook.
    On a more general level contemporary culture
leads people to think that they can control life and death
by taking the decisions about them into their own hands.
A tragic expression of all this is the spread of euthanasia,
justified by the motive of avoiding costs
that bring no return and weigh heavily on society.
    Euthanasia is proposed
to eliminate malformed babies,
the disabled, the elderly,
and the terminally ill.
There are even more furtive
but no less serious forms of euthanasia
to increase the availability of organs for transplants,
without respecting the objective criteria
for verifying the death of the donor.

16. Demography is often used to justify attacks against life.
In the rich countries
there is a disturbing decline or collapse of the birth rate,
while poorer countries generally have a high rate
of population growth,
difficult to sustain because of their poverty.
    In the face of this overpopulation in poorer countries
  —instead of programs of development
and a fair distribution of production and resources—
anti-birth policies are enacted.

Contraception, sterilization, and abortion
are certainly part of the reason for the sharp decline in the birth rate,
and it is not difficult to be tempted to use the same means
where there is a "demographic explosion."
　　Some of the powerful of the earth
　　act like the pharaoh of old,
　　　who, haunted by the birth rate of Israel,
　　　ordered every male child born of Hebrew women to be killed.
They, too, fear that the growth of the poorest people
are a threat for their well-being
and the peace of their own countries.
They prefer to promote and impose
a massive program of birth control,
and even the help they would be willing to give is
on the unjust condition of accepting an anti-birth policy.

17. Humanity today offers us a truly alarming spectacle,
if we consider the scientifically
and systematically organized attacks on life,
done with the approval of certain health-care personnel.
We are in fact faced by a "conspiracy against life."
The mass media are often implicated in this conspiracy,
presenting contraception, sterilization, abortion, and even euthanasia
as a mark of progress and a victory of freedom,
while describing those who are pro-life
as enemies of progress and freedom.

• "Am I my brother's keeper?" (Gn 4:9): A Perverse Idea of Freedom

18. The Lord's question to Cain, "What have you done?"
reaches beyond the murder itself
to his motives and their consequences.
　　Decisions that go against life
　　sometimes arise from difficult or even tragic situations
　　and profound suffering, loneliness, poverty, depression,
　　and anxiety about the future—
　　circumstances that can mitigate considerably
　　subjective responsibility and consequent culpability.
But today the problem goes far beyond
these personal situations.
It is a problem at the cultural, social, and political levels,
where these crimes against life tend to be interpreted
as legitimate expressions of personal freedom.
　　In this way the process that led to the discovery
　　of the idea of "human rights" is reaching a turning point
　　and is marked by a surprising contradiction.

In an age when the rights of the person are proclaimed
and the value of life publicly affirmed,
the very right to life is trampled upon and denied
at the moments of birth and death.
>On one hand there is a growing moral sensitivity
>alert to the value of every individual as a human being
>without any distinction of race, nationality, religion,
>political opinion, or social class.
>On the other hand these proclamations
>are contradicted in practice.
How can these solemn affirmations
be reconciled with the widespread attacks on human life
and the refusal to accept those
who are weak, needy, elderly, or just conceived?
>These attacks go directly against respect for life;
>they threaten the very meaning of democratic coexistence,
>and our cities risk becoming societies of people
>who are rejected, marginalized, uprooted, and oppressed,
>instead of communities of "people living together."
How can we fail to see
that the solemn affirmation of human rights
in distinguished international assemblies
is a merely futile exercise
when the selfishness of the rich countries is not unmasked,
when their help to poorer countries
is made dependent on birth control?
>Should we not question the economic models,
>often adopted by states,
>that cause and aggravate injustice and violence,
>degrading whole peoples?

19. The roots of this contradiction can be found
in the mentality of a culture and morality
that — to begin with — carries the concept of subjectivity
to an extreme,
distorting it by recognizing the rights only of those
who enjoy full or incipient autonomy
and who emerge from a state of total dependency on others.
>How can we reconcile this approach
>with the exaltation of the human person
>as one who is "not to be used"?
>The theory of human rights is based precisely
>on the affirmation that the human person
>—unlike animals and things—
>cannot be subjected to domination by others.

In this mentality one tends to equate personal dignity
with verbal, explicit, or at least perceptible communication.
In this world there is no place for the unborn or dying
or for anyone at the mercy of others and totally dependent on them,
capable of communicating through the silent language
of profound sharing of affection.
    In this case it is force
        that decides in interpersonal relations and social life —
        the exact opposite of what a state ruled by law
        should affirm.
Another root of this contradiction
between affirmation and practice
lies in a notion of freedom
that exalts the individual in an absolute way
giving no place to solidarity, openness to others,
or service of them, asking like Cain:
"Am I my brother's keeper?"
    Yes, human beings are their brother's and sister's keepers.
    God entrusts us to one another.
    Our freedom has a relational dimension;
        we find our fulfillment through the gift of self to others.
Freedom destroys itself
and leads to the destruction of others
when it no longer respects its link
to the objective truth about good and evil
but refers only to a person's subjective opinion,
selfish interest, and whim.

20. This view of freedom leads to the point
    of rejecting one another.
    Everyone else is an enemy from whom one has to defend oneself.
    Society becomes a mass of individuals only,
    and individuals want only their own interests to prevail.
    Any reference to common values and a binding truth is lost;
    social life ventures onto the shifting sands of complete relativism.
    Everything becomes negotiable, even the right to life.
        The same happens at the level of politics and government.
        The right to life is denied on the basis of a parliamentary vote
        or the will of one part of the people — even if it is a majority.
    "Right" ceases to be such, as it is no longer firmly founded
    on the inviolable dignity of the human person
    but is subject to the will of the stronger party.
    In this way democracy moves toward
    a form of totalitarianism.
    The state is no longer a "common home."

It arrogates to itself the right to dispose of the life
of the weakest and most defenseless members,
from the unborn child to the elderly,
in the name of a public interest
that really is nothing but the interest of one part.
 Democratic legality seems to be maintained,
  but what we have is only the tragic caricature of legality.
To claim the right to abortion, infanticide, and euthanasia
and to recognize that right in law
means to attribute to human freedom
a perverse and evil significance:
that of an absolute power over others and against others.
It is the death of true freedom.

- *"And from your face I shall be hidden" (Gn 4:14): The Eclipse of the Sense of God and the Human Being*

21. The deepest roots of the struggle
between the "culture of life" and the "culture of death"
lie even deeper than this perverse idea of freedom.
At the heart of this human tragedy lies
the eclipse of the sense of God and of the human being
typical of secularism,
sometimes putting even Christian communities to the test.
 When the sense of God is lost,
  the sense of humanity tends to be lost as well,
  just as the systematic violation of the moral law
  darkens our capacity to discern God.
Cain, having killed Abel, is afraid
that he will have to "hide his face" from God
and that his fault is "greater than he can bear."
It is only before God
that one can admit one's sin and recognize its seriousness.

22. "When God is forgotten,
the creature itself becomes unintelligible" (GS 36).
We are no longer able to see ourselves
as "mysteriously different" from other creatures.
We are reduced — though at a high stage of perfection —
to being a "thing," no longer able to grasp
our "transcendent" character.
 Life is no longer considered a splendid gift from God,
  but rather life becomes a mere thing,
  subject to our control and manipulation.
  Birth and death, too, become things
  to be merely "possessed" or "rejected."

Once all reference to God has been removed,
everything else becomes distorted.
Nature itself, from being *mater* (mother),
is reduced to "matter,"
subject to every kind of manipulation.
   The very idea that there is a truth of creation
   and a plan of God for life that must be acknowledged
   tends to disappear in the direction
   a certain technical and scientific way of thinking
   appears to be taking.
Something similar seems to happen
when in their concern about this "freedom without law"
some people are led to a "law without freedom";
they consider it unlawful to interfere with nature,
practically making it into God.
   Losing contact with God
   is the deepest root of modern humanity's confusion.
   By "living as if God did not exist"
   we lose sight not only of God,
   but also of the mystery of the world
   and the mystery of our own being.

23. The eclipse of the sense of God and ourselves
    leads to materialism, which breeds
    individualism, utilitarianism, and hedonism.
    There is a switch from "being" to "having."
    The only goal is the pursuit
    of one's own material well-being.
    So-called quality of life is primarily seen
    as economic efficiency, inordinate consumerism,
    physical beauty, and pleasure,
    to the neglect of the more profound interpersonal,
    spiritual, and religious dimensions of existence.
       In such a context suffering is an inescapable burden.
       When it cannot be avoided,
       life appears to have lost all meaning,
       and the temptation grows to claim the right
       to suppress it.
    In this climate the body is reduced
    to a complex of organs, functions, and energies
    to be used for pleasure and efficiency.
    Sexuality, too, is depersonalized and exploited.
    From being the sign of love
    it becomes a means of self-assertion
    and the selfish satisfaction of personal desires and instincts.

The unitive and procreative meanings
inherent in the very nature of the conjugal act
are distorted and falsified.
Procreation becomes an "enemy" to be avoided.
If a child is welcomed it is because one desires a child "at all costs,"
and not because one is open to the richness of the other,
the richness the life of the child represents.
  Others are not considered for what they "are,"
  but for what they "have."

24. The eclipse of the sense of God and humanity
is at the heart of the individual conscience,
but it is also a question of the "moral conscience" of society.
It too is responsible,
because it tolerates or fosters the "culture of death,"
creating and consolidating actual "structures of sin."
Good and evil are confused
precisely in relation to the fundamental right to life.
  Yet all the efforts to silence it
  fail to stifle the voice of the Lord
  in the conscience of every individual,
  and it is from there that a new journey of love can begin.

• *"You have come to the sprinkled blood" (cf. Heb 12:22, 24):
  Signs of Hope and Invitation to Commitment*

25. The blood of every human being,
and not only the voice of the blood of Abel,
cries to God, the source and defender of life.
The voice of the blood of Christ
cries out in an absolutely singular way.
  This is "the sprinkled blood" that redeems, purifies, and saves,
  crying out more graciously than the blood of Abel.
  It expresses and requires a more radical justice,
  and above all it implores mercy.
The blood of Christ, revealing the Father's love,
shows how precious humanity is in God's eyes
and how priceless is the value of human life.
  As we sing at the Easter Vigil:
  "How precious must the human being be
  in the eyes of the Creator,
  if we gained so great a Redeemer."
Christ's blood reveals to us our greatness
and our vocation: the sincere gift of self.
Whoever drinks this blood in the Eucharist
is drawn into the dynamism of Jesus' love and gift of life,

bringing to fulfillment in us the original vocation to love,
which belongs to everyone.
  It is from this blood of Christ
  that we draw the strength to commit ourselves
  to promoting life.
  That blood is our hope,
  as "death is swallowed up in victory" (1 Cor. 15:54–55).

26. It would be one-sided, therefore, and discouraging,
    if we condemned the threats to life
    without accompanying them
    by the presentation of the positive signs at work
    in humanity's present situation.
    It is often hard to see those positive signs,
    perhaps because the media do not give them sufficient attention.
      But many initiatives
      to help the weak and defenseless have sprung up;
      many married couples are willing to accept children;
      many families are willing to accept abandoned children
      and others who have been left alone.
    Centers in support of life offer moral and material assistance
    to mothers in difficulties tempted to have recourse to abortion.
      Medical science continues to discover remedies
      for the unborn and the terminally ill.
      Agencies bring the benefits of the most advanced medicine
      to countries afflicted by poverty and endemic diseases.
      National and international associations of physicians
      bring quick relief to peoples
      affected by disasters, epidemics, and wars,
      though a just international distribution of medical resources
      is still far from being a reality.
      All are signs of a growing solidarity
      and a greater respect for life.

27. Initiatives are taken to raise social awareness
    in defense of life where laws permit abortion and euthanasia.
    When those movements — in accordance with their principles —
    act resolutely but without violence,
    they promote a wider consciousness of the value of life.
      How can we fail to mention
      the daily gestures of unselfish love and care
      that countless people make,
      guided by the example of Jesus
      "the good Samaritan" (cf. Lk 10:29–37).
    The church has always been in the front line
    of providing this charitable help.

In their love for God
so many of her sons and daughters
have dedicated themselves
— in traditional and ever new forms —
to the weak and needy.
    Among these signs of hope
    is also the ever growing sensitivity
    that opposes war
    as a means of resolving conflicts between nations,
    and finds effective "nonviolent" means
    to counter armed aggression.
Then there is evidence of a growing opposition
to the death penalty,
even when such a penalty is seen as a kind of
"legitimate defense" on the part of society.
Modern society has the means of effectively suppressing crime
by rendering criminals harmless
without definitively denying them the chance to reform.
    Another welcome sign is the growing attention paid to
    the quality of life and ecology
    and the reawakening of a reflection on issues of bioethics
    and ethical problems affecting human life.

28. We find ourselves in the midst of a conflict
    that affects us all
    with the inescapable responsibility of choosing
    to be unconditionally pro-life.
        Moses' invitation rings loud and clear:
            "I have set before you life and death,
            blessing and curse; therefore choose life,
            that you and your descendants may live" (Dt 30:15, 19).
    This call urges us to give our own existence
    a basic orientation that finds its full meaning
    when nourished by faith in Christ, who dwelt among us
    that "they may have life
    and have it abundantly" (Jn 10:10).

II. I CAME THAT THEY MAY HAVE LIFE: The Christian Message concerning Life

- *"The life was made manifest, and we saw it" (1 Jn 1:2): With Our Gaze Fixed on Christ, "The Word of Life"*

29. Faced with threats to life
    one might feel overwhelmed and powerless.
    At such a time we should profess our faith in Jesus Christ.

The Gospel of Life consists in the proclamation of the person of Jesus,
who made himself known by saying
"I am the way, and the truth, and the life" (Jn 14:6).
    Jesus told Martha, Lazarus' sister:
    "I am the resurrection and the life" (Jn 11:25–26).
Through the words, the actions, and the very person of Jesus Christ,
we are given the complete truth concerning the value of human life,
loving, serving, defending, and promoting it.
    In Christ the Gospel of Life
    —already present in the Old Testament—
    and written in the heart of every man and woman,
    is definitively proclaimed and fully given.

30. Hence, with our eyes fixed on the Lord Jesus,
    we wish to hear from him once again "the words of God" (Jn 3:34)
    and meditate anew on the Gospel of Life.

    • *"The Lord is my strength and my song, and he has become
      my salvation" (Ex 15:2): Life Is Always a Good*

31. In the Old Testament Israel discovered
    the preciousness of its life in the eyes of God
    in the events of the Exodus,
    the center of the Old Testament faith experience.
        When Israel was threatened by extermination,
        the Lord was revealed as savior.
    Thus coming to know the value of its own existence,
    Israel grew in its understanding
    of the meaning and value of life itself.
        It is the problem of suffering
        that puts this faith to the test.
        But even when this darkness is deepest
        faith points to a trusting acknowledgment of the mystery:
            "I know that you can do all things
            and that no purpose of yours can be thwarted" (Job 42:2).

    • *"The name of Jesus . . . has made this man strong" (Acts 3:16):
      In the Uncertainties of Human Life, Jesus Brings Life's
      Meaning to Fulfillment*

32. The experience of Israel is renewed
    in the experience of all the "poor"
    who meet Jesus of Nazareth.
    All who suffer because their lives are in some way "diminished"
    hear the good news of God's concern for them,
    realizing that their lives, too, are a gift
    carefully guarded in the hands of the Father (cf. Mt 6:25–34).

The crowds of the sick and the outcasts who follow him
find in his words and deeds
a revelation of the great value of their lives.
From the beginning the church proclaims Christ
as the one who "went about doing good
and healing all who were oppressed by the devil" (Acts 10:38).
The words and deeds of Jesus and the church
affect every person's life
in its moral and spiritual dimensions.
In an encounter with Jesus
we discover the authenticity of our own existence.

33. From beginning to end
Jesus' life is marked by uncertainty.
It is accepted with a joyful "yes" by Mary,
but others look for the child "to destroy him" (Mt 2:13).
> Life's contradictions and risks
> were fully accepted by Jesus;
> he lived poverty throughout his life
> until the culminating moment of the cross.
It is by his death that he revealed the value of life
inasmuch as in his self-giving on the cross
he becomes the source of new life for all (cf. Jn 12:32).
> On his journey through life,
> he is guided by the certainty
> that his life is in the hands of his Father:
> "Father, into your hands I commend my spirit" (Lk 23:46).
Truly great must be the value of human life
if the Son of God has taken it up,
and made it the instrument of the salvation of all humanity.

- *"Called . . . to be conformed to the image of his Son"
  (Rom 8:28–29): God's Glory Shines on the Face of
  Every Man and Woman*

34. Life is always a good. Why is life a good?
This question is found everywhere in the Bible,
and from the very first pages
it receives a powerful and amazing answer.
> Man and woman, formed from the dust of the earth,
> are traces of God's glory!
All is created in relation to them,
all things are made subject to them,
and they are bonded in a special way to their Creator:
> "Let us make man and woman in our image,
> after our likeness" (Gn 1:26).

Man and woman alone, among all visible creatures
are "capable of knowing and loving their Creator" (GS 12).
The life bestowed on us is much more than mere existence in time;
it is a drive toward fullness of life.
It is the seed of an existence
that transcends the very limits of time.

35. In the Bible's second account of creation,
God breathes into the human being.
Made by God and bearing within ourselves God's breath,
we are naturally drawn to God,
and our hearts will remain restless until they rest in God.
    The glory of God shines on the face of man and woman.
    In them the Creator found rest.

36. Sin marred God's plan.
Humanity rebels against its Creator
and ends up worshiping creatures,
not only deforming the image of God in themselves
but also replacing relationships of communion
by distrust, indifference, hostility, and murderous hatred.
    At the coming of the Son of God in flesh
    God's image shines forth anew,
    being the perfect image of the Father.
The plan given to Adam finds its fulfillment in Christ.
All who commit themselves to Christ are given the fullness of life;
the divine image is restored, renewed,
and brought to perfection in them.

• *"Whoever lives and believes in me shall never die" (Jn 11:26):
The Gift of Eternal Life*

37. The life the Son of God came to bring
cannot be reduced to our earthly life.
Sometimes Jesus refers to the life
he came to bring simply as "life."
At other times he speaks of "eternal life,"
evoking a perspective beyond time.
    The life Jesus promises is eternal
    because it is a full participation in the life
    of the one who is the "Eternal One."
To know God and God's Son is to accept
the loving communion of the Father, the Son, and the Spirit
into one's own life.

38. Eternal life is the life of God's very self
and at the same time the life of the children of God.

Here the Christian truth about life becomes most sublime.
Consequences arise from this for human life here on earth,
in which eternal life already springs forth.
  Our instinctive love for life
  finds a new breadth and depth
  in the divine dimensions of this good.
Our love for life cannot be reduced to self-expression
and relationships with others;
it develops in a joyful awareness
that life can become the place where God is manifest to us,
where we meet and enter into communion with God.

  • *"From one person in regard to another person I will demand
    an accounting" (Gn 9:5): Reverence and Love for Every
    Human Life*

39. Our life comes from God.
    It is God's gift, image, and imprint,
    a sharing in God's life.
      Life is the Lord's; we cannot do with it what we will.
      That is what God made clear to Noah after the flood:
        "For your own life blood, too, I will demand an accounting,
        and from one person in regard to another person
        I will demand an accounting for human life" (Gn 9:5).
    Human life is in God's loving hands.
    God exercises power over life not arbitrarily
    but as a caring mother who accepts,
    nurtures, and takes care of her child.
      Israel sees in the history of peoples
      and the destiny of individuals
      no mere chance or blind fate,
      but the loving plan of God,
      bringing together all the possibilities of life
      and opposing the powers of death.

40. The sacredness of life gives rise to its inviolability,
    written from the beginning in humanity's heart and conscience,
    an inviolability that is at the heart
    of the "ten words" in the covenant of Sinai (cf. Ex 20:13):
    "You shall not kill" (Ex 20:13),
    thus prohibiting in Israel's later legislation
    all personal injury inflicted on another (cf. Ex 21:12–27).
      This sense of the value of life does not find as yet
      the refinement found in the Sermon on the Mount,
      for it provides severe forms of corporeal punishment
      and even the death penalty.

It culminates in the positive commandment
obliging us to be responsible for our neighbor
as for ourselves:
"You shall love your neighbor as yourself" (Lev 19:18).

41. In his answer to the rich young man's question,
"Teacher, what good must I do, to have eternal life?"
Jesus reaffirms the commandment
"You shall not kill" in all its force.
    Jesus asks his disciples to go even further:
        "Every one who is angry with his brother or sister
        shall be liable to judgment" (Mt 5:21–22).
The requirements already foreseen in the Old Testament
—to defend life when it is weakened or threatened,
in the case of foreigners, widows,
orphans, the sick, and the poor,
including children in the womb (cf. Ex 21:22, 22:20–26)—
assume with Jesus new force and urgency.
    A stranger is no longer a stranger,
    as the parable of the good Samaritan shows (Lk 10:25–37).
    Even an enemy ceases to be an enemy;
    the height of this love is to pray for one's enemy,
    and be in tune with the love of God,
    who lets the "sun rise on the evil and on the good" (Mt 5:44–45).
We are required to show reverence and love
for every person and the life of every person:
"You shall love your neighbor as yourself."

- *"Be fruitful and multiply, and fill the earth and subdue it"*
  (Gn 1:28): Our Responsibility for Life

42. God entrusts to every person the task
of defending and promoting life.
Called to till and look after the garden of the world
we have a specific responsibility for the environment
in which we live.
    It is the ecological question
    —ranging from the preservation of the natural habitat
    of the different species of animals and other forms of life
    to "human ecology" properly speaking—
    which finds in the Bible clear and strong ethical direction
    leading to a solution
    that respects the great good of life, of every life.
The dominion granted to humankind by the Creator
is not an absolute power.
The Creator imposed a limitation from the beginning,

symbolically expressed by the prohibition
"not to eat of the fruit of the tree" (cf. Gn 2:16–17).
    We are subject not only to biological laws,
    but also to moral ones.

43. God made humanity to share
in responsibility for human life as such,
a responsibility that reaches its highest point
in the giving of life through procreation by man and woman,
so participating in God's "creative work" (GS 50).
    A new person born is born in the image and likeness of God.
    "Indeed, God alone is the source of that 'image and likeness'
    which is proper to the human being
    as it was received in creation.
    Begetting is the continuation of creation."*
Aware of this Eve exclaims
at the first birth of a human being on this earth:
"I have begotten a man with the help of God" (Gn 4:1).
    In procreation God's own image and likeness
    is transmitted, thanks to the creation of the immortal soul.
As co-workers with God man and woman — joined in matrimony —
become partners in a divine undertaking,
but this task of accepting and serving life involves everyone,
above all when it is at its weakest.

- *"For you formed my inmost being" (Ps 139:13):*
   The Dignity of the Unborn Child

44. Human life is at its most vulnerable
when it enters this world
and when it leaves it to embark upon eternity.
    The Old Testament does not say anything
    about protecting human life at its beginning,
    of life not yet born or of life nearing its end,
    since attacking life in that way is completely foreign
    to the way of thinking of the people of God.
In the Old Testament sterility is dreaded as a curse,
and numerous offspring are seen as a blessing.
    This is more than anything else
    because of the certainty that life has its origin in God.
    Many biblical passages speak lovingly of conception,
    of the forming of life in the mother's womb,
    and of the intimate connection between
    the initial moment of life and the action of God the Creator.

---

*John Paul II, *Letter to Families*, 9; cf. Pius XII, *Humani Generis* (August 12, 1950).

"Before I formed you in the womb, I knew you,
   and before you were born, I consecrated you" (Jer 1:5).
"You have fashioned and made me....
You clothed me with skin and flesh,
you knit me together with bones and sinews.
You granted me life and steadfast love" (Job 10:8–12).
How can anyone think that this process of the unfolding of life
could be separated from the wise and loving work of the Creator
and left prey to human caprice?

45. The New Testament confirms the recognition
of the value of life from its very beginning.
The value of the person from the moment of conception
   is celebrated in the meeting
   between the Virgin Mary and Elizabeth,
   and the meeting between the two children
   they carry in the womb.
It is in their meeting that the redemptive power
of the presence of the Son of God becomes operative.
   It is John in Elizabeth's womb
   who, leaping for joy, recognizes the Lord
   in Mary's womb.

- *"I kept my faith even when I said, 'I am greatly afflicted'"*
  (Ps 116:10): Life in Old Age and at Times of Suffering

46. It would be anachronistic to expect the Bible
to make reference to present-day issues concerning
respect for the elderly and sick,
or to condemn explicitly attempts to hasten their end by force.
In Holy Scripture old age is characterized by dignity
and surrounded by reverence.
   In old age, how should we face
   the inevitable decline of life?
   How should we act in the face of death?
Our life is in the hands of God in life, in sickness, and in death;
we have to entrust ourselves completely
to the "good pleasure of the Most High."
   Illness does not drive believers to despair,
   but makes them cry out in hope:
      "O Lord, my God, I cried to you for help,
      and you have healed me" (Ps 30:2–3).

47. Jesus shows great concern for our bodily life.
In the mission he gives to his disciples
healing the sick goes hand in hand
with the proclamation of the Gospel.

The life of the body in its earthly state
is no absolute good;
we might even be asked to give it up for a greater good.
   Jesus did not hesitate to sacrifice himself,
   making his life an offering to the Father
   and to those who belong to him (cf. Jn 10:17).
So do John the Baptizer, Stephen,
and a countless host of martyrs.
   No one, however, can arbitrarily choose
   whether to live or to die;
   the Creator is the absolute Master of such a decision.
   It is in God that
   "we live and move and have our being" (Acts 17:28).

• *"All who hold her fast will live" (Bar 4:1):*
  From the Law of Sinai to the Gift of the Spirit

48. The truth of life is revealed by God's commandment.
   It is not only ensured by the specific commandment
   "you shall not kill";
   the entire law of God serves to protect life.
      God's covenant with God's people
      is closely linked to the perspective of life.
      God's commandment is the path of life.
         "If you keep God's commandments,
         then you shall live and multiply,
         and the Lord God will bless you " (Dt 30:15–16).
   What is at stake is not only the existence of the people of Israel,
   but the whole world of today and tomorrow,
   the existence of the whole of humanity.
      It is thus that the law as a whole
      fully protects human life.
      It would be hard to be faithful to the commandment
      "you shall not kill," without observing the other "words of life."
   It is by listening to the word of God
   that we are able to bring forth fruits of life and happiness:
      "All who hold her fast will live,
      and those who forsake her will die" (Bar 4:1).

49. Israel's history shows how difficult it is
   to remain faithful to the law of life
   inscribed in human hearts and given on Sinai.
      The prophets remind people
      that the Lord is the source of life,
      pointing an accusing finger at those
      who show contempt for life and violate people's rights.

But while condemning offenses against life,
the prophets are also concerned to awaken hope
for a new principle of life and a "new heart":
    "A new heart I will give you,
    and a new spirit I will put within you" (Ez 36:25–26).
It is in the coming of Jesus that the law is fulfilled
and the new heart given through his Spirit.
He does not deny the law but brings it to fulfillment,
summing up the law and the prophets
in the golden rule of mutual love (cf. Mt 7:12).
    This is the new law,
    "the law of the Spirit of life in Christ Jesus" (Rom 8:2),
    expressed fully in the example of Jesus,
    who gave his life for his friends (cf. Jn 15:13),
    the gift of self for one's brothers and sisters.

- *"They shall look upon him whom they have pierced" (Jn 19:37): The Gospel of Life Is Brought to Fulfillment on the Tree of the Cross*

50. In the early afternoon of Good Friday
    "there was darkness over the whole land" (Lk 23:44) —
    a symbol of the conflict between good and evil.
        Today we find ourselves in a conflict
        between the "culture of death" and the "culture of life."
    This darkness does not overcome the glory of the cross.
    Jesus is nailed on the cross, mocked, jeered, and insulted,
    and yet amid all this, seeing him breathe his last,
    the Roman centurion exclaims:
    "Truly this man was the Son of God!" (Mk 15:39).
        He asked his Father to forgive his persecutors;
        he told the criminal:
        "Today you will be with me in paradise" (Lk 23:43).
        After his death tombs opened,
        and people were raised (Mt 27:52).
    The salvation wrought by Jesus
    is the gift of life and resurrection.
        By looking upon the one who was pierced
        we meet the sure hope of finding freedom and redemption.

51. "When Jesus had received the vinegar,
    he said, 'It is finished,' and he bowed his head,
    and gave up his spirit" (Jn 19:30).
        This "giving up" of the spirit describes Jesus' death,
        but it also seems to allude to the "gift of the Spirit"
        by which Jesus ransoms us from death

and opens before us a new life.
It is the very life of God we now share,
the life which through the sacraments of the church
is continually given to God's children.
From the cross, the source of life,
the "people of life" is born and increases.
In this way Jesus proclaims that life finds its center,
its meaning, and its fulfillment when it is given up.
Let us learn not only to obey the commandment
not to kill human life,
but also to revere life, to love and to foster it.

III. YOU SHALL NOT KILL: God's Holy Law

- *"If you would enter life, keep the commandments" (Mt 19:17):
  Gospel and Commandment*

52. The first precept from the ten commandments
that Jesus quotes to the young man who asks him what to do is
"you shall not kill" (Mt 19:18).
God's commandment is never detached from God's love;
it is always a gift meant for our growth and joy.
The Gospel of Life is both a gift from God
and an exacting task for humanity.
In giving us life God demands that we
love, respect, and promote life.
We are rulers and lords not only over things,
but especially over ourselves,
and — in a certain sense — over the life we have received
and are able to transmit.
Our lordship is, however, not absolute,
but ministerial and to be exercised with wisdom and love,
sharing in God's wisdom and love.
And this comes about through obedience to God's holy law.
We are the "ministers of God's plan" (HV 13).

- *"From one person in regard to another person I will demand
  an accounting for human life" (Gn 9:5): Human Life Is Sacred
  and Inviolable*

53. Human life is sacred because from its beginning
it involves "the creative action of God."
"You shall not kill" is a divine commandment.
God is the absolute Lord of the life of the human being.
The inviolability of human life
reflects the Creator's inviolability.

God is the *goel*, the defender of the innocent (cf. Gn 4:9–15).
Only Satan can delight in the death of the living.

54. The precept "you shall not kill" is strongly negative.
It implies, however, a positive attitude of absolute respect for life.
It leads to promotion of life and to progress along the way of love,
which gives, receives, and serves.
    The people of the covenant slowly matured
    while preparing for Jesus' proclamation
    that the commandment to love one's neighbor
    is like the commandment to love God:
    "On these two commandments
    depend all the law and prophets" (Mt 22:36–40) —
    words repeated by Paul (Rom 13:9) and John (1 Jn 3:15).
The oldest nonbiblical Christian document, the Didache,
categorically repeated the commandment "you shall not kill."
It spoke about two ways, the way of life and the way of death.
It said of the way of death:
    "The way of death is this:
        'They show no compassion for the poor,
        they do not acknowledge their Creator,
        they kill their children and by abortion
        cause God's creatures to perish....
        May you be able to stay away from all these sins.'"
The church always considered murder
one of the most serious sins.

55. Yet there are in fact situations
in which values proposed by God's law
seem to involve a genuine paradox.
    This happens for example in the case
    of legitimate defense,
        when the right to defend one's own life
        and the duty not to harm someone else's life
        are difficult to reconcile in practice.
The Old Testament's and Jesus' commandment
of love of neighbor
presuppose love of oneself:
"Love your neighbor as yourself" (Mk 12:31).
No one can renounce the right to self-defense
out of lack of love for life or for self.
    This can be done only in virtue of a heroic love
        that deepens the love of self into a radical self-offering,
        of which the self-offering of Jesus is a sublime example.
Moreover "legitimate defense
can be not only a right but a grave duty,

for someone responsible for another's life
the common good of the family or the state" (CCC 2265).
It does happen that the need to render aggressors
incapable of causing harm involves taking their lives —
an outcome attributable to the aggressors.

56. In this context we have to place
the problem of the death penalty.
In the church and civil society there is a growing tendency
to apply it in a very limited way or to abolish it completely.
This problem should be viewed in the context of a penal justice
ever more in line with the dignity of the human person
and God's plan for humanity and society.
The violation of personal and societal rights
must be adequately punished as a condition for the offender
to regain the exercise of his or her freedom.
In this way the public order is defended,
public safety is ensured, and the offender is offered an incentive
to change and be rehabilitated.
The nature and extent of the punishment
ought not to go to the extreme of executing the offender,
except in cases of absolute necessity:
in other words, when it would not be possible otherwise
to defend society.
Today, however, as a result of steady improvements
in the organization of the penal system,
such cases are very rare if not practically nonexistent.

57. If such care should be taken
to respect the life of criminals and unjust aggressors,
how much more is this true
in the case of weak and defenseless human beings.
Faced with the weakening of the moral sense
in individuals and in society
as regards the taking of innocent life
the church's papal magisterium seconded by that of the bishops
has spoken with increasing frequency
in defense of the sacredness and inviolability of human life.
Therefore by the authority that Christ
conferred upon Peter and his successors
and in communion with the bishops of the Catholic Church,
I confirm that the direct and voluntary killing
of an innocent human being is always gravely immoral.
To deprive innocent human beings of their lives
can never be licit either as an end in itself
or as means to a good end.

As far as the right to life is concerned,
every innocent human being is absolutely equal to all others.
"It makes no difference whether one is the master of the world
or the 'poorest of the poor'" (VS 96).

- *"Your eyes beheld my unformed substance" (Ps 139:16):*
  The Unspeakable Crime of Abortion

58. The Second Vatican Council defines abortion,
together with infanticide, as an "unspeakable crime" (GS 51).
The perception of its gravity has become progressively obscured.
Its acceptance in the popular mind
is a sign of a crisis of the moral sense.
    As the prophet says:
    "Woe to those who call evil good" (Is 5:20).
There is widespread use of ambiguous terminology
especially in the case of abortion,
such as the term "interruption of pregnancy,"
which tends to hide its true nature.
This playing with words is maybe itself a sign
of an uneasiness of conscience.
No word has the power to change things:
procured abortion is direct killing.
    We are dealing with the murder
    of a human being at the very beginning of life,
    lacking even that minimal form of defense
    consisting of the cries and tears of a newborn baby.
Sometimes the mother herself makes the decision,
not out of selfish reasons or out of convenience,
but to protect her own health
or a decent standard of living for her family.
Sometimes it is feared that the child would live in such conditions
that it would be better not to be born.
    These and similar reasons can never justify
    the deliberate killing of an innocent human being.

59. In addition to the mother others might decide
upon the death of the child in the womb.
The father may be to blame,
or the pressure of the wider family circle and friends.
Moral responsibility lies with all those
who directly or indirectly obliged her to have the abortion.
    Doctors and nurses who put their skills
    at the service of death also are responsible,
    like the legislators who promote or approve abortion laws
    and the administrators of abortion centers.

Responsibility lies with those who spread sexual permissiveness
or a lack of esteem for motherhood
and those who do not support effective family policies.
  Then there is the international network
  that systematically campaigns for the legalization of abortion
  even beyond the responsibility of individuals
  and giving it a distinctly social dimension.
We are facing what can be called a "structure of sin"
that opposes unborn life.

60. Some people justify abortion by claiming
    that for a certain number of days
    the result of conception cannot be considered
    a personal human life.
      But from the time of fertilization
      a life of a new human being is begun,
      from the first instant there is established
      what this living being will be: a person.*
    Even if the presence of a spiritual soul
    cannot be ascertained by empirical data,
    scientific research provides a valuable indication
    of a personal presence at the first moment of a human life.
      Furthermore, even the mere possibility
      that a human person is involved
      would suffice for an absolute prohibition
      of killing a human embryo.
    Over and above all scientific and philosophical affirmations,
    the church has always taught
    that "the human being is to be respected and treated as a person,
    from the moment of conception."†

61. The texts of Sacred Scripture never address
    the question of deliberate abortion,
    though they show great respect for the human being
    in the mother's womb as belonging to God.
      Christian tradition, confronted with abortion
      in the Greco-Roman world, radically opposes it,
      as shown by the Didache mentioned earlier (cf. 54),
      a condemnation confirmed by early Christian authors
      like Athenagoras and Tertullian.
    Throughout Christianity's two-thousand-year history
    this same doctrine has constantly been taught.

---

*Congregation for the Doctrine of the Faith, *Declaration on Procured Abortion* (November 18, 1974), nos. 12–13.
†Congregation for the Doctrine of the Faith, Instruction on Respect for Human Life in Its Origin and on the Dignity of Procreation, *Donum Vitae*, I.1.

62. Pius XI, Pius XII, John XXIII,
the Second Vatican Council, and Paul VI
all reaffirmed the same doctrine.
Therefore, *I declare that direct abortion,*
that is, abortion willed as an end or as a means,
always constitutes a grave moral disorder.

63. This evaluation of the morality of abortion
must also be applied to
recent forms of intervention on human embryos,
which inevitably involve the killing of those embryos.
   We uphold as licit procedures carried out on the human embryo
   that respect its life, do not involve disproportionate risks,
   and are directed to its healing, improvement, or survival;
   but the use of embryos for experimentation
   constitutes a crime against their human dignity.
This moral condemnation also regards procedures
that exploit living human embryos and fetuses
— sometimes specifically "produced" for this purpose
by in vitro fertilization —
either to be used as "biological material"
or as provider of organs or tissue for transplants
in the treatment of certain diseases.
   Special attention must be given to the evaluation
   of prenatal diagnostic techniques
   that enable the early detection of anomalies
   in the unborn child.
These techniques are morally licit
when they do not involve disproportionate risks
for the child and the mother
and are meant to make early therapy possible
or to favor the acceptance of the child not yet born.
   To use these techniques for eugenic purposes
   — as not infrequently happens —
   is utterly reprehensible,
   since it presumes to measure
   the value of human life
   only within the parameters
   of "normality" and "physical well-being,"
   thus opening the way
   to euthanasia and infanticide.
So many of our brothers and sisters
suffering from serious disabilities
live their lives with courage and serenity
when shown acceptance and love.

The church is close to those married couples
who willingly accept gravely disabled children
and who adopt those abandoned by their parents.

- *"It is I who bring both death and life"* (Dt 32:39):
  The Tragedy of Euthanasia

64. The experience of dying is today marked by new features.
When pleasure and well-being are considered to be life's only value
and suffering is seen as an unbearable setback,
death is "senseless" when it suddenly interrupts life
but it becomes a "liberation" when life is filled with pain.
    When they deny their fundamental relationship with God,
    people think they are their own rule and measure,
    with the right to demand that society guarantee them
    the ways and means of deciding what to do with their lives.
In the developed countries science and medical practice
today can sustain and prolong life in situations of extreme frailty;
they can resuscitate patients
and make organs available for transplants.
    In this context euthanasia is a temptation,
    which is one of the more alarming symptoms
    of the "culture of death."
It occurs above all in prosperous societies
marked by an excessive preoccupation with efficiency,
which considers the growing number
of elderly and disabled people,
often isolated by their families and by society,
as intolerable and burdensome.

65. Euthanasia in the strict sense is an action or omission
which of itself and by intention causes death,
with the purpose of eliminating all suffering.
    It must be distinguished from the decisions
    to forgo so-called aggressive medical treatment,
    medical procedures that are
    disproportionate to any expected results,
    or that impose an excessive burden
    on the patient and his or her family.
To forgo these extraordinary or disproportionate means
is not equal to suicide or euthanasia.
    In this context arises the issue of whether it is licit to use
    painkillers and sedatives to relieve the patient's pain
    when this involves the risk of shortening life.
While praise may be due to the person
who accepts suffering in order to remain lucid

or as a believer to share consciously in the Lord's passion,
such "heroic" behavior cannot be considered the duty of everyone.
    It is licit to relieve pain with narcotics
    even when the result is decreased consciousness
    and a shortening of life,
    "if no other means exist, and if, in the given circumstances,
    this does not prevent the carrying out
    of other religious and moral duties."*
In such a case death is neither willed nor sought;
there is simply a desire to ease pain.
Yet it is not right to deprive the dying person of consciousness
without a serious reason.
People ought to be able to satisfy their moral and family duties
and to prepare for their meeting with God.
    Taking into account these distinctions,
    in harmony with my predecessors,
    and in communion with the bishops of the Catholic Church,
    I confirm that euthanasia
    is a grave violation of the law of God.
Euthanasia is a practice that involves the malice
proper to suicide or murder.

66. The church has always rejected suicide as a gravely evil choice.
It involves the rejection of love of self
and the obligation of justice and charity toward one's neighbor,
the communities one belongs to, and society as a whole.
    Suicide is the rejection
    of God's sovereignty over life and death.
To assist someone who intends to commit suicide
and to help carrying it out can never be excused.
    Even when not motivated by a selfish refusal
    to be burdened with the life of someone who is suffering,
    euthanasia is a perversion of "mercy."
    True compassion leads to sharing another's pain;
    it does not kill the person whose suffering we cannot bear.
    This is even more true when family members are involved.
Euthanasia becomes more serious
when a person has not requested it
and never consented to it.
    It is the height of injustice
    when people assume the power
    to decide who ought to live and who ought to die.
    God alone has the power over life and death.

*Pius XII, Address to Physicians, III (February 24, 1957).

When people seize this power,
they inevitably use it for injustice and death.
The life of the weak is put in the hands of the strong,
and mutual trust is undermined.

67. The human heart confronted with suffering and death,
especially when faced with the temptation to give up in desperation,
requests above all companionship, sympathy, and support —
> a plea for help to keep on hoping
> when all human hopes fail.
> Our faith promises and offers a share
> in the victory of the risen Christ.
Saint Paul expressed this newness
in terms of belonging to the Lord:
>> "If we live, we live to the Lord;
>> if we die, we die to the Lord;
>> so then, whether we live or whether we die,
>> we are the Lord's" (Rom 14:7–8).

- *"We must obey God rather than any human authority" (Acts 5:29): Civil Law and the Moral Law*

68. There is a trend to demand a legal justification
for the present-day attacks on life,
as if they were rights the state must acknowledge
— at least under certain circumstances —
with the safe and free assistance of medical personnel.
> Some claim that the relative good of an unborn child
> or seriously disabled person should be compared with
> and balanced against other goods.
> It is said that only someone directly involved
> can correctly do this and decide on the morality of the choice —
> and that the state should respect this choice.
Then again it is claimed that civil law cannot demand that everyone
live according to moral standards
higher than what all the citizens themselves acknowledge and share.
The law should express the majority opinion,
recognizing that people have — in certain extreme cases —
the right to abortion and euthanasia.
> A prohibition would lead to illegal practices
> carried out in a medically unsafe way.
> The law would not be enforceable
> and undermine ultimately the authority of all laws.
More radical views even go so far
as to hold that in a modern and pluralistic society
people should be allowed the freedom

to dispose of their own lives
as well as of the lives of the unborn.

69. It is held that in the democratic culture of our time
the legal system should take into account and accept
what the majority considers moral and actually practices.
    It is believed that if in a democratic system
    an objective truth shared by all is in fact unattainable,
    the autonomy of the citizens should be acknowledged.
    In other words the only determining factor
    should be the will of the majority,
    whatever this may be.
So we are facing two opposed tendencies:
on the one hand individuals claim complete freedom of choice,
and the state should guarantee maximum freedom.
    On the other hand it is held that
    — in the exercise of one's duties —
    respect for the freedom of the other requires
    that one set aside one's own convictions
    in order to satisfy every demand of the other
    that is recognized and laid down by the law.
Individual responsibility would be turned over to civil law,
with a renouncing of personal conscience,
at least in the public sphere.

70. At the root of all these tendencies
lies the ethical relativism of our present-day culture,
a relativism many think an essential condition of democracy,
for it guarantees tolerance and mutual respect.
    Objective moral norms are then considered
    as leading to authoritarianism and intolerance.
It is true that crimes have been committed in the name of "truth,"
but equally so in the name of "ethical relativism."
    Everyone's conscience rightly rejects
    those crimes against life of which our century
    has had such a sad experience.
    But would these crimes cease to be crimes if,
    instead of being committed by unscrupulous tyrants,
    they were legitimated by popular consensus?
Democracy cannot substitute for morality
or be a panacea for immorality.
Democracy is a "system,"
a means and not an end.
    The value of democracy
    — considered by the church as a positive "sign of the times" —
    stands or falls with the values it embodies and promotes.

The basis of these values cannot be changeable "majority" opinions,
but only the acknowledgment of an objective moral law,
written as the "natural law" in the human heart.
   If the fundamental principles
   of the moral law were to be shaken
   — by an obscuring of the collective conscience —
   the democratic system itself would be shaken
   and reduced to a mere mechanism for regulating
   different and opposing interests.
   It would not be able to ensure peace
   without an objective moral grounding.
   The most powerful would make democracy an empty word.

71. The future of society and the development of democracy
    depend on the rediscovery of the innate human and moral values
    no one, no majority, and no state can create, modify, or destroy.
       There is a need to recover the relationship
       between civil and moral law.
       "In no sphere of life can the civil law
       take the place of conscience
       or dictate norms concerning things
       outside its competence" (*Donum Vitae*, III).
    The purpose of civil law is to guarantee
    an ordered social coexistence in true justice.
    For that reason it must ensure
    that in the first place the fundamental right to life
    of every innocent human being is respected.
       The legal toleration of abortion and euthanasia
       can in no way be claimed
       to be based on the respect for the conscience of others,
       precisely because society has the right and the duty
       to protect itself against abuses
       that can occur in the name of conscience
       and under the pretext of freedom.
    Any government that refused to recognize these human rights
    would not only fail in its duty;
    its decrees would lack binding force.

72. Thomas Aquinas wrote,
    "Every human law can be called a law
    insofar as it derives from the natural law.
    But if it is somehow opposed to the natural law
    then it is not really a law
    but the corruption of law" (ST, Ia–IIae, q. 95, a. 2).
       This applies in the very first place to the source
       of all other rights, the right to life.

Laws that legitimize the direct killing of innocent human beings
through abortion or euthanasia are in opposition to this right to life.
    This is the case even when euthanasia
    is requested with full awareness of the person involved.
    Any state that makes such a request legitimate,
    authorizing it to be carried out,
    would be legalizing suicide-murder,
    thus lessening respect for life
    and destroying mutual trust.

73. There is a clear and grave obligation
    to oppose such laws by conscientious objection.
        Christians have the duty to obey
        legitimate public authorities,
        but they must obey God
        rather than human beings (cf. Acts 5:29).
    In the case of a law permitting abortion or euthanasia,
    it is never licit to obey it or
        "to take part in a propaganda campaign
        in favor of such a law, or vote for it."*
    A problem can arise when there is the possibility
    of voting for the restriction of an existing pro-abortion law.
    In such a case people known
    for their opposition to procured abortion
    could vote in favor of such a law to limit the harm done.

74. Unjust laws raise difficult questions
    for morally upright people as regards to cooperation.
        The choices to be made are sometimes difficult;
        prestigious positions and careers might be at stake.
    One should recall here the general principles
    concerning cooperation in evil actions.
    It is never licit to cooperate formally in evil,
    not even by appealing to the freedom of others
    or to the fact that the law permits the action.
        To refuse to take part in committing an injustice
        is not only a moral duty;
        it is also a basic human right,
        a right that as such should be acknowledged
        and protected by civil law.
    Those who have recourse to conscientious objection
    must be protected not only from lawsuits

---

*Congregation for the Doctrine of the Faith, *Declaration on Procured Abortion* (November 18, 1974), no. 22.

but also from other negative effects
on the legal, disciplinary, financial, and professional plane.

- *"You shall love your neighbor as yourself" (Lk 10:27):*
  "Promote" Life

75. The negative moral commandments
indicate the minimum we must respect,
beneath which we cannot lower ourselves.
> They are the beginning and the first stage
> of a further journey toward freedom.

76. The commandment "you shall not kill"
is a point of departure.
It leads us to promote and serve life actively.
> With the gift of his Spirit,
> Christ gives new content and meaning
> to our being entrusted to one another.
> The Spirit becomes the new law.

77. Jesus laid down his life for us,
and we ought to lay down our lives
for our brothers and sisters (1 Jn 3:16).
> We are committed to ensure a service of love
> to our neighbors, defending and promoting their lives,
> especially when they are weak or threatened.

IV. YOU DID IT TO ME:
For a New Culture of Human Life

- *"You are God's own people, that you may declare the wonderful*
  deeds of him who called you out of darkness into his marvelous
  light" (1 Pet 2:9): A People of Life and for Life

78. The church received the Gospel of Life
— an integral part of which is Christ himself —
as a gift, a proclamation, and a source of joy and salvation.
The church has received it as a gift from Jesus, sent by the Father,
"to preach good news to the poor" (Lk 4:18).

79. We are the people of life,
ransomed by the "Author of Life."
Through baptism we have been made part of him,
renewed by the grace of the Spirit.
> We have been sent.
> We have been sent as a people
> with the obligation to be at the service of life.

We have a community commitment
that does not lessen our individual responsibility.

- *"That which we have seen and heard we proclaim*
  also to you" (1 Jn 1:3): Proclaiming the Gospel of Life

80. Jesus is the only Gospel;
    we have nothing further to say
    or any other witness to bear.
    To proclaim Jesus is to proclaim life,
    the eternal life given to us.
      We feel a need to proclaim this good news
      that exceeds every human expectation.
    Our gratitude and joy
    impel us to share this message with everyone.

81. This involves above all the core of this Gospel,
    the proclamation of a God who is close to us,
    who calls us to profound communion with God,
    awakening in us the hope of eternal life.
      It is the affirmation of the inseparable connection
      between person, life, and bodiliness.
    It is the presentation of human life
    as God's gift, the fruit and sign of God's love.
      It is the proclamation that Jesus
      has a unique relationship with every person,
      which enables us to see in every human face
      the face of Christ.
    It is the call for a "sincere gift of self"
    as the fullest way to realize personal freedom.
      It also involves making clear
      all the consequences of this Gospel:
      human life is sacred and inviolable,
      procured abortion and euthanasia
      are absolutely unacceptable.
    The meaning of human life is found in giving and receiving love,
    and in this light human sexuality and procreation
    reach their true and full significance.

82. Teachers, catechists, and theologians
    have the task of emphasizing the reasons
    for our respect for human life.
      It is in all this that we shall find
      important points of contact and dialogue with nonbelievers.
    With so many opposing and negative points of view,
    all of us — and above all those who are bishops —
    have to announce all this "in season and out of season" (2 Tim 4:2).

We need to make sure that this sound doctrine is taught
in theological faculties, seminaries, and Catholic institutions.
We should not fear hostility or unpopularity,
and we should avoid all ambiguity.
We must be in the world but not of the world (cf. Jn 16:33).

- *"I give thanks that I am fearfully, wonderfully made" (Ps 139:14):
Celebrating the Gospel of Life*

83. As "people for life" we must celebrate the Gospel of Life.
We need to foster a contemplative outlook,
seeing in life a deeper meaning,
accepting it as a gift,
and seeing in each person God's living image.
    This outlook will encourage us
    when confronted with those who are sick, suffering,
    outcast, or at death's door.
We cannot but respond
with songs of joy, praise, and thanksgiving
for the priceless gift of life.

84. We must celebrate eternal life,
from which all life flows.
In our daily prayer as individuals and as a community
we bless and praise God,
who knitted us together in our mother's womb (Ps 139:13).
    God granted us a dignity that is near to divine (Ps 8:5–6),
    while the celebration of the paschal mystery
    and the sacraments make us sharers
    in the life of the crucified and risen Christ.

85. We also need to appreciate and make good use
of the symbols and traditions of different cultures and peoples
that express their joy for life.
    That is why I propose that a "Day for Life"
    be celebrated each year in every country,
    with attention to issues like abortion and euthanasia.

86. The Gospel of Life is to be celebrated above all
in daily living filled with self-giving love for others.
It is in this context that heroic actions are born,
made up of gestures of sharing, big and small,
with the particularly praiseworthy example
of the donation of organs.
    Part of this daily heroism
    is the silent witness of all those brave mothers
    who devote themselves to their own family.

They do not always find support in the world around them;
on the contrary the media often do not encourage motherhood,
calling its values of fidelity, chastity, and sacrifice obsolete.
     We thank you, heroic mothers, for your invincible love!

- *"What does it profit, my brothers and sisters, if someone says
  I have faith, while not having the works?" (Jas 2:14):
  Serving the Gospel of Life*

87. Our promotion of human life
    must be accomplished through the service of charity.
    We must care for the other as a person
    for whom God has made us responsible.
         This service cannot tolerate bias and discrimination.
         We need to show care for all life.
    Every Christian community should continue to write
    the history of charity, developing programs of support for life.

88. All this involves education
    and the promotion of vocations to service,
    particularly among the young.
         Centers for natural methods of regulating fertility
         should be promoted
         as a help to responsible parenthood.
    Marriage and family counseling agencies
    and centers for unmarried mothers and couples in difficulties
    offer a valuable help by their work.
         Communities for treating drug addiction,
         residential communities for minors or the mentally ill,
         care and relief centers for AIDS patients,
         associations for solidarity
         especially with the disabled, the terminally ill, and elderly
         — all are eloquent expressions of what charity is able to devise
         in order to give new hope and practical possibilities for life.
    The role of hospitals, clinics, and convalescent homes
    needs to be reconsidered,
    so that they might become places
    where pain and death are understood in their Christian meaning.

89. A unique responsibility belongs to health-care personnel.
    They are the guardians and servants of human life,
    but in today's climate they are often tempted
    to become manipulators of life and death.
         Their absolute respect for every innocent human life
         requires the exercise of conscientious objection
         as regards procured abortion and euthanasia.
    "Causing death" can never be considered medical treatment.

Biomedical research too, promising great benefits for humanity,
must always reject experimentation
that under the guise of helping people actually harms them.

90. Volunteer workers have a special role to play.
The Gospel of Life has to be taken into account in politics;
individuals, families, and groups, all have a responsibility
in shaping society and developing projects
so that the life of all is defended and enhanced.
Civic leaders, called to serve the people and the common good,
have the duty to support life through legislation.
In a democratic system the sense of personal responsibility
can never be renounced.
Though laws are not the only means
of protecting human life,
nevertheless they play
an important and sometimes decisive role
in influencing patterns of thought and behavior.
The church knows that it is difficult to defend life by law
in a pluralistic society,
but the church encourages political leaders
not to give in and to make those choices
that will lead to the reestablishment of a just order
in the defense and promotion of life.
But that is not enough;
a good family policy must be the basis
of all social policies,
taking into account labor, urban,
residential, and social service policies.

91. Population growth is another important issue.
Public authorities have a responsibility to intervene
to orient the demography of the population.
But they have to take into account
the responsibility and rights of married couples,
beginning with the right to life.
It is morally unacceptable that they encourage or impose
contraception, sterilization, and abortion to regulate birth.
Nationally and internationally
they must strive for solutions
by establishing a true economy of communion
and sharing of goods,
so that everyone can share equitably in the goods of creation.
Service of the Gospel of Life is a complex and immense task,
requiring cooperation with other churches
and the followers of other religions.

- *"Your children will be like olive shoots around your table"*
  (Ps 128:3): The Family as the "Sanctuary of Life"

92. Within the "people of life and the people for life"
    the family has a decisive responsibility
    as a natural community of life and love,
    the parents being the co-workers with God's love.
    It is the "sanctuary of life,"
    where life is welcomed and protected
    and where it can develop
    in authentic human growth.
    The family is the domestic church,
    proclaiming, celebrating, and serving
    the Gospel of Life.
    It is in raising children that the family fulfills
    its mission to proclaim the Gospel of Life,
    teaching the children
    the true meaning of suffering and death
    and fostering assistance and sharing
    toward sick and elderly family members.

93. The family celebrates the Gospel of Life
    through daily individual and family prayer,
    in living together in a life of love and self-giving.
    An expression of solidarity between families
    is a willingness to adopt or take in children
    abandoned by their parents.
    In cases of extreme poverty
    adoption-at-a-distance
    should also be considered,
    helping the family
    without the children having to be uprooted
    from their natural environment.

94. Special attention must be given to the elderly,
    who are often regarded as useless and left to themselves.
    It is important to preserve or to reestablish
    a sort of covenant between the generations —
    something required by the divine commandment
    to honor one's father and one's mother (cf. Ex 20:12).
    Elderly people themselves have a contribution to make
    to the Gospel of Life,
    as sources of wisdom and witnesses of love and hope.
    In all this the family needs to be helped
    to meet the problems of the day
    by the community and the state.

- *"Walk as children of the light" (Eph 5:8):*
  Bringing about a Transformation of Culture

95. We must build a new culture of life
    that confronts today's problems affecting life.
    The purpose of the Gospel is, in fact,
    to transform humanity from within and to make it new.
    We need to begin within our Christian communities themselves.

96. The first step is forming consciences
    in regard to the inviolable worth of human life
    and reestablishing the connection between life and freedom.
      There is no true freedom
        where life is not welcomed and loved,
          and there is no fullness of life except in freedom.
    In the formation of conscience is the necessary link
    between freedom and truth.
    Only by admitting our innate dependence on God
    can we live and use our freedom and at the same time
    respect the life and freedom of every other person.
      When God is denied, human life also ends up being rejected.

97. There is a need for education
    about the value of life from its very origins.
    We have to help the young
    to accept and experience sexuality and love
    according to their true meaning and in their interconnection.
      The trivialization of sexuality
        is among the principal factors
        that lead to the contempt for new life.
      Only a true love is able to protect life.
    There is a duty to offer adolescents and young adults
    an authentic education in sexuality and in love;
    this involves training in chastity as a virtue
    and learning respect for the "spousal" meaning of the body.
      This education involves the training of married couples
        in responsible procreation,
        with openness to new life and the service of it,
        even if — for serious reasons and with respect to the moral law —
        they choose to avoid new birth for the time being.
    If they control the impulses of instinct and passion
    and respect the biological laws inscribed in their persons,
    they can legitimately use natural methods of regulating fertility
    in the service of responsible procreation.
      These methods are becoming more and more accurate.
      An honest appraisal of them

should dispel certain prejudices
that are still widely held.
The church is grateful to those who devote themselves
to the study and spread of these methods.
    This education should also consider suffering and death.
    Even pain and suffering have meaning and value.
    In this regard I have called for the yearly celebration
    of the "World Day of the Sick."
Death is anything but an event without hope,
it is the door that opens on eternity;
for those who believe it is a participation
in the death and resurrection of Christ.

98. The cultural change we are calling for
    asks for the primacy of being over having,
    of the person over things.
    Others are not rivals but brothers and sisters,
    to be loved for their own sakes.
        In this mobilization for a new culture
        no one must feel excluded;
        everyone has an important role to play.
    Catholic intellectuals have a special role to play,
    as do all those involved in mass media.

99. In this transformation of culture
    women play a unique and decisive role.
    It depends on them to promote a "new feminism,"
    rejecting the temptation to imitate models of "male domination"
    and affirming the true genius of women in life and society
    in order to overcome all discrimination, violence, and exploitation.
    I ask them to "reconcile people with life."
        Motherhood involves a special communion
        with the mystery of life;
        it gives life room, respecting it in its otherness.
    I would like to say a special word to women
    who have had an abortion.
    The church is aware of the many factors
    that may have influenced your decision,
    and it does not doubt that in many cases
    it was a painful and even shattering decision.
    The wound in your heart may not yet have healed.
    Certainly what happened was and remains terribly wrong.
    But do not give in to discouragement
    and do not lose hope.
        Try to understand what happened
        and face it honestly.

The Father of mercies is ready
to give you his forgiveness and peace
in the sacrament of reconciliation.
Nothing is definitively lost,
and you will be able to ask forgiveness from your child
who is now living in the Lord.
With the help of others and as a result of your experience
you can be among the most eloquent defenders
of the right to life.

100. There is an enormous disparity
between the powerful resources available
to the forces promoting the "culture of death"
and the means of those working for a "culture of life and love."
But God is with us.
Prayer is needed;
Jesus himself showed that prayer and fasting
are the most effective weapons
against the forces of evil (cf. Mt 4:1–11).

101. The Gospel of Life
is not for believers alone; it is for everyone.
To be actively pro-life is to contribute
to the renewal of society through the promotion
of the common good.
Only respect for life can be the foundation of democracy and peace.

CONCLUSION

102. The one who accepted "Life" in the name of all
and for the sake of all was Mary, the Virgin Mother.
    Mary, like the church of which she is the type,
    is a mother of all those reborn in life.

  • *"A great portent appeared in heaven, a woman clothed
    with the sun" (Rev 12:1): The Motherhood of Mary and
    of the Church*

103. In the book of Revelation,
the "woman clothed with the sun" was with child.
The church, too, bears within herself the Savior of the world.
    Like Mary, the church lives her motherhood in suffering
    through the birth pangs and the labor of childbirth,
    that is to say, in constant tension with the forces of evil
    that roam the world.

- *"And the dragon stood before the woman . . . that he might devour the child when she brought it forth" (Rev 12:4): Life Menaced by the Forces of Evil*

104. Here, too, Mary helps the church realize
     that life is always at the center of the great struggle
     between good and evil, between light and darkness.
     In a way her threatened child
     is a figure of every person, every child,
     especially every helpless baby whose life is threatened,
     because by his incarnation
     "the Son of God has united himself
     in some fashion with every person" (GS 22).

- *"Death shall be no more" (Rev 21:4):
  The Splendor of the Resurrection*

105. Mary's whole life is pervaded by the certainty
     that God is near to her.
     The same is true of the church,
     and Mary is its comfort in its struggle against death.
     In the "New Jerusalem," that new world
     toward which human history is traveling,
     "death shall be no more."
     And on our way, we, the pilgrim people, look to her who is for us
     "a sign of sure hope and solace" (LG 68).
     O Mary, Mother of the Living,
     to you do we entrust the cause of life.

12

That They May Be One

Ut Unum Sint

May 25, 1995

The Catholic Church is linked with the other Christian communities by a true union in the Holy Spirit. The more closely we live our common Christian vocation and pray in common, the nearer we will be to "converting" to Christian unity. The fruits of our renewed and continued dialogue will be a recovered sense of friendship, solidarity in the service of humankind, and an increase in communion. The bishop of Rome has a particular responsibility in all this; in exercising his primacy and faithful to this mission he is open to the new situation.

INTRODUCTION

1. With the approach of the year 2000,
   the year of the great jubilee,
   the call for Christian union,
   to which the Second Vatican Council committed itself,
   is finding an ever greater echo in the hearts of believers.
   > The witness of the martyrs of our century,
   > including those in churches and ecclesial communities
   > not in full communion with the Catholic Church,
   > gives new force to this call.
   Christ calls his disciples to unity.
   As I stated before on Good Friday 1994,
   having meditated upon the Way of the Cross
   prepared by my venerable brother Bartolomew,
   the ecumenical patriarch of Constantinople,
   the believers in Christ cannot remain divided.
   > They must profess the same truth about the cross,
   > if they want to overcome the world's attempts

to reduce to powerlessness the mystery of redemption
in their anti-Christian claim
that the cross is unable to provide either vision or hope
and that the human being is nothing but an earthly thing
who must live as if God did not exist.

2. Believers cannot fail to meet this challenge,
breaking down — with God's help —
the walls of division and distrust
and overcoming obstacles and prejudices
that hinder the proclamation of the Gospel of Salvation.
    I thank God for the progress made,
    but Christians should not underestimate
    the longstanding misgivings,
    misunderstandings, and prejudices,
    often made worse by complacency,
    indifference, and ignorance.
The commitment to ecumenism
must be based on conversion, prayer,
and the purification of past memories.
Inspired by love and with the grace of the Holy Spirit
the Lord's disciples are called to reexamine their painful past
and the hurt it causes even today.
    A calm, clear-sighted, and truthful vision is needed
    to acknowledge mistakes made
    and to free the mind, inspiring everyone with a new willingness
    to proclaim the Gospel to all.

3. At the Second Vatican Council the Catholic Church
committed itself to the path of the ecumenical venture,
heeding the Spirit of the Lord and interpreting the "sign of the times."
    The experiences of recent years
    have made the church more aware of its identity and mission.
    It confesses the weaknesses of its members,
    not ceasing to do penance,
    while exalting still more the power of the Lord.
Taught by history, the church wants
to free itself from every human support,
to live the Gospel Beatitudes, and to seek nothing
but the freedom to proclaim the Gospel.
    I myself intend to promote any initiative
    to make the Catholic witness understood
    in its purity and consistency,
    especially at the threshold of the new millennium,
    an exceptional occasion
    to ask the Lord for the unity of all Christians.

This encyclical is meant to be a pastoral contribution,
encouraging the efforts of all who work for unity.

4. I do this as the bishop of Rome,
   the successor of the apostle Peter,
   convinced that I am obeying the Lord
   and aware of my human frailty.
   > Christ asked Peter
   > to strengthen his brothers and sisters (Lk 22:32),
   > while he made his human weakness clear to him.
   In Peter's human weakness it becomes clear
   that the pope depends on God's grace and prayer:
   "I have prayed for you that your faith may not fail" (Lk 22:32).
   > The bishop of Rome prays himself
   > for that conversion indispensable for "Peter"
   and asks all to share in his prayer for this conversion!

Chapter One
THE CHURCH'S COMMITMENT TO ECUMENISM

God's Plan and Communion

5. The Catholic Church bases its commitment
   to gather all Christians into unity on God's plan.
   It is not a reality closed in on itself.
   It is sent to make present the mystery of communion
   and to gather all people and all things into Christ
   in order to be for all a sacrament of unity.
   > The prophet Ezekiel,
   > using the simple sign of two broken sticks
   > — first divided and then joined together —
   > expressed the divine will to "gather from all sides"
   > God's scattered people (Ez 37:16–28).
   The Gospel of John describes how
   > "Jesus would die ... to gather into one
   > the scattered children of God" (11:52).
   Paul explained in his letter to the Ephesians
   how Jesus' cross broke down all hostility:
   "to what was divided, he brought about unity" (2:14–16).

6. The unity of divided humanity is the will of God.
   For this reason God sent God's Son,
   so that by dying and rising he might give us the Spirit of love.
   > On the eve of his death on the cross
   > Jesus himself prayed to his Father
   > "that they may be one," a living communion.

This is the basis not only of our duty,
but also of our responsibility before God and God's plan.
How is it possible to remain divided
if Jesus through his death
has broken down the walls of division?
> Our division contradicts the will of Christ,
> provides a stumbling block to the world,
> and damages the Good News.

The Way of Ecumenism: The Way of the Church

7. As the Second Vatican Council noted:
The Lord of the Ages follows out the plan of grace,
making divided Christians regret their divisions
and making them long more for unity.
> Everywhere large numbers have felt the impulse of this grace
> increasing also among our separated brothers and sisters.
Those taking part in this ecumenical movement
—invoking the triune God and confessing Jesus their Lord and Savior—
join not merely as individuals,
but as members of the corporate groups
they regard as their and, indeed, God's churches;
they long to be one visible, truly universal church of God (cf. UR 1).

8. The Second Vatican Council exhorted
"all the Catholic faithful to recognize the signs of the times
and to participate actively in the work of ecumenism" (UR 4).
> The Catholic Church embraces with hope
> the commitment to ecumenism as a duty,
> sure that "our hope does not disappoint us"
> for "God's love has been poured into our hearts
> through the Holy Spirit" (Rom 5:5).

9. The unity Jesus prayed for at the hour of his passion,
"that they may be one" (Jn 17:21),
is at the very heart of Christ's mission.
It belongs to the essence of the community of his disciples.
God wills the church, because God wills unity
as an expression of the whole depth of God's love (agape).
> This unity does not consist merely
> in the gathering of people as a collection of individuals.
> It is a unity constituted by the profession of faith,
> the sacraments, and hierarchical communion.
The faithful are one,
because in the Spirit they are in communion with the Son,
sharing his communion with the Father.

The communion of Christians is the manifestation in them
of the grace that makes them share in God's own communion,
which is God's eternal life.
> Christ's prayer "that they may be one"
> asks the Father that all may clearly see
> "what is the plan of the mystery hidden for ages
> in God who created all things" (Eph 3:9).
To believe in Christ means to desire unity;
to desire unity means to desire the church;
to desire the church means the communion of grace
corresponding to the Father's plan and Christ's prayer:
"that they may be one."

10. In the present situation of lack of unity
and the quest for full communion
the Catholic faithful are challenged by the Lord of the church.
> The Council states that the church of Christ
> "subsists in the Catholic Church,
> which is governed by the successor of Peter
> and by the bishops in communion with him,"
> but it acknowledges at the same time that:
> "many elements of sanctification and truth
> can be found outside its visible structure.
> These elements, however,
> as gifts properly belonging to the church of Christ,
> possess an inner dynamism toward Catholic unity" (LG 8).
The Holy Spirit has not refrained from using those elements
as means of salvation, which derive their efficacy
from the fullness of grace and truth
entrusted to the Catholic Church (cf. UR 3).

11. The Catholic Church has been preserved in unity
for the two thousand years of its history,
endowed with all the means God wished for the church,
notwithstanding grave crises, infidelities of its ministers,
and the daily faults of its members.
> Weakness, mediocrity, sins, and betrayals
> cannot destroy God's plan of grace;
> "the powers of death shall not prevail against it" (Mt 16:18).
The Catholic Church does not forget
that many among its members cause God's plan
to be discernible only with difficulty.
> "People of both sides were to blame" (UR 3),
> not only "the other side."
The elements of sanctification and truth
in other Christian communities

constitute the basis of the communion,
though imperfect, between them and the Catholic Church.
   To the extent that these elements are found in them
   the one church of Christ is present in them;
   there is a certain, though imperfect communion.
      The Catholic Church "recognizes that in many ways
      it is linked" (LG 15) to them,
      by a true union in the Holy Spirit.

12. The Council listed many of those elements,
   like the honoring of Sacred Scripture,
   the belief in God the Father, and Christ, God's Son,
   baptism, and other sacraments, the episcopacy, the Eucharist,
   devotion to the Virgin Mother, prayer, and other spiritual benefits.
      They share with us in the Holy Spirit,
      who gives them gifts and graces,
         to the point of their shedding their blood.
   The Council, speaking of the Orthodox churches,
   states that through the celebration of the Eucharist
   "the church of God is built up and grows in stature" (UR 15).
   Truth demands that all this be recognized.

13. "All those justified by faith through baptism
   are incorporated into Christ.
   They have a right to be honored as Christians
   and regarded as brothers and sisters in the Lord" (UR 3).
      All positive elements
      in other churches and ecclesial communities
      belong by right to the one church of Christ.
         Their sacred actions can truly engender a life of grace
         and are capable of providing access
         to the community of salvation.
   These are important texts for ecumenism.
   There is no ecclesial vacuum
   beyond the boundary of the Catholic community.
   Many elements of great value,
   parts of the means of salvation and the gifts of grace,
   are also found in other Christian communities.

14. It is not a matter of getting all those scattered riches together
   in order to arrive at a church
   that God has in mind for the future.
   The tradition in the East and the West believes
   that in the Pentecost event
   God already manifested the church in its final reality—
   a reality already given.

We are now in the last times.
> The elements of this already-given church exist
> in their fullness in the Catholic Church
> and without this fullness in the other communities
> where certain features at times
> have been more effectively emphasized.

Ecumenism is directed to making this partial communion
grow toward full communion.

Renewal and Conversion

15. The Council stresses the need for conversion.
Conversion is an essential element of every new beginning.
"There can be no ecumenism worthy of the name
without a change of heart" (UR 7), personally as well as communally.
Each one has to change his or her way of looking at things.
> Thanks to ecumenism we have been enriched
> by new horizons,
> seeing the Spirit at work in other Christian communities,
> discovering their holiness and commitment.

The consequence is a greater sense of the need for repentance
and a better awareness of exclusions that harm charity,
of refusals to forgive, of pride, of condemning "the other side,"
and of disdain born of an unhealthy presumption.

16. The Council, connecting renewal, conversion, and reform,
states that Christ summons the church
—as an institution of human beings—
to a continual reformation
when the influence of events or the times
has led to deficiencies (cf. UR 6).
> By a frank dialogue
> communities can help each other to look at themselves
> in the light of the apostolic tradition,
> asking themselves whether they truly express
> all that the Holy Spirit transmitted through the apostles.

As for the Catholic Church, I have frequently done this,
as for example on the anniversary of the baptism of Kievan Rus',
on the commemoration of Saints Cyril and Methodius,
and more recently by approving the
"Directory for the Application of Principles and Norms on Ecumenism."

17. Numerous documents and statements
provided other Christian communities
with useful tools for the ecumenical movement
and the conversion that it must inspire.

They are signs of the progress made
and a source of hope for the future.
> The increase of fellowship is one of the most
> important aspects of ecumenism
> and an essential guarantee for its future.
Catholics cannot forget that ecumenism
is a consequence of the church's reexamination of itself
during the Second Vatican Council.
> John XXIII refused to separate renewal from ecumenism;
> Paul VI sealed this commitment
> by renewing the dialogue with the patriarch of Constantinople.
Other Christian communities played a part
in the great debates of the Council.

The Fundamental Importance of Doctrine

18. According to John XXIII and the Council,
    formulating doctrine is one of the elements
    of a continuing reform.
    It is not a question of changing the faith
    or of accommodating it
    to the preferences of a particular age;
    in matters of faith compromise
    is in contradiction with God who is Truth.
    > A "being together" that betrayed the truth
    > would be opposed to God's nature
    > and the human heart's need for truth.

19. Even so, doctrine needs to be understandable;
    that is why Cyril and Methodius translated
    the ideas of the Bible and Greek theological concepts
    in the very different context of the Slavs,
    wanting to make the Word of God
    "accessible in each civilization's own forms of expression" (SA 11).
    > I myself told the Aboriginal peoples of Australia:
    > "You do not have to be divided into two parts....
    > Jesus calls you to accept his words and his values
    > into your own culture."*
    Meant for all humanity, faith must be translated into all cultures.
    The expression of truth can take different forms.
    The renewal of these forms becomes necessary
    for the sake of transmitting the Gospel to the people of today
    in its unchanging meaning.
    "This renewal has notable ecumenical significance" (UR 6).

---

*Address to the Aboriginal Peoples (November 29, 1986), 12.

Who is responsible for doing this?
The Council's answer is:
"It extends to everyone,
according to the ability of each,
whether it be exercised in daily Christian living
or in theological and historical studies" (cf. UR 5).

20. The ecumenical movement is not just an "appendix,"
but an organic part of the church's life and work.
John XXIII saw this, and he noted:
    "What unites us is much greater
    than what divides us."
The more faithful Christians live the purity of the Gospel
the more they foster and practice Christian unity.
To the degree that they enjoy communion
with the Father, the Word, and the Holy Spirit,
the better they will achieve mutual communion (cf. UR 7).

The Primacy of Prayer

21. Public and private prayer for the unity of Christians
should be considered as the soul of the whole ecumenical movement.
    It is love that gives the desire for unity,
    even in those who have never been aware of the need for it.
    If we love one another, we strive to perfect our communion.
Love finds its most complete expression in common prayer.
When those who are not in perfect communion
come together to pray,
their prayer is the soul of the ecumenical movement,
a very effective means of asking for unity,
and a genuine expression of what binds us together.
    This remains true even if the prayer is not for union
    but for other intentions such as peace.
The common prayer of Christians is an invitation
to Christ himself to visit them:
"Where two or three are gathered in my name,
there I am in the midst of them" (Mt 18:20).

22. In the fellowship of prayer Christ is truly present;
he prays "in us," "with us," and "for us,"
leading our prayer in the Spirit,
who established the church in its original unity
in the Upper Room in Jerusalem.
    If Christians, though divided,
    can grow more united in common prayer,
    they will grow in the awareness
    of how little divides them,

and they will find themselves together
in that community of the church
that Christ constantly builds up in the Holy Spirit,
despite all human weakness and limitation.

23. Fellowship in prayer will lead us
to look at the church and Christianity in a new way.
The ecumenical movement was born
out of the negative experience
of appealing to one's church
when proclaiming the one Gospel —
a contradiction that could not escape those
who listened to the message of salvation.
This obstacle has not yet been overcome,
but we are on the way to full unity.
Our common prayer is proof of this,
gathering together as we do
in the name of Christ, who is One.
He is our unity.

24. It is a joy to see that ecumenical meetings
almost always include and indeed culminate in prayer.
The week of Prayer for Christian Unity
and so many other occasions
bring Christians to pray together.
The Council made it the special responsibility of the pope
to make pilgrimages to the various churches
in the different continents and countries.
My own visits have always included
ecumenical meetings and common prayer
with our brothers and sisters
seeking unity in Christ and in his church,
in Canterbury Cathedral,
in Scandinavia, in North and South America, in Africa,
and at the headquarters of the World Council of Churches.
How could I forget taking part in the eucharistic liturgy
in the Church of Saint George at the ecumenical patriarchate
and the service at Saint Peter's in Rome
with my venerable brother Patriarch Dimitrios I,
when we recited the Nicene-Constantinopolitan Creed together?

25. I am not the only one who became a pilgrim;
many church and ecclesial community leaders
have visited me in Rome, joining in public and private prayer.
There is no significant event
that does not benefit from Christians

coming together and praying.
The list of them would be too long to mention.
These exchanges and prayers
have already written pages and pages
of our "Book of Unity," to which we must constantly return,
rereading it to draw new inspiration and hope.

26. Prayer will make us discover anew
the truth of the words: "You have one Father" (Mt 23:9);
"You have one teacher, and you are all brothers and sisters" (Mt 23:8).
    Ecumenical prayer expresses all this.
    When Jesus prayed to the Father,
    "That they may be one . . . as we are one,"
    he opened vistas closed to human reason,
    implying a likeness between the union of the divine persons
    and the union of God's children in truth and charity.
The change of heart needed for unity
flows forth from prayer,
and its realization is guided by it.

27. Praying for unity is not reserved
only to those who actually experience the lack of it;
it is a concern that cannot be absent
in the prayer of anyone in personal dialogue with the Lord.
    A model of this prayer is Blessed Marta Gabriella,
    whom I beatified on January 25, 1983,
    and who offered her whole life as a Trappistine Sister
    in meditation and prayer for Christian unity.

Ecumenical Dialogue

28. Prayer — the "soul" of ecumenical renewal
and the yearning for unity —
is the basis and support for everything
the Council calls "dialogue."
    Dialogue is rooted in the nature and dignity
    of human beings,
    unable to find themselves
    except through a sincere gift of themselves.
It is an indispensable step toward human self-realization.
Though the concept might appear
to be only something intellectual or of the mind,
all dialogue implies the human person as human person,
in his or her entirety;
dialogue between communities involves the subjectivity of each.
    Dialogue is not simply an exchange of ideas;
    in some way it always is an "exchange of gifts" (cf. LG 13).

29. That is why every effort should be made
    to eliminate words, judgments, and actions
    that are not true or fair
    and make mutual relations difficult.
        In all this reciprocity is required.
        It is a precondition for starting a dialogue.
        Passing from discord and conflict,
        the parties should recognize each other as partners,
        presupposing in the other a desire for reconciliation.
        Any display of mutual opposition must disappear.

30. The Second Vatican Council laid the bases
    for the Catholic Church's participation in ecumenical dialogue.
    Observers of other churches and ecclesial communities
    were deeply involved in the events of the Council.
    Many meetings and common prayer
    helped bring about the conditions for dialogue
    and showed the readiness of the Catholic episcopate and the Holy See
    to engage in dialogue.

Local Structures of Dialogue

31. This dialogue is the duty not only of the Holy See
    but also of individual local churches.
        Special commissions have been set up
        at bishops' conferences and synods
        with similar structures in individual dioceses.
    These initiatives are a sign
    of the Catholic Church's commitment to ecumenism.
    Dialogue became one of the church's priorities.
        The methods of dialogue have improved,
        and being familiar with the method
        that makes dialogue possible
        is useful for all the faithful.

32. The inquiry into truth is to be free,
    in accord with the dignity of each person,
    and each person's social nature.
    It is to be carried on with the aid of instruction,
    communication, and dialogue,
    with people explaining to each other the truth they have discovered,
    or think they have discovered (cf. DH 3).
        Ecumenical dialogue is of essential importance,
        with the various communions coming together for common prayer,
        examining their faithfulness to Christ's will for the church,
        and undertaking the tasks of renewal and reform (cf. UR 4).

Dialogue as an Examination of Conscience

33. The common quest for truth forms consciences
    and directs efforts to promote unity.
    It should be inspired by and submissive to Christ's prayer for unity.
       Dialogue and prayer are closely related;
       dialogue depends on prayer,
       and prayer is the ever more mature fruit of dialogue.

34. Dialogue also serves as an examination of conscience.
    In his first letter John wrote:
       "If we say we have no sin, we deceive ourselves,
       and the truth is not in us.
       If we confess our sins, God is faithful and just,
       and will forgive our sins
       and cleanse us from all unrighteousness" (1:8–9).
    Acknowledging our condition as sinners
    should mark the spirit that we bring to ecumenical dialogue.
       All the sins of the world,
       including those against the church's unity
       —those of the pastors no less than those of the lay faithful—
       were gathered up in Christ's saving sacrifice.
    Even after the many sins that have divided Christians
    Christian unity is still possible,
    provided that we are conscious of having sinned
    and of our need for conversion.
       Not only our personal sins must be forgiven,
       but also the social sins,
       the "sinful structures" that have contributed
       and still contribute to division.

35. The Council's Decree on Ecumenism is permeated
    by the spirit of conversion;
    ecumenical dialogue becomes a "dialogue of conversion,"
    and thus a "dialogue of salvation."
       This dialogue is not only horizontal,
       restricted to meetings,
       exchanges of points of view, and sharing gifts.
       It also has a vertical thrust,
       directed to the Redeemer of the world;
       it acknowledges that we are people who have sinned
       and creates in this way the space where Christ can act.

Dialogue as a Means of Resolving Disagreements

36. In dialogue one can compare different points of view
    and examine disagreements.

Catholic theologians faithful to the church's teaching
should do this humbly and charitably with love for truth.
   The whole body of doctrine should be presented,
   in a way that is correct, fair, and understandable,
   and at the same time takes into account
   the way of thinking and the actual experiences
   of the other party (UR 11).
Full communion requires the acceptance of the whole truth,
without reductionism or facile agreement.
If serious questions are not resolved,
   they will return at another time.

37. Catholics should remember
    that there exists a "hierarchy" of truths.

38. In dialogue the problem
    of the different formulations of doctrine will arise.
    Different words can say the same thing,
    as has been proved by recent common declarations
    signed by my predecessors and by myself on Christology.
       Dogmatic declarations are distinct
       from the changeable concepts of a given time,
       though they may bear traces of such conceptions.
       Dogmatic declarations communicate revealed truth
       and will always do so if interpreted correctly.
    The ecumenical dialogue has led to surprising discoveries:
    intolerant polemics and controversies
    made incompatible statements
    of what was really the result
    of two different ways of looking at the same reality.
       We need to find the formula
       that will enable us to capture the full reality
       and help us to move on.
    Ecumenism helps Christian communities
    to discover the richness of the truth;
    what one finds "in others" can serve all.

39. Dialogue finally makes us face real disagreements in faith,
    disagreements that should be faced in a spirit of charity,
    and with full respect for one's own conscience
    and that of the others,
    in all humility and love for the truth.
       The two essential points of reference are:
       Sacred Scripture and the tradition of the church.
       Catholics have the help
       of the church's living magisterium.

Practical Cooperation

40. Mutual knowledge, common prayer, and dialogue
presuppose and call for every form of cooperation at all levels,
pastoral, cultural, and social,
as well as that of witnessing to the Gospel message.
> This cooperation is a manifestation of Christ himself.
> It is a school of ecumenism, a road to unity,
> and a form of common Christian witness.

Chapter Two
THE FRUITS OF DIALOGUE

Brother/Sisterhood Rediscovered

41. Thanks to the Spirit of Truth
for all what has been said about ecumenical dialogue
since the Second Vatican Council.
> An overall view of the last thirty years
> helps us to see the many fruits
> of this common conversion to the Gospel.

42. Our vocabulary has changed:
we no longer speak of "separated brethren"
but of "other Christians,"
or of "others who have received baptism."
The communities to which those Christians belong are called
"churches and ecclesial communities
that are not in full communion with the Catholic Church."
> There is a greater awareness
> that we all belong to Christ,
> as I observed so often during ecumenical celebrations.
> Communities are helping each other,
> places of worship are lent out, scholarships are offered,
> and Christians intervene for each other if need be.
Christians have been converted to a mutual charity
that embraces all Christians.
In the case of violence charity prevails,
though not every conflict has been transformed.
> This new spirit is not rooted in philanthropy,
> but in the oneness of baptism.

Solidarity in the Service of Humanity

43. Christian leaders are more and more
taking a stand together in the name of Christ
on important issues like justice, peace, and the future.

The united voice of Christians often
has more impact than one isolated voice.
Not only the leaders, but many Christians, by reason of their faith,
join in projects to change the world
instilling respect for the rights and needs of everyone,
especially the poor, the lowly, and the defenseless.
This is the way of the Gospel,
and I have encouraged before every effort
made in this direction.

Approaching One Another through the Word of God and through Divine Worship

44. Significant progress has also been made with regard to the Word of God.
I am thinking of the ecumenical translations of the Bible.
Anyone remembering the past, especially in the West,
will appreciate this step forward.

45. Corresponding to the liturgical renewal in the Catholic Church,
others have made efforts to renew their worship.
Some celebrate the Lord's Supper more frequently,
the cycles of liturgical readings are essentially the same,
prominence has been given to the liturgy and liturgical signs
(like images, icons, vestments, light, incense, gestures),
and courses on liturgy have been introduced.
All these are signs of a coming together.
It is not yet possible to celebrate together the same liturgy,
but the burning desire to do so
is itself a common prayer of praise and supplication
Who could even have imagined such a thing a century ago?

46. It is a source of joy to note
that Catholic ministers are able — in certain particular cases —
to administer the sacraments to Christians
who are not in full communion with the Catholic Church.
Catholics too can request these same sacraments
from ministers of churches
in which these sacraments are valid.
The conditions for this reciprocity have been laid down
and should be respected.

Appreciating the Endowments Present among Other Christians

47. Dialogue engages the whole person;
it is a dialogue of love.
Catholics should recognize the riches of Christ
and virtuous works in the lives of others bearing witness to Christ.

48. Our direct contact with others
    has made us aware of the witness
    other Christians bear to God and to Christ,
    "even to the shedding of blood" —
        a witness that can contribute
        to the edification of Catholics.
    Whatever is truly Christian never conflicts with faith
    and can result in a better realization of the mystery
    of Christ and the church.

The Growth of Communion

49. The result of these contacts is
    the growth of communion
    and commitment to full unity.
    The saving elements in other churches and ecclesial communities
    are not static, but by their nature they are a force to reestablish unity.
        The quest for unity is not a matter of choice or expediency,
        but a duty springing from the nature of Christian community.
    The dialogues start from the degree of communion already present,
    reducing the matters in dispute.

Dialogue with the Churches of the East

50. The Second Vatican Council strengthened
    the bonds with the churches from the East.
    The observers there present stated publicly
    their common willingness to seek to reestablish communion.
        The Council, for its part,
        expressed its affection for the churches of the East,
        their possession of true sacraments
        — above all the priesthood and the Eucharist —
        whereby we are still joined in a close relationship (cf. UR 15).
    The Council acknowledged
    their great liturgical and spiritual tradition
    and their own way of expressing their teaching,
    in the conviction that legitimate diversity
    in no way opposes unity,
    but enhances the splendor of the church,
    contributing to its mission.
        The Council asked those dedicated
        to restoring the full communion
        to evaluate these facts correctly.

51. Though the process has been slow and arduous,
    the Council's approach has proved fruitful,
    both for the dialogue of charity and for doctrine,

in the framework of the Commission for the Theological Dialogue
between the Catholic Church and the Orthodox Church.

Resuming Contacts

52. I resumed the contacts John XXIII and Paul VI had
with the ecumenical patriarchate of Constantinople,
sealed during the last days of the Council
in a solemn act of mutual forgiveness
and a firm commitment to strive for communion.
    Paul VI visited Benedictos, the Orthodox patriarch of Jerusalem,
and Patriarch Athenagoras at the Phanar (Istanbul).
I considered it one of the first duties of my pontificate
to renew personal contact with Dimitrios I,
the successor of Patriarch Athenagoras.
On my visit to him in 1979 we decided to begin a dialogue
between the Catholic Church and all the Orthodox churches
in communion with the See of Constantinople.
    I received him with great joy
when he returned my visit in 1987.

53. These regular contacts help the exchange of information
in view of fraternal coordination.
Praying together accustoms us once more
to live side by side, thus accepting the Lord's will for the church.
    Two further telling events should be mentioned:
the 1984 jubilee
of the eleventh centenary of Saints Cyril and Methodius,
who were from a Byzantine church in communion with Rome,
and whom I declared patrons of Europe,
together with Saint Benedict,
who had been declared Patron of Europe by Pope Paul VI.
I did this not only to reaffirm
the truth about Christianity in Europe,
but also to provide an important topic for the dialogue
between the East and the West.

54. The second event is the celebration
of the millennium of the baptism of Rus' (988–1988) in Kiev.
The baptism of Saint Vladimir
was a key event in the evangelization of the world.
The Slav nations owe their faith to this event,
as do the peoples living beyond the Ural mountains,
as far as Alaska.
    The church must breathe with both lungs!
In the first millennium this expression related
to Rome and Byzantium.

From the time of the baptism of Rus'
it now includes the entire church.
The unity sought is that of unity in legitimate diversity.

Sister Churches

55. The unity the Second Vatican Council's decree
Unitatis Redintegratio (Decree on Ecumenism)
has in mind as a model
is the unity of the first millennium.
    The structures of the church in the East and the West
    evolved in reference to the apostolic heritage
    going back to the Pentecost event,
    when the church began its journey
    centered around Peter and the Eleven.
Its unity was maintained within those structures
through the bishops in communion with the bishop of Rome.
    It is that unity, thus structured,
    to which we must look.
    Those particular churches remained in unity
    with family ties "as between sisters" (UR 14).

56. After the Second Vatican Council
and the lifting of mutual excommunications,
the local churches around their bishops
are again usually referred to as "sister churches."
    The structures that existed before the separation
    are a heritage of experience
    that guides our common path
    to reestablish full communion.
After the separation — during the second millennium —
the Lord did not cease to bless the church;
but the mutual estrangement
between the churches of the East and the West
deprived them of the benefits
of mutual exchanges and cooperation.
    Full communion should be reestablished,
    an effort that calls for our good will and prayer
    and steadfast cooperation.
    Saint Paul urges us:
    "Bear one another's burdens!" (Gal 6:2).

57. Our declared purpose is to reestablish
full unity in legitimate diversity.
By baptism we are one in Christ (cf. Gal 3:28);
in virtue of the apostolic succession
we are even more so by the priesthood and the Eucharist.

For centuries we lived like "sister churches,"
holding ecumenical councils together;
the Lord is enabling us now to rediscover ourselves
as "sister churches."
On the threshold of the third millennium
we are seeking again the full communion
that will be so fruitful for the church.
From the beginning the church of the West
has drawn from the treasury of the churches of the East.
One part of this treasury is monastic life,
the privileged means for the evangelization of peoples.
The Council does not limit itself to the similarities
between the churches of the East and the West.
It does not hesitate to say
that sometimes one tradition expressed certain aspects of revelation
in a clearer manner than the other.
As a result the various theological formulations
are often to be considered
as complementary rather than conflicting,
enriching each other.

58. The Second Vatican Council drew pastoral consequences
useful for the everyday life of the faithful
and for the promotion of the spirit of unity,
offering to all Eastern brothers and sisters
the means of salvation through participation in the sacraments
and in other sacred functions and objects (UR 26).
This orientation was incorporated
into the two Codes of Canon Law.*
Pastors should instruct the faithful with care
in this important and sensitive matter.

Progress in Dialogue

59. The Joint International Commission for the Theological Dialogue
between the Catholic Church and the Orthodox Church
has worked steadily at the reestablishing of full communion,
which will find its fulfillment
in the common celebration of the Eucharist.
Substantial progress has been made,
and the two churches can already profess together
that common faith in the mystery of the church
and the bond between faith and sacraments,
acknowledging that,

*Cf. *Code of Canon Law Canon* 844, nos. 2 and 3; *Code of Canons of the Eastern Churches,* Canon 671, nos. 2 and 3.

"in our churches apostolic succession is fundamental
for the sanctification and the unity
of the people of God."*

60. More recently the Joint International Commission
took a significant step forward
with regard to the method to be followed
in reestablishing full communion
between the Catholic Church and the Orthodox Church
on the basis of the doctrine of "sister churches."
    A recognition of the right of the Eastern churches
    to have their own structure and their own apostolate,
    as well as their actual involvement in the dialogue,
    will promote mutual esteem
    and foster their commitment to work for unity.
    This step taken, there are already signs
    of a lessening of tensions.
With regard to those Eastern Catholic churches
in communion with the Catholic Church,
the Council expressed its esteem
for their entire heritage.

61. The Catholic Church desires nothing less
than full communion between East and West,
inspired by the experience of the first millennium.
    The first Councils are an eloquent witness
    to enduring unity in diversity.
Restoring this unity after almost a thousand years
is a task for both churches
in a dialogue guided by the Holy Spirit.

Relations with the Ancient Churches of the East

62. Since the Second Vatican Council
the Catholic Church has restored fraternal relations
with the ancient churches of the East
that rejected the Councils of Ephesus and Chalcedon.
They sent their observers to the Council,
and their patriarchs visited the bishop of Rome,
meeting as brothers after a long time.
    In relation to Christology
    we have been able to declare our common faith
    in Jesus Christ, true God and true man.

---

*"The Sacrament of Order in the Sacramental Structure of the Church, with Particular
Reference to the Importance of the Apostolic Succession for the Sanctification and the
Unity of the People of God," June 26, 1988, 1; *Information Service*, 68 (1988): 173.

Pope Paul VI did that together with His Holiness Shenouda III,
the Coptic Orthodox pope and patriarch,
and with His Beatitude Jacoub III,
the Syrian Orthodox patriarch of Antioch.
   I myself reconfirmed this Christological agreement
   with Pope Shenouda and also with a view to pastoral cooperation,
   with the Syrian patriarch of Antioch Mor Ignatius Zakka I Iwas.
In 1993 I affirmed
with Abuna Paulos, the venerable patriarch of the Ethiopian Church,
that we share the one faith in Christ handed down from the apostles.
   And more recently I signed with joy
   a common Christological declaration
   with the Assyrian patriarch of the East,
   His Holiness Mar Dinkha IV.

63. These important achievements are the fruit
    of theological investigation and fraternal dialogue.
       They show that the path followed is the right one,
       and that we can hope to solve the other disputed issues.

Dialogue with Other Churches and Ecclesial Communities in the West

64. The Council's Decree on Ecumenism in its great plan
    for the reestablishment of unity among all Christians
    also speaks of relations
    with the churches and ecclesial communities of the West.
       It states that those churches and communities
       — separated from Rome at the end of the Middle Ages —
       are bound to the Catholic Church because of all the centuries
       that the Christian people lived in ecclesiastical communion;
       but also that there are weighty historical,
       sociological, psychological, and cultural differences,
       as well as theological and doctrinal ones (cf. UR 19).

65. The Catholic Church and those churches and communities
    that have their origin in the Reformation have common roots.
    They share the fact that they are "Western" in character;
    their diversity does not prevent interaction and complementarity.
       The ecumenical movement
       began in the churches and ecclesial communities of the Reform,
       at practically the same time
       that the ecumenical patriarchate expressed the hope
       of some kind of cooperation among Christian communities.
    The prayer of Christ speaks to everyone in the same way
    both in the East and the West.

66. The Second Vatican Council did not attempt
    to give a description of post-Reformation Christianity,
    as these churches differ not only from the Catholic Church
    but also among themselves.
        Besides, the Council observed
        that not all of them desired peace with the Catholic Church.
        Yet the Council called for dialogue
        and proposed some considerations
        that could serve as a basis and motivation for it.
    Those Christians confess Jesus Christ as God and Lord
    and the sole Mediator between God and humanity
    unto the glory of the Father, the Son, and Holy Spirit (UR 20).
        They promote love and veneration for the Sacred Scriptures,
        though they think differently from us
        about the relationship between Scriptures and church.
    We have the sacrament of baptism in common
    as a sacramental bond of unity.
    Though this sacrament is only "a beginning, a point of departure,"
    it is directed toward a complete confession of faith
    and a complete participation in eucharistic communion (UR 22).

67. At the time of the Reformation
    disagreements emerged with regard to the church,
    the sacraments, and the ordained ministry.
    The Council asked for dialogue on those issues.
        The post-Reformation communities
        —because of the lack of the sacrament of orders—
        have not preserved the genuine
        and total reality of the eucharistic mystery (cf. UR 22).

68. The spiritual life of these brothers and sisters
    is nourished by faith in Christ;
    it is strengthened by the grace of baptism
    and the hearing of God's Word.
    It is expressed in prayer, in family life,
    and in worship
    that sometimes kept features of the ancient, common tradition.
        The Council expressed its appreciation
        for the sense of justice and charity,
        human development, and the promotion of peace.
    There is room for dialogue in this vast area.

69. Hopes have been acted upon
    and dialogue has started.
        A "Joint Working Group" with the World Council of Churches
        was begun;

> Catholic theologians were admitted
> to the World Council's Commission on Faith and Order.
> In the dialogue — on issues like baptism, the Eucharist,
> ordained ministry, sacramentality,
> authority, and apostolic succession —
> unexpected possibilities for resolving these questions
> have come to light,
> while at the same time it has become obvious
> that certain questions needed more study.

70. All this work was accompanied by prayer for unity —
a prayer that, far from being limited to some specialists,
has come to be shared by all the baptized.

Ecclesial Relations

71. Thanking God for this progress made,
we should mention some other encounters.
Paul VI visited the World Council of Churches in 1969,
John Paul I expressed his desire to continue on this path,
and the Lord enabled me to carry on this work.

> A significant part of my pastoral visits
> has a precise "ecumenical priority"
> especially in respect to the post-Reformation communities.

72. In this regard I would like to mention especially
— without minimizing my other visits —
my visits to Germany (1980 and 1987),
the United Kingdom (1982), Switzerland (1984),
and the Scandinavian and Nordic countries (1989).

> We met in joy and experienced
> the Lord's presence among us.

I would like to mention how during eucharistic celebrations
I presided over in Finland and Sweden
Lutheran bishops approached the celebrant
— dictated by fraternal charity and marked by deep clarity of faith —
wishing to receive his blessing,
showing their desire for the time
that Lutherans and Catholics
will be able to share the same Eucharist.
With love I blessed them.

> I met the same sentiments in Canada (1984)
> and at the "Ecumenical Meeting of the Word"
> on the theme of the family in Columbia, South Carolina (1987),
> in the United States, where one notices
> a great ecumenical openness....

Achievements of Cooperation

74. The consistency and honesty of intentions
    are verified by their application to real life.
    What has been outlined
    is fertile ground not only for dialogue
    but also for practical cooperation
    with a lively sense of justice
    and a true neighborly charity.
    > Active faith has brought forth many organizations
    > for the relief of spiritual and bodily stress,
    > the education of youth, the advancement of social conditions,
    > and the promotion of peace throughout the world.
    With increasing frequency Christians are working together
    to defend human dignity, to promote peace,
    to apply the Gospel to social life,
    and to bring the Christian spirit to the world of science and the arts.
    > They find themselves even more united
    > to meet the sufferings and needs of our time:
    > hunger, natural disasters, and social injustice.

75. For Christians this cooperation
    is never mere humanitarian action;
    it has it roots in the Lord's words:
    "For I was hungry and you gave me food" (Mt 25:35).
    > This united action
    > reveals to the world the face of Christ.
    Disagreements still have their negative influence,
    but such cooperation will facilitate the quest for unity.

76. How can I fail to mention the ecumenical interest in peace,
    expressed in prayer and action
    by an ever greater number of Christians
    and from within a steadily growing theological inspiration?
    Do we not believe in Jesus Christ, the Prince of Peace?
    > During the World Day of Prayer in Assisi
    > Christians of the various churches and ecclesial communities
    > prayed with one voice for peace;
    > and that same day—in a parallel way—
    > we prayed together with Jews
    > and representatives of non-Christian religions
    > for that same peace.
    We prayed for peace in Europe at Assisi in 1993
    and for peace in the Balkans in Saint Peter's in 1994.
    > It is with joy that we see
    > that Christians are challenged by the issue of peace.

Continuing and Deepening Dialogue

77. What we have achieved up to now
cannot suffice for Christians who profess
that the church is one, holy, catholic, and apostolic.
The ultimate aim is full visible unity
among all the baptized.
> All the results so far obtained
> are only a stage of the journey.

78. The Christian communities should help one another
so that the full content of the heritage of the apostles
may be present in them.
> On the basis of a certain fundamental doctrinal unity
> as regards baptism, Eucharist, ministry, and authority,
> we have to advance to visible unity
> shown in a real and concrete way
> and expressed in the common celebration of the Eucharist.
This journey requires patient and courageous efforts,
and we should take care not to impose on each other burdens
beyond what is strictly necessary (cf. Acts 15:28).

79. It is already possible to identify the areas
in need of fuller study
before a true consensus of faith can be reached:
    1) the relation between Sacred Scripture and Sacred Tradition;
    2) the Eucharist, as the Body and Blood of Christ;
    3) Ordination;
    4) the magisterium of the church, entrusted to the pope
        and the bishops in communion with him;
    5) the Virgin Mary, as Mother of God
        and Icon of the Church.
On this journey our faith requires us
to avoid both false irenicism
and indifference to the church's ordinances.
> It also asks us to reject
> a half-hearted commitment,
> prejudicial opposition, and defeatism.
To uphold this vision of unity
does not mean to put a brake
on the ecumenical movement.
On the contrary, it means preventing it
from settling for apparent solutions
that would lead nowhere.
> The obligation of the respect for truth is absolute;
> it is the law of the Gospel.

Reception of the Results Already Received

80. While we continue the dialogue
on new subjects at a deeper level,
the results already achieved should be received
as a common heritage.
> For this to come about the whole people of God
> needs to be involved.
> Matters of faith require universal consent
> from the bishops to the lay faithful,
> all of whom have received the same Spirit.
A critical process is needed
that analyzes and tests the results
with the tradition of faith
received from the apostles
and lived out in the community of believers
gathered around their bishop.

81. The results of this process
must be made known by competent persons.
Theologians and theological faculties
should exercise their charism in this regard.
> A definitive judgment is up to the bishops
> and the Holy See.
In all this one always has to keep in mind the distinction
between the deposit of faith and its formulation.

Continuing Spiritual Ecumenism and Bearing Witness to Holiness

82. The commitment to ecumenism is a deep challenge;
it calls for a serious examination of conscience
and a "dialogue of conversion,"
conversion to the will of the Father.
> It is only in this way that we will find the strength
> to conclude successfully the pilgrimage of ecumenism,
> beyond a mere cordial understanding or sociability.
> The bond of "koinonia" must be forged.
All Christian communities have to ask themselves
whether they have been faithful to the Father's plan for the church.

83. All Christian communities know
that obeying the Father's will and overcoming the obstacles
are not beyond their reach, thanks to the power given by the Spirit.
All of them in fact have martyrs for the faith,
because of their radical attachment to Christ and to the Father.
> Is that same attachment
> not at the heart of the "dialogue of conversion"?

84. We Christians have a common martyrology,
    with many more martyrs in our own century
    than one might think.
        The fact that one can die for one's faith
        shows that the demand of faith can be met.
        In martyrdom our communion is already perfect.
    Martyrs are not the only proofs of the power of grace;
    so are the saints who at the end of their life
    are in communion with Christ,
    coming from all churches and ecclesial communities.
    This holiness is our foremost common heritage.
        This heritage of the saints
        belonging to all communities
        proves the transcendent power of the Spirit
        and God's victory over division.
    If communities are able truly "to be converted,"
    God will do for them what God did for their saints.

85. God always brings good even out of situations
    that are an offense to God's plan.
    The Holy Spirit has allowed conflicts to serve in some circumstances
    to make explicit certain aspects of the Christian vocation,
    just as it happens in the lives of the saints.

Contribution of the Catholic Church to the Quest for Christian Unity

86. The Vatican Council's documents *Lumen Gentium*
    and *Unitatis Redintegratio* state that
    the one church of Christ subsists in the Catholic Church (LG 8, UR 4).
        In it is the fullness of the means of salvation (UR 3).
        Full unity will come when all share in this fullness.

87. We must walk the path to full unity,
    helping each other and striving to give each other
    what each one needs to grow toward this fullness.
        I spoke above of how the Catholic Church is aware
        that we have received much from the witness given by
        other churches and ecclesial communities
        to certain common Christian values —
        a mutual enrichment that has to be taken into account.
        Let me say it once more:
            "We must take every care to meet the legitimate desires
            and expectations of our Christian brethren,
            coming to know their way of thinking
            and their sensibilities. . . .

The talents of each must be developed
for the utility and the advantage of all."*

The Ministry of Unity of the Bishop of Rome

88. Among all the churches and ecclesial communities
the Catholic Church is conscious of having preserved
the ministry of the successor of the apostle Peter,
the bishop of Rome, whom God established as its
"perpetual and visible principle and foundation of unity" (LG 23)
and whom the Spirit sustains
in order that he may enable all the others
to share in this essential good.
    As Pope Saint Gregory the Great said,
    my ministry is that of the "servant of servants"
    safeguarding against the division of power and ministry,
    a division that would be
    against the meaning of power in the Gospel.
        Jesus, the Head of the church, said,
        "I am among you as one who serves" (Lk 22:27).
As I acknowledged on my visit
to the World Council of Churches in Geneva in 1984,
the Catholic Church's conviction
that it has preserved in the ministry
of the bishop of Rome
the visible sign and guarantor of unity
constitutes a difficulty for most Christians,
whose memory is marked by certain painful recollections.
    To the extent that we are responsible for these,
    I join Paul VI in asking forgiveness.

89. It is significant and encouraging
that the question of the primacy of the bishop of Rome
is now studied or will be studied in the near future.
    It is encouraging that this question
    is now an essential theme in the dialogues
    that the Catholic Church is engaging in
    with other churches and ecclesial communities,
    and in the ecumenical movement as a whole.

90. It is at Rome that Peter concludes his journey following Christ,
giving his greatest proof of love and fidelity.
Paul, too, gives his supreme witness at Rome.
The church of Rome became in this way
the church of Peter and Paul.

---

*Address to the Cardinals and the Roman Curia (June 28, 1985), 4.

In the New Testament Peter has an eminent place;
the Acts of the Apostles describes that place:
"Peter...and the Eleven" (2:14; cf. 2:37, 5:29).

91. The Gospel of Matthew outlines Peter's mission:
"You are Peter,
and on this rock I will build my church" (16:17–19).
Luke states that Christ urged Peter
to strengthen his brothers and sisters,
reminding him of his own human weakness
and need of conversion (cf. 22:31–32).
   The same role of Peter
   —linked with an affirmation of his weakness—
is confirmed in the Fourth Gospel.
      "Simon, son of John, do you love me more than these?
      Feed my sheep" (cf. Jn 21:15–19).
And in Paul's first letter to the Corinthians
the Risen Christ appears first to Peter,
and then to the Twelve (cf. 15:5).
   The weakness of Peter and of Paul shows
   how the church is founded upon the power of grace.
   The mercy Peter needs himself
   is related to his ministry of mercy.

92. Paul heard from the Lord himself:
"My power is made perfect in weakness,"
and he can consequently say:
"When I am weak, I am strong" (2 Cor 12:9–10).
A basic characteristic of Christian experience.
   The bishop of Rome exercises his ministry
   —originating in the manifold mercy of God—
   as the heir to Peter's mission in the church,
   experiencing the bitter taste
   of his personal weakness and helplessness.
His ministry is completely at the service
of God's merciful plan
and must always be seen as such.

93. Peter's successor knows that he must be
a sign of mercy, born of Christ's own mercy.
   To a world caught in sin and evil
   the church is called to show
   that God's mercy can convert hearts to unity
   and to communion with God.

94. This service of unity,
rooted in divine mercy,

is within the College of Bishops entrusted to one
who is to lead the people to peaceful pastures.
> The mission of the bishop of Rome
> within the college of all the pastors
> is "keeping watch" like a sentinel,
> so that the true voice of Christ the Shepherd
> may be heard in all the particular churches.

All the churches are in full and visible communion
because all the pastors are in communion with Peter
and therefore united in Christ.
> The bishop of Rome is the first servant of unity,
> a primacy exercised on various levels,
> including vigilance over the handing down of the Word,
> the celebration of liturgy and the sacraments,
> the church's mission, discipline, Christian life,
> the common good, and the unity of faith.

He can also declare ex cathedra
—under conditions laid down by the First Vatican Council—
that a certain doctrine belongs to the deposit of faith.*
> Bearing witness to the truth in this way,
> he serves unity.

95. All this must be done in communion
with the whole body of bishops,
who are also "vicars and ambassadors of Christ" (LG 27).
> The bishop of Rome is a member of the "college"
> and the bishops are his brothers in ministry.

As bishop of Rome I am fully aware
that Christ desires the full and visible communion
of all those communities in which his Spirit dwells.
I am convinced that I have a special responsibility in this regard
and that I should heed the request to exercise the primacy,
finding a way to be open to a new situation
without renouncing what is essential to its mission.
> For a whole millennium Christians were united
> in communion of faith and life,
> and when disagreements arose
> it was by common consent
> that the Roman See acted as moderator.

In this way primacy exercised its office of unity.
It is my desire to exercise that ministry,
though what should have been a service
has sometimes manifested itself in a very different light.

---

*Cf. First Vatican Ecumenical Council, Dogmatic Constitution on the Church of Christ, *Pastor Aeternus.*

I insistently pray the Holy Spirit to shine his light
upon all the pastors and theologians of our churches.

96. This is an immense task, which we cannot refuse
and which I cannot carry out by myself.
    Could not the real but imperfect communion we have
    persuade church leaders and theologians
    to leave useless controversies behind,
    to listen to Christ's plea,
        "That they may all be one,
        so that the world may believe
        that you have sent me" (Jn 17:21)?

The Communion of All Particular Churches with the Church of Rome: A Necessary Condition for Unity

97. The Catholic Church holds
that the communion of the particular churches
with the church of Rome
is — in God's plan — an essential requirement
of the full and visible communion,
of which the Eucharist is the highest sacramental manifestation.
    The function of Peter,
    in the Acts of the Apostles the one who speaks
    in the name of the apostolic group
    and serving the unity of the community
    while respecting the authority of James,
        must continue in the church under its sole head Jesus Christ.
Do not many involved in ecumenism
feel the need for such a ministry?

Full Unity and Evangelization

98. The ecumenical movement in our century
has had a missionary outlook:
    "That they may all be one,
    so that the world may believe" (Jn 17:21)
    and that the Father may be glorified.
As Paul VI wrote:
    "Yes, the destiny of evangelization is certainly bound up
    with the witness of unity given by the church" (EN 77).
How can we proclaim the Gospel of reconciliation
without being committed to the reconciliation of Christians?
    When nonbelievers meet missionaries
    who do not agree among themselves
    though they appeal to Christ,
        will they be in a position to receive the true message?

99. The lack of unity represents an obstacle
    for the proclamation of the Gospel.
    That is why I consider the ecumenical task
    as one of the pastoral priorities of my Pontificate.
    It is a matter of the love that God has in Jesus Christ
    for the whole of humanity.
    To stand in the way of that love
    is an offense against him.
    May the unity of the churches
    become a sign of hope and a consolation
    for all humankind.

EXHORTATION

100. The best preparation for the new millennium
     is a renewed commitment to apply the teaching of Vatican II
     to the life of every individual and of the whole church.
     The Council is the great beginning
     — the Advent as it were —
     of the journey leading us to the third millennium.
     That is why I thought it necessary
     to reaffirm the ecumenical convictions of that Council.
     The Holy Spirit is active in this endeavor,
     leading the church to the realization of the Father's plan,
     and the will of Christ, as expressed in his prayer.

101. I exhort my brother bishops
     to be mindful of this commitment.
     It belongs to their responsibilities
     — as described in the two Codes of Canon Law —
     to promote the unity of all Christians.
     All the faithful are asked to do
     everything possible to strengthen the bonds of communion.

102. At the approach of the new millennium the church asks
     the grace to strengthen its own unity
     and to make it grow toward full communion
     with other Christians.
     How is it to obtain this grace?
     By prayer, by thanksgiving, and by hope in the Spirit.
     And should we ask if all this is possible,
     then the answer will be the one of Mary of Nazareth,
     who said: "With God nothing is impossible."

103. I, John Paul, servant of the servants of God,
     venture to make Paul's words my own

as I say to the faithful of the Catholic Church
and to my brothers and sisters
of all the other churches and ecclesial communities:
  "Mend your ways,
    encourage one another,
    and the God of love and peace will be with you" (2 Cor 13:11).

13

Faith and Reason

Fides et Ratio

September 14, 1998

In this encyclical John Paul II insists on the relationship between faith and other human knowledge. It is by faith in revelation that the human mind transcends what it can naturally know, reaching the ultimate truth about self, the world, and God. There is, however, an intimate wisdom link between faith and reason, a link that should not be lost, neither by the theologian nor by the scientist or philosopher. Thomas Aquinas is proposed as the model of one who realized that link in his thinking. This encyclical offers John Paul's response to the postmodern nihilistic tendencies of our age.

Faith and reason are like two wings
on which the human spirit rises
to know the truth about itself.

Introduction: "KNOW YOURSELF"

1. All through time and all over the world
   men and women have been on a journey
   of unfolding consciousness.
       The more they know reality,
       the more they understand their own uniqueness,
       and the more pressing becomes the question
       of the meaning of all things and of their own existence.
   The admonition "Know Yourself,"
   carved above the temple door at Delphi,
   witnesses to this basic insight.
       Even a quick glance at ancient history
       shows how in different regions,

periods, and cultures in the world
the questions:
"Who am I?"; "Where do I come from?"
"Where am I going?"; "Why is there evil?"
"What is there after this life?"
have been arising.
We find them in the sacred writings of Israel,
in age-old Indian and Chinese writings,
and in ancient Greek literature and philosophy.
The answers to them determine the direction that lives take.

2. The church is no stranger to this quest.
From the moment she received
— through the Paschal mystery —
the ultimate truth about human life,
she has made her pilgrim way through this world
proclaiming that Jesus Christ is
"the way, and the truth, and the life" (Jn 14:6).
It made her a partner in humanity's struggle to arrive at the truth,
while being aware
that every truth is but a step toward that fullness
which will appear at the Final Revelation of God:
"For now I see in a mirror dimly,
but then face to face" (1 Cor 13:12).

3. Philosophy — or the love of wisdom —
is one of the noblest ways to ask the question of life's meaning
and to sketch an answer.
Philosophy had a powerful influence on culture
in the West and the East.
In fact every people has its own treasure of wisdom,
as is evident in the way they organized
their national — and international — legal systems.

4. These fundamental elements of knowledge
spring from the *wonder* and astonishment
people experience when they discover themselves
as part of the world, together with others,
and as having a common destiny.
Without that *wonder* life would be deadly boring
and in the end unlivable.
Philosophizing, the human intellect
produced rigorous, logical, organic, and systematic
systems of thought, at different times and in different cultures.
In one's "philosophical pride"
one was often tempted to see these partial and imperfect views

as fully explaining all of reality, overlooking the lasting priority
of philosophical *enquiry.*
Beyond the different schools of thought,
there exists a core of philosophical insight
that is shared by all — in a kind of implicit philosophy —
    such as the principles of non-contradiction, finality, and causality;
    the notion of human freedom;
    and the capacity to know God, truth, and goodness.
It is this core knowledge — in a measure — common to all,
called *right reason* (or *recta ratio*),
that should serve as a shared reference point.

5. The reason I want to reflect upon philosophy
   is that the church has always considered philosophy
   as a way to come to know truths about human life
   and as a help to understand and to communicate the faith.
     I even judge it necessary to do so, because modern philosophy,
     focusing attention on the human person
       in philosophy, anthropology, logic,
        the natural sciences, history, linguistics, and so forth,
       seems to have forgotten that men and women
       are always called to a truth that transcends them.
   Under the weight of so much knowledge
   reason has — little by little — lost the capacity
   to lift its gaze any higher.
     This has led to agnosticism, relativism, and widespread skepticism,
     even as regards truths once judged certain.
       The legitimate plurality of positions
       gave way to a pluralism in which all positions are equally valid,
       even if they contradict one another.
     Everything is reduced to opinion;
     there is a sense of being adrift
     and — also under the influence of some Eastern thought —
     a lack of confidence in truth.

6. I write you, my brother bishops,
   because I share with you the mission
   to "proclaim the truth openly" (2 Cor 4:2),
   and to be witnesses to it (cf. LG 25).
     I do it because certain fundamental Catholic truths
     risk being distorted and denied,
     leaving especially the younger generation
     with a sense of having no valid points of reference.
   Many people stumble through life to the very edge of the abyss,
   without knowing where they are going,
   valuing only things that do not last.

It is why I have felt both the need and the duty
to address this theme of philosophy's original vocation
on the threshold of the third millennium of the Christian era.

Chapter One
THE REVELATION OF GOD'S WISDOM

Jesus, Revealer of the Father

7. The church bears a message coming from God (2 Cor 4:1–2),
    a message that has its origin
    not in the church's own thinking, but in God.
    At the beginning of our faith we met Christ
    through whom we have access to the Father
    in the Holy Spirit (cf. DV 2).
    This knowledge of God
    perfects all we can know of the meaning of life.

8. The First Vatican Council and the Second Vatican Council stressed
    the supernatural character of God's revelation,
    in reaction to the widespread opinion
    that such a type of knowledge was irrational
    and consequently impossible.

9. "There are two different orders of knowledge,
    faith and reason" (GS 59).
    Reason depends on our senses and our experience.
    Faith, guided and enlightened by the Holy Spirit,
    recognizes the "fullness of grace and truth" (Jn 1:14)
    which God has willed to reveal in history,
    and definitively through his Son,
    Jesus Christ (cf. 1 Jn 5:9; Jn 5:31–32).

10. In revelation God speaks to men and women
    as friends (Ex 33:11; Jn 15:14–15),
    living among them (cf. Bar 3:38),
    inviting them into communion by deeds and words
    and finally in and through Christ,
    who is the fullness of all revelation (cf. DV 2).

11. In Jesus God's revelation took flesh in time and history,
    the importance of which I would like to stress
    two thousand years later.
    In our time, the final days,
    God has spoken to us in the Son (cf. Heb 1:1–2).
    Jesus Christ, the Word made flesh,
    sent as a human being to human beings,

speaks the words of God (cf. Jn 3:34)
and completes the work of salvation,
which his father gave him to do (cf. Jn 5:36; 17:4).
To see Jesus is to see his father (Jn 14:9).
Jesus perfected revelation through his words, deeds, signs, and wonders,
but especially through his death and resurrection,
and finally by his sending of the Spirit.
> For the People of God
> history becomes a path to be followed to the end.

12. In Jesus Christ the eternal enters time,
the Whole is hidden in the part.
> In Christ all have access to the Father,
> all are offered the truth about their own life
> and about the goal of history.
Where else might the human being find an answer to dramatic questions
such as pain, the suffering of the innocent, and death,
if not in Christ's passion, death, and resurrection?

Reason before the Mystery

13. Revelation remains charged with mystery!
Jesus revealed the face of the Father,
but our vision of God remains impaired
by the limits of our understanding.
> Faith is the obedience we must render
> God's self-revelation (DV 4).
Entrusting oneself in this way to God
is a moment of fundamental decision,
engaging the whole person, intellect and will,
realizing one's personal freedom to the full.
> The act of faith is the most important act in human life;
> it is here that freedom reaches the certainty of truth
> and chooses to live in that truth.
Revelation offers signs
to assist reason to understand the mystery.
> Take the sacramental character
> of the sign given in the Eucharist.
> Christ is truly present and alive in it,
> working through his Spirit.
> But as Thomas Aquinas said:
>> "What you neither see nor grasp,
>> faith confirms for you, leaving nature far behind."

14. Revelation is a point of reference,
both for philosophy and theology.
It stirs the human mind to ceaseless effort,

extending the range of its knowledge,
and yet admitting with Saint Anselm
that God is greater "than all that can be conceived."

15. The truth found in Jesus of Nazareth
enables all men and women
to embrace the "mystery" of their own life.
    It summons them to be open to the transcendent,
        while respecting both their autonomy as creatures and their freedom.
Christian revelation is the true guiding star
to find one's way in the world
with its intellectual and technocratic restrictions.
    Given by God, it offers the possibility
        to know God's plan of love that began with creation.
It gives to those who can look beyond themselves and their concerns
the possibility of taking possession of their lives
by following the path of truth.
    "The word is very near to you;
        it is in your mouth and in your heart" (Dt 30:11–14).
Revelation is not the product of human reason;
it is something gratuitous, an expression of God's love.
    We meet this truth in history
        as an anticipation of the definitive vision of God
        reserved for those who seek God with a sincere heart.
Philosophy and theology both point to the "path of life" (Ps 16:11)
leading to the full and lasting joy of the contemplation of the triune God.

Chapter Two
I BELIEVE IN ORDER TO UNDERSTAND

"Wisdom Knows All and Understands All" (Wis 9:11)

16. The wisdom books in Sacred Scripture
describe the wise person
as the one who loves and seeks truth (see Sir 14:20–27).
    Those books are not only based on the faith of Israel.
    Voices from Egypt and Mesopotamia
    also come to life in those texts.
The desire for knowledge is characteristic of all people.
    The unity between the knowledge of reason
    and the knowledge of faith
    is a typical characteristic in the biblical books.
        In them all that happens in the world
        is observed, analyzed, and assessed rationally,
        but also with faith.

The God of Israel is seen as acting in all events.
"The human mind plans the way,
but the Lord directs the steps" (Prov 16:9).
In the light of reason
human beings can know what path to take,
but they can follow that path to the end
only if they search for it within the horizon of faith.

17. There is no reason for competition between reason and faith;
each contains the other,
and each has its own scope for action.
God and the human being
are in a unique relationship.
The human heart yearns for what lies beyond,
knowing that there is an answer to every question.

18. With God's revelation Israel could plumb depths
that reason tried in vain to reach.
The chosen people understood
that if reason wants to be true to itself,
it must respect certain basic rules:
- human knowledge is a journey that allows no rest;
- not everything on that path is the fruit of personal conquest;
- reason must recognize God's transcendent love and providence.
Abandoning these rules human beings risk failure
by not paying attention to the things that matter,
and ending up as "fools."
And when we claim that "God does not exist" (cf. Ps 14:1)
we show how wrong we are as regards the truth of things,
their origin and their destiny.

19. The Book of Wisdom speaks of nature revealing God.
"For from the greatness and beauty of created things
comes a corresponding perception of their Creator" (Wis 13:5).
The "book of nature" is a first step of divine revelation
that can lead to knowledge of the Creator.
If people fail to recognize God,
it is not because they lack the means;
it is because of their sinful unwillingness.

20. In this way reason is valued without being overvalued.
Faith allows reason to know correctly
what it seeks to understand.
Human beings reach the deeper meaning of everything,
especially of their own existence,
by reason enlightened by faith.
"The fear of the Lord is the beginning of knowledge" (Prov 1:7).

21. In the Bible people could understand themselves
    only as "being in relation"
       with self, others, the world, and God.
       Though sometimes weary
       when trying to understand God's mysterious designs,
       they do not give up.
       Created as "explorers" (cf. Eccl 1:13)
       they continue to lean on God,
       reaching out to all that is beautiful, good, and true.

22. Saint Paul explains this insight in his letter to the Romans.
    Through all that is created
    "the eyes of the mind"
    can come to know God (cf. Rom 1:20).
       Originally reason could reach without difficulty
       beyond nature to its Creator.
       Sin diminished this possibility.
          Our first parents thought that they could ignore
          the knowledge which comes from God.
       The eyes of the mind were no longer able to see clearly;
       reason became its own prisoner.
       It was Christ who came to free it.

23. Saint Paul writes how "the wisdom of this world"
    opposes "the wisdom of God"
       revealed in Jesus Christ.
       Revelation disrupts our usual thinking.
          Every human philosophy
          is challenged by Jesus' death on the cross.
       To reduce the Father's saving plan to human logic
       is doomed to fail.
          "Has not God made
          the wisdom of the world foolish?" (1 Cor 1:20).
    Christ's cross shows the gratuitous nature of love.
    Reason cannot do away with the love shown by the cross,
    and the cross gives human logic the ultimate answer it seeks.
       The "foolishness" of the cross
       is the critique of those who believe they possess the truth
       when in fact they ran it aground
       on the reef of a system of their own making.
    The preaching of Christ crucified and risen
    is the reef on which the link
    between philosophy and religion can break up.
       It is also the reef beyond which
       the two can begin a journey
       on the boundless ocean of truth!

Chapter Three
I UNDERSTAND IN ORDER TO BELIEVE

Journeying in Search of Truth

24. In Athens Saint Paul found an altar dedicated to "an unknown God."
From this starting point he spoke about God as Creator,
as the one who gives life to all, and as the one
"who is not far from each one of us" (Acts 17:26–27):
    a truth the church has always treasured,
    recalling it on Good Friday, when praying:
    "You created humankind
    so that all might long to find you,
    and have peace when you are found."
Literature, music, painting, sculpture, architecture,
every other work of our creative intelligence,
and especially philosophy show this universal human desire.

25. All human beings desire to know
what is true or not.
If they discover something that is false,
they reject it.
If they discover the truth,
they feel themselves rewarded.
No one wants to be deceived.
    Truth is not only a question of theory,
    but also of practice,
    looking for the good which is to be done.
        This truth
        — essential to growth as mature, adult persons —
        is to be found not by turning in on oneself
        but by being open to levels that transcend the person.

26. "Does life have a meaning?"
You do not need philosophers or the Book of Job
to ask questions like that.
    Our daily pain and the riddles of life
    are enough to make anyone ask questions like that,
    if only because of our unavoidable death.
Is death the end,
or is there something beyond this life?

27. No one can avoid asking these questions.
The answer we give will determine whether we think it possible
to reach universal and absolute truth.
    If something is true, then it must be true
    for all people and for all times.

People are looking for a final explanation.
There comes a moment that our personal existence
must be anchored in something final,
a truth beyond all doubt.

The Different Faces of Human Truth

28. The human being might be defined
    as the one who seeks the truth.
       Life cannot be grounded upon doubt, uncertainty, or deceit.
       It would constantly be threatened by fear and anxiety.

29. A search so deeply rooted in human nature
    cannot be completely vain and useless.
       One does not ask questions
       about something one knows absolutely nothing about.
    Scientists who try to explain something
    will not give up until they find an answer.
       The same is true of the ultimate questions.
       The thirst for truthful answers to them
       is so deeply rooted in the human heart
       that ignoring them would cast our existence in jeopardy.

30. There are different kinds of truth.
       1. Most of them depend on
          immediate evidence confirmed by experimentation.
          This is the kind of truth in everyday life
          and in scientific research.
       2. Philosophical truth is obtained
          by the speculative power of the human intellect.
       3. Finally, there are the religious truths
          of the different religious traditions,
          to some degree grounded in philosophy.
    Philosophical truths are not only
    the domain of professional philosophers.
    All men and women direct their lives
    according to their own philosophies.
       At this point we might ask the question
       about the link between philosophy and religion,
       about philosophy and Jesus Christ,
          but before doing that,
          one last thing has to be noted about philosophy.

31. Human beings do not live alone!
    Born into a family they enter a society,
    a language, traditions, and truths
    they believe almost instinctively.

Those truths might be called into doubt,
and after a personal critical inquiry "recovered,"
but many more truths remain simply believed
than those acquired by personal verification.
Who would be able to assess all the scientific findings
or the information that comes to us
or walk personally the paths
that led to human wisdom and religion?
The human being looking for truth lives by belief!

32. Believing we entrust ourselves to others.
Belief can seem to be an imperfect form of knowledge,
to be perfected through personally acquired evidence,
but belief is often humanly richer than mere evidence,
because it involves a personal relationship,
entrusting oneself to others.
   The truth attained in this way
   has to do with the truth of the person we trust,
   and with what the person reveals from deep within
   in a faithful self-giving, linked to truth.
      Martyrs witness to all this;
      neither suffering nor death could ever lead them
      to abandon the truth they had discovered
      in their relationship to Jesus Christ.

33. It is the nature of the human being
   to seek a deeper truth
   that explains the meaning of life —
      truth that is attained not only by reason,
      but also by trusting other people
      who can guarantee its authenticity.
   To entrust oneself and one's life to another person
   and the decision to do so
   are among the most important human acts.
      Reason needs to be sustained
      by dialogue and sincere friendship.
      Friendship has always been considered
      as one of the best contexts for philosophical enquiry.
   Christian faith meets those who search in this way,
   offering them the possibility of reaching their goal,
   immersing them in the order of grace,
   enabling them to share in Christ's mystery
   and the knowledge of the triune God.

34. The truth revealed in Christ
   does not oppose the truth discovered by philosophy.

Revelation and philosophy together
lead to truth in its fullness.
God guarantees the unity of this truth,
as revealed in the natural order of things
and in the way God is revealed
as the Father of Jesus Christ.
    "Truth is in Jesus" (cf. Eph 4:21; Col 1:15–20).
    Christ is the *eternal* Word in which all things were created
    and the *incarnate* Word revealing the Father (cf. Jn 1:14, 18).

35. We must now explore more directly the relationship
between revealed truth and philosophical learning.

Chapter Four
THE RELATIONSHIP BETWEEN FAITH AND REASON

Important Moments in the Encounter of Faith and Reason

36. From the very beginning Christian proclamation
engaged the philosophy of its time.
    In Athens Paul held discussions
    with "certain philosophers" (Acts 17:18).
    Speaking to pagans the first Christians could refer
    not only to Moses and the prophets;
    they had to refer to the natural knowledge of God
    and to the voice of conscience
    given to everyone (cf. Rom 1:19–21; 2:14–15),
    though it often had lapsed into idolatry (cf. Rom 1:21–32).
That is why Paul linked his thinking with that of the philosophers
who long opposed the myths and mystery cults
and were respectful of divine transcendence.
    The classical Greek philosophers
    had always tried to purify the notion of God
    of mythological and polytheistic elements
    linking religion with reason.
Unmasking superstitions, they offered the fathers of the church
a basis to start to proclaim and understand the God of Jesus Christ.

37. Though Christianity adopted Greek philosophy
we should not forget the early Christians' caution
when it came to other elements of the pagan cultural world.
    Paul warned the Colossians:
        "See to it that no one captivates you
        with an empty, seductive philosophy according to human tradition,
        according to the elemental powers of the world
        and not according to Christ" (2:8).

A warning very pertinent to our own days,
when we think of the various occult superstitions
among believers who lack a critical sense.

38. The first Christians were sometimes called
    "illiterate and uncouth,"
    because they were not interested in philosophy.
        Their first preoccupation was to proclaim the Gospel
        that gave them such a satisfying answer
        that delving into philosophy seemed to them
        something remote and outmoded.
    Through the Gospel truth was accessible to everyone;
    people from every race, status, or gender had access to it.
        The former elitism was over.
        Access to God could not be denied to anyone.
        Among the many paths one could take,
        the saving one leads to the revelation of Jesus Christ.
    Saint Justin (d. 165) was a pioneer in engaging Greek philosophy,
    calling the Gospel "the only sure and profitable philosophy."
        Clement of Alexandria (d. 215) considered philosophy
        as a preparation for the Gospel.
            God's revelation does not need philosophy's support,
            but it can help to protect it against illogical attacks.

39. Origin (d. 254) is an outstanding example
    of a Christian thinker adopting philosophy in a critical way.
        He used elements of Plato's thought
        to defend the Gospel message against attacks,
        constructing an early form of Christian theology.

40. Saint Augustine (d. 430), disappointed by the philosophies of his time,
    converted when he found the truth of the Christian faith.
        He preferred the followers of Plato
        to the other philosophers of his time,
        though they had ignored "the Word made flesh."
    He succeeded in producing
    the first great synthesis of philosophy and theology,
    confirming and sustaining the great unity of knowledge,
    confirming and sustaining what he found in the Bible
    by his profound philosophical thinking.
        Augustine's synthesis remained for centuries
        the most illustrious one in the West,
            and reinforced as it was by his personal life and holiness,
            it was a prelude to further developments.

41. The Fathers in the East and West
    went different ways in the use of philosophy,

but they never identified their message
with the philosophies they used.
    They confronted the relationship
    between philosophy and faith critically.
Not being naive,
they reached the most profound speculation
because they lived their faith.
    They did much more than just transpose
    the truths of faith in philosophical terms.
In fact they disclosed what had remained
implicit and preliminary in those philosophies.
    They showed how reason could find its way out of myth,
    opening itself to the transcendent in a more appropriate way.
They fully welcomed reason as open to the absolute,
filling it with the richness drawn from revelation.
      The Fathers were not afraid
      to recognize the points of concurrence,
      but were not blind to the differences.

42. For Saint Anselm (d. 1109) reason is not asked
    to pass judgment on faith—something it is incapable of doing—
    but to find meaning and to discover explanations
    to help everyone to come to an understanding of faith.
    The love for truth and the desire for it
    will spur reason on to go further and further,
    even if it knows that in the final instance
    it will be able to reach only a certain perception
    of a reality that is beyond its comprehension.
Saint Anselm confirmed the harmony between faith and reason.

The Enduring Originality of the Thought of Saint Thomas Aquinas

43. Saint Thomas deserves a special place in this development,
    not only because of his thought, but also because of his dialogue
    with Arab and Jewish thought of his time.
    He gave pride of place to the harmony between reason and faith,
    arguing that both come from God,
    and that nature, philosophy's proper concern,
    could help to understand divine revelation.
Faith has no fear of reason;
it seeks it, building upon and perfecting it.
    Helped by faith, reason is set free from the disobedience of sin,
    finding the strength to rise to the knowledge of the Triune God.
Stressing the supernatural character of faith,
Thomas did not overlook its reasonableness.

Thomas is a master of thought,
  a model of the right way to do theology,
  "a pioneer in reconciling the secularity of the world
  and the radicality of the Gospel,"
  as Pope Paul VI noted
  at the seventh centenary of his death in 1974.

44. Saint Thomas showed the primacy of wisdom,
  a gift of the Holy Spirit, opening the way to know divine realities.
    According to him this wisdom
    is different from the wisdom acquired by study.
    Wisdom "comes from on high."
  It is also different from faith, since faith accepts divine truth as it is,
  while the gift of wisdom enables one to judge
  — "connaturally" — according to the divine truth.
    Saint Thomas does not overlook the other forms of wisdom,
    philosophical wisdom based on the work of the intellect
    and theological wisdom based on revelation.
  According to Saint Thomas,
  "Whatever its source, truth is of the Holy Spirit."*
    Thomas, called an "apostle of truth," sought truth
    wherever it might be found,
    recognizing its universality and objectivity.
      His realism was not about "what seems to be"
      but about "what is."

The Drama of the Separation of Faith and Reason

45. From the beginning of the first universities,
  Saint Albert the Great and Saint Thomas recognized
  the autonomy that science and philosophy needed
  to perform well and play their proper roles.
    This legitimate distinction, however,
    led gradually to a fateful separation.
      Eventually a philosophy emerged that
      — because of its exaggerated rationalism —
      was separate from and independent of faith.
    It led to a distrust of reason,
    which led some to focus more on faith
    and others to deny its rationality altogether.

46. Modern philosophy moved further and further away
  from Christian revelation, often explicitly opposing it.
    Various forms of atheistic humanism
    tried to rationalize even the mystery

---

*Summa Theologiae, I-II, 109 1 ad 1.

of the death and resurrection of Christ,
regarding faith as alienating and damaging
the development of full rationality.
They even presented themselves as new religions
leading to totalitarian political and social systems disastrous for humanity.
Scientific positivistic science
did not only abandon the Christian vision,
but often rejected any metaphysical and moral vision.
Lacking any ethical reference point,
certain scientists are in danger of losing the human person
as the center of their concerns.
Sensing the opportunities of technological progress,
some of them fall victim to a market-based logic
and the temptation of a quasi power over nature
and even over the human being.
The final outcome is nihilism, a philosophy of nothingness.
Search became an end in itself;
life is no more than an occasion for fleeting sensations and experiences,
leaving no place for any definitive commitment.
All is short-lived and provisional.

47. In modern culture philosophy was relegated to a marginal role.
It was replaced by other forms of rationality
directed toward utilitarian ends, like enjoyment or power.
In my first encyclical I wrote about the danger of all this.
People became afraid of the work of their hands,
the work of their intellects, and the tendencies of their wills.
What all this activity yields is not only taken away from them;
it even turns against them.
Consequently people live increasingly in fear.
They are afraid that part of what they produce
can turn radically against them.
In the wake of these shifts,
some philosophers abandoned the search for truth,
looking only for some subjective certainty or pragmatic practicality.

48. The history of philosophy shows a growing separation
between faith and philosophical reason.
However, even in the thinking of those
who contributed to this separation,
at times some precious and fruitful insights are found
on perception and experience,
on the imaginary and the unconscious,
on personhood and intersubjectivity,
on freedom and values,
on time, history, and death.

But this does not mean that the link between reason and faith
should not be carefully reexamined.
Each without the other
is impoverished and weakened.
Reason without faith risks losing sight of its final aim.
Faith without reason risks ending up in myth and superstition.

Chapter Five
THE MAGISTERIUM'S INTERVENTIONS
IN PHILOSOPHICAL MATTERS

The Magisterium's Discernment as Service of the Truth

49. The church has no philosophy of her own.
Nor does she canonize any philosophy.
Philosophy must remain faithful
to its own principles and methods
even when it engages theology.
Philosophy, by its own nature seeking truth
and having the means to find it,
cannot but respect revealed truth.
History shows that philosophy can go wrong.
It is not the magisterium's task
to intervene, correcting those errors;
yet it is its duty to respond
when those errors threaten
the right understanding of revealed truth.

50. The church's magisterium should indicate
which philosophical presuppositions and conclusions
contradict Christian doctrine.
It has the responsibility of expressing a judgment
as to whether the basic tenets of the different schools of philosophy
are compatible or incompatible with the demands
of the word of God
and theological enquiry.
Many philosophical opinions
are the direct concern of the church,
such as those regarding God, the human being,
human freedom, and ethical behavior,
because they touch directly
the revealed truth of which she is the guardian.
In making this discernment,
we bishops have the duty to be "witnesses to the truth,"
a service every philosopher should appreciate.

51. This discernment should not be seen as primarily negative,
    but above all for promoting further philosophical enquiry.
        Philosophers are the first to understand the need for self-criticism,
        the correction of errors, and the extension of their frame of thinking.
    No human philosophy can legitimately claim
    to embrace the totality of truth,
    nor the complete explanation of the human being,
    of the world, or the human being's relationship with God,
    wounded and weakened as human reason is by sin.
        The need for critical discernment
        is even the more urgent
        considering the proliferation of systems, methods,
        concepts, and philosophical theses.
    The church knows that "the treasures of wisdom and knowledge"
    are hidden in Christ (Col 2:3),
    and consequently intervenes
    in order to stimulate philosophical enquiry
    lest it stray from the path of truth.

52. All through the centuries,
    the church intervened to make its mind known
    with regard to certain philosophical teachings.
        It did so more frequently since the middle of the last century
        because not a few Catholics responded to modern thought
        with philosophies of their own.
            The censures were delivered even-handedly
            against *fideism* and *radical traditionalism*
            for their distrust of reason;
            against *rationalism* and *ontologism*
            for their exaggeration of natural reason,
            attributing to it knowledge only faith could give.
        The dogmatic constitution *Dei Filius* of the First Vatican Council,
        which collected the positive elements of this debate,
        remains the point of reference for Christian thinking in this regard.

53. Those pronouncements had less to do
    with individual philosophical statements
    than with the role of reason in the understanding of faith.
        The First Vatican Council showed
        how faith and reason, revelation and the natural knowledge of God,
        are at the same time inseparable *and* distinct.
            "There are two orders of knowledge,
            distinct not only in their point of departure,
            but also in their object" (DF IV; DS 3015; cf. GS 59).
        There was the need to react against *rationalism,*
        affirming the transcendence of faith;

and against *fideism*, stressing the unity of truth
and the contribution reason can make
to the knowledge of faith.
"...The same God who reveals the mysteries
and bestows the gift of faith
has also placed in the human spirit the light of reason.
This God could not deny himself,
nor could the truth ever contradict the truth" (DF IV; DS 3017).

54. In our own century the magisterium warned several times
against the same type of rationalism.
Pius X warned against modernism
with its *phenomenist, agnostic,* and *immanentist* claims.
Marxism and atheistic *Communism* were rejected.
Pius XII warned in his encyclical *Humani Generis*
against *evolutionism, existentialism* and *historicism,* but added:
"Catholic theologians and philosophers...
cannot afford to ignore these more or less erroneous opinions.
Rather they must come to understand...
because even in these false theories some truth is found at times."*
More recently there was a warning
against the danger of an uncritical adoption
of some opinions and methods drawn from Marxism
by some liberation theologians.

55. Today these problems have returned in a new way.
It is no longer a question of some individuals.
The distrust of reason is to some extent so common
that there is even talk at times of "the end of metaphysics."
In theology, too, the older temptations reappeared.
Rationalism is gaining ground,
taking philosophy as the norm for theological research,
especially when theologians are uncritically swayed
by current parlance and culture poorly grounded in reason.
So too *fideism,* which denies the role of reason
when understanding faith and the possibility of belief in God.
One form of this *fideistic* tendency is "biblicism,"
making Sacred Scripture the only criterion of truth
and eliminating the doctrine of the church.
Scripture is not the church's only point of reference.
The church derives the "supreme rule of her faith"
from the unity the Holy Spirit has created between
Sacred Tradition, Sacred Scripture, and the magisterium of the church
in such a way that none of the three can survive without the others.

Humani Generis, AAS 42 (1950): 562–63.

        Moreover, when studying Sacred Scripture,
        one should always remember the various possible approaches
        to arrive at the full meaning of the text.

56. There are signs of a widespread distrust
    of universal and absolute statements,
    especially among those who think that truth
    is a question of a general consensus,
    and not of a consonance
    between intellect and objective reality.
        It is not surprising that in a world
        divided over so many specialized fields as ours
        the knowledge of the ultimate meaning of life is a hard issue.
    Yet, in the light of faith,
    which finds in Jesus Christ this ultimate meaning,
    I encourage all, Christian or not,
    to trust in the power of human reason
    to continue to search for it.
        Faith is the advocate of reason!

The Church's Interest in Philosophy

57. The magisterium does not only correct and warn.
    It also asks for a renewal of philosophical research,
    suggesting the direction to be taken.
        Pope Leo XIII in his letter *Aeterni Patris*
        insisted on the incomparable value
        of the philosophy of Saint Thomas Aquinas.
            Saint Thomas, distinguishing between faith and reason,
            unites the two in a mutual friendship.

58. His letter renewed the study of Saint Thomas's thought,
    historical studies flourished, medieval thought was rediscovered,
    and Thomistic schools arose.
        The most important scholars at the Second Vatican Council
        were products of these developments.

59. Even before this Thomistic revival,
    Catholic philosophers had been at work,
    keeping alive the great tradition
    of uniting faith and reason.

60. In its constitution *Gaudium et Spes*
    the Second Vatican Council has a chapter on philosophy,
    on the dignity and freedom of the human person
    created in the image of God,
    on the transcendent capacity of human reason,
    and on atheism.

I took its main statement
— "The truth is that only in the mystery of the incarnate Word
does the mystery of man take on light" (GS 22; cf. RH 8) —
as a constant reference point for my teaching:
The Council requires candidates for the priesthood
to study philosophy based upon the philosophical heritage,
taking into account currents of modern philosophy.
I myself stressed several times the importance of this study
for those who one day have to address
the aspirations of the modern world.
These recommendations are of importance
for Christian education as a whole.

61. These directives have not always been followed.
Catholic schools and some theologians have not only overlooked
the importance of studying Scholastic philosophy,
but even of philosophy itself.
There are various reasons for this disenchantment:
- contemporary philosophy abandoned the study of ultimate issues;
- there was a misunderstanding of the role of the "human sciences."
The Second Vatican Council stressed the value of scientific research,
but this should not be at the cost of philosophy.
Inculturation is another factor.
The young churches brought in
a wealth of traditions, modes of thinking,
and expressions of popular wisdom.
But the study of these traditional ways
must go hand in hand with philosophical research
to bring out their wisdom and their link with the Gospel.

62. I wish to repeat that the study of philosophy
is fundamental and indispensable
in the formation of candidates for the priesthood.
The Fifth Lateran Council (1512–17) decided not without reason
to precede the study of theology by the study of philosophy.
This order enabled the development of modern philosophy.
The dismantling of that order has created serious gaps
in both priestly education and theological research.

63. For the above reasons it has seemed urgent to me
to address in this encyclical the church's interest in philosophy
and the magisterium's duty to discern and promote
a philosophical thinking not at odds with faith,
discerning what link, if any, theology should forge
with the philosophies of the world today.

Chapter Six
THE INTERACTION BETWEEN PHILOSOPHY
AND THEOLOGY

The Knowledge of Faith and the Demands
of Philosophical Reason

64. God's word addresses all people,
    and they all by nature are philosophers.
        Theology, as a reflection on
        and a scientific elaboration of God's word,
        relates to philosophy.
    I have no wish to direct theologians to particular methods;
    that is not the magisterium's task.
    But I wish to recall the tasks of theology
    and the needed recourse to philosophy.

65. Theology listens to revelation (*auditus fidei*), which is found in
        Sacred Tradition, Sacred Scripture,
        and the church's living magisterium.
    It responds to it by its inquiry and understanding (*intellectus fidei*).
        Philosophy contributes to this response
        with its study of knowledge and language,
        its understanding of the concepts and thought forms
        of the philosophical systems
        used in the church's tradition by the magisterium
        and by the great masters in theology.

66. The divine Truth in Sacred Scriptures
        and the church's teaching
        enjoys an innate intelligibility and consistency.
    Intellectus fidei expounds this Truth,
        bringing to light its redemptive meaning
        for the individual and for humanity,
        culminating in the person of Jesus Christ
        and his Paschal mystery.
        By their faith believers share in this mystery.
    Dogmatic theology needs philosophy
        to be able to discuss theological issues
        such as the use of language when speaking
        of God, the Trinity, Creation,
        the relationship between God and the human being,
        in a critical and understandable way.
    Moral theology uses concepts
        like conscience, freedom, responsibility, and guilt
        in part defined by philosophical ethics.

Consequently theology presupposes and implies
in the mind of the believer a natural knowledge
of the world and of the human being.

67. *Fundamental theology* justifies and explains
the relationship between faith and philosophical thought.
    It should show how there are truths naturally known
    that achieve their fullest meaning in the light of faith,
    like for example the natural knowledge of God.
        Faith, though not based on reason,
        can certainly not do without it;
        and reason needs to be reinforced by faith
        to discover horizons it cannot reach on its own.

68. *Moral theology* needs philosophy even more
to be able to apply the Gospel prescriptions to life.
    It requires a sound philosophical vision
    of human nature and society,
    as well as of the general principles of decision-making.

69. One might object that theologians should nowadays pay more attention
to other kinds of human knowledge
    such as history, the sciences,
    and the wisdom contained in people's traditions,
    and not so much to a Greek and Eurocentric philosophy.
        The Second Vatican Council acknowledged
        that there is some truth in this claim (GS 15).
        Yet we have the duty to go beyond the particular and concrete
        to demonstrate the universality of faith.
        What counts is
        "not what people think but what the objective truth is."*

70. From the beginning the universal message of the Gospel
was preached to different cultures.
    Saint Paul responded to the problem by writing:
        "You who were once far off
        have been brought near in the blood of Christ.
        For he is our peace, who has made us both one,
        and has broken the wall that separated us" (Eph 2:13–14).
    Called from different places and traditions
all are called in Christ to share in the one family of God.
    In this way faith created something new.
    Deeply rooted in their experience cultures show their openness
    to the universal and the transcendent,
    though offering different paths to the truth.

---

*Thomas Aquinas, *De Caelo*, 1, 22.

Appealing to older traditions,
they witness to the manifestation of God in nature.

71. Cultures share the dynamics of human life.
Like human beings they change and advance,
assimilating new experiences;
    open to mystery and the desire for knowledge,
    they have the capacity to receive divine revelation.
Cultures pervade the living of Christian faith,
which in turn gradually shapes them.
    Again and again the Pentecost event is repeated;
    hearing the Good News they say:
        "We hear them telling in our own tongues
        the mighty works of God" (Acts 2:7–11).
The Gospel allows people to preserve their cultural identity.
The community of the baptized is marked by a universality
that can embrace every culture,
bringing what is implicit in them to the full light of truth.
    No culture can become the criterion of truth.
    The Gospel is not opposed to any culture;
    it delivers cultures from the disorder caused by sin,
    and at the same time calls them to the fullness of truth.

72. Christianity met Greek philosophy first,
but other cultures' approaches to philosophy are not excluded.
    As we come into contact with new cultural worlds,
    there are new tasks of inculturation
    not unlike those faced by the church in the first centuries.
I am thinking of the East, and especially of India,
which looks for an experience that would liberate the spirit
from the shackles of time and space.
    It is up to Indian Christians
    to draw from their rich heritage
    the elements compatible with their faith
    in order to enrich Christian thought,
    keeping in mind the following criteria:
        1. the universality of the human spirit
           and its basic needs in any culture;
        2. the perennial value of the heritage
           that the church providentially gained
           from her inculturation in the Greco-Latin worlds;
        3. the legitimate defense of the uniqueness of Indian thought.
What has been said here of India
is no less true of the great cultures of China,
Japan, and the other Asian countries,
and also for the mainly orally transmitted cultures of Africa.

73. Theology's starting point is God's word.
Its final goal is the understanding of that word,
which increases with each passing generation,
    while philosophy helps to understand God's word better,
    and at the same time is helped to explore paths
    reason would not have found by itself.

74. The fruitfulness of this relationship is confirmed
in the great theologians of the past and the present.

Different Stances of Philosophy

75. First there is *philosophy independent of revelation,*
an autonomous enterprise that
— though handicapped by the weakness of human reason —
should be supported and strengthened.
    It should remain open — at least implicitly —
    to the supernatural.
        If it does not have that openness it does damage to itself,
        excluding access to a deeper knowledge of truth.

76. Then there is *Christian philosophy.*
This does not mean an official church philosophy,
but a philosophy in line and in union with faith.
    1. In this philosophy faith purifies reason,
       and it liberates reason from presumption,
       a typical temptation of philosophers.
           This humility allows them to tackle questions
           like the problem of evil and suffering,
           the personal nature of God, the meaning of life,
           and existence itself,
           all problems difficult to solve without revelation.
    2. Revelation proposes to this philosophy some truths
       that reason alone would not have been able to discover,
       though they are not of themselves inaccessible to reason,
           like a free and personal, creating God,
           the reality of sin in its relation to suffering,
           the proclamation of human dignity, equality, and freedom,
           the importance of history,
           and also the need
           to study the rationality of Sacred Scripture.
       These questions broaden reason's scope and action,
       stimulating for a good part contemporary philosophy.

77. The next position is *theology calling upon philosophy.*
Theology presupposes and requires in its research
philosophy's contribution and a philosophically formed reason.

The fathers of the church and medieval theologians
consequently adopted non-Christian philosophies.
This confirms philosophy's relative autonomy.
  Still, philosophy, like theology,
    may come under the authority of the magisterium
    insofar as its teaching is used
    in our search to understand revelation.

78. It should be clear by now
    why the magisterium shows Saint Thomas Aquinas
    as the model for theological studies.
      In his thinking faith and reason
      showed the most elevated synthesis.

79. Finally I intend to point out
    how philosophy should relate today to theology
    and even more fundamentally to the word of God.
      Revelation does not debase philosophy,
      but offering the fullness of light,
      it illumines its path.
        It is the place where faith and human cultures meet,
        guided by the authority of truth.

Chapter Seven
CURRENT REQUIREMENTS AND TASKS

The Indispensable Requirements of the Word of God

80. Sacred Scripture offers a vision of the human being and the world
    of exceptional philosophical density.
      It is there that we learn that what we experience
      is not absolute, nor is it uncreated or self-generating.
      God alone is the absolute;
      we are created in God's image,
      and every creature depends on God.
        Forgetting that basic fact distorts
        the rational search for the meaning of life.
    The Bible tells us that moral evil comes from sin
    and points to Jesus Christ,
    the perfect realization of human existence,
    as its response to the problem of the meaning of life.
      The sacred text rejects in this way
      all forms of relativism, materialism, and pantheism.
    According to the Bible's "philosophy,"
    life has meaning and finds its fulfillment in Jesus Christ.

This mystery pushes philosophy to its limits,
breaking down the walls in which it risks being imprisoned.
    In the Incarnate Word,
    human and divine nature are safeguarded
    in all their autonomy,
    and yet their unique bond is revealed,
    without confusion of any kind.

81. One of the main issues of our current situation
is the "crisis of meaning."
    We are overwhelmed by a fragmentation of knowledge,
    such a maelstrom of data and facts,
    that many wonder whether it makes any sense
    to ask even about meaning,
    often leading them to skepticism, indifference, or nihilism.
        Reference to the transcendent was lost
        to a human spirit locked up in itself.
To be in line with the Word of God
philosophy needs first of all to rediscover
its wisdom (*sapiential*) dimension, that is to say,
its search for the ultimate and overarching meaning of life.
    If the ever growing human technology is not ordered
    to something greater than a mere utilitarian end,
    it becomes a potential destroyer of the human race.
        A philosophy that denies the possibility
        of such an ultimate meaning
        is not only ill-adapted to its task, but false.

82. Next to this "sapiential" function
a second requirement is that philosophy
verifies the human capacity *to know the truth*.
    Sacred Scripture always assumes that the individual
    — even if guilty of duplicity and mendacity —
    can know and grasp the clear and simple truth,
    expressing objective reality.

83. The two requirements mentioned above imply a third one.
Philosophy should have *a genuinely metaphysical range*.
    I want to say here only that reality and truth
    do transcend the world of sense experience.
        Philosophy needs to vindicate the human being's capacity
        to know the transcendent,
        God's self, the ultimate foundation
        of the moral good and the person's spiritual nature.
At the end of the millennium we face the challenge
to move from *phenomenon* to *foundation*,

from mere human experience to the spiritual core
of the human being's interiority and spirituality.
   A philosophy that shuns metaphysics
   would be no help in the understanding of revelation.
I insist so strongly on this metaphysical element
because I think it is the only way out
of today's crisis in large sectors of philosophy
and its consequent behavioral mistakes.

84. The study of hermeneutics* and the analysis of language
   can be helpful in the understanding of faith,
   bringing to light the structures of thought, speech, and meaning.
      But when they restrict themselves to that,
         not considering whether reason can discover the essence of reality,
         they not only degrade reason, they disqualify themselves.
            Faith presupposes that human language
            can express divine and transcendent reality
            in a universal — though analogical — way.
Were this not so, human language would not be able
to say anything about God.

85. All this might seem to be a daunting task
   for those involved in philosophical research.
      That is why I wish to reaffirm that the human being
      can come to a unified and united vision of knowledge.
         The fragmentation of knowledge
         that keeps people from this vision
         is a serious concern to the church.
Philosophers who want to respond to these demands
should develop their thought
in continuity with the great tradition
of the ancients, the fathers of the church, Scholasticism,
and modern and contemporary philosophy.
      This appeal to tradition is more than a remembrance of the past;
      it is a recognition of a cultural heritage
      that belongs to the whole of humanity.
Rooted in tradition philosophy and even more so theology
will be able to develop new ways of thinking.

86. This insistence on the need for a continuity
   intends to ward off the dangers hidden
   in the following currents of thought prevalent today.
      Eclecticism is the approach of some
      who choose ideas from different philosophies,

---

*The science and methodology of interpretation, especially of scriptural text.

without attention to their coherence,
their place within a system, or their historical context.

87. *Historicism* denies the lasting validity of truth,
holding that what is true in one period
may not be true in another period.
   In theology historicism appears mostly as "modernism,"
   in which some theologians use only the newest opinions and terms,
   ignoring a critical evaluation of them in the light of tradition.

88. *Scientism* denies the validity of any knowledge
but that of the positive sciences.
   Religious, theological, ethical, and aesthetic knowledge
   are mere fantasy and products of emotion.
   Science should dominate all aspects of life
   through its technological progress.
This scientistic outlook invaded and changed cultures
because of its undeniable scientific triumphs,
but it neglects the great problems of philosophy,
and it impoverishes human thought.
   Leaving no space for ethics
   it made many think that anything technically possible
   is also morally admissible.

89. No less dangerous is *pragmatism,*
making its choices without reference to ethical principles.
   Whether an action is permissible is decided
   by the vote of a majority,
   without any reference to unchanging values.

90. The philosophies mentioned lead to the rejection
of the meaningfulness of being,
to *nihilism,* the denial of all objective truth,
and to conflict with the word of God:
   a denial of the humanity, the identity,
   and the dignity of the human being.
It erases from the human face
the marks of its likeness to God.
Once this truth is denied, freedom is an illusion.
   Truth and freedom go hand in hand
   or together they perish in misery.

91. This overview does not offer a complete picture,
and it does not want to deny the different ways
in which our philosophical heritage has enriched knowledge.
   However, since the last century, the principle of immanence,
   central to the rationalist argument,

began to question claims once thought undeniable,
resulting in *irrationalism* as a response.
What is today called "postmodernism"
has remained somewhat ambiguous,
but it is a current of thought that merits attention.
   According to some postmodernists,
   the age of philosophic certainty is irrevocably past.
      Human beings must learn, they say, to live without belief
      that a transcendent meaning embraces their lives.
      Instead, they teach, we live in an age
      when every "truth" is provisional.
This nihilism is partly understandable when one considers
the experience of radical evil that marks our age,
which has resulted in the destruction of a previous generation's
unwarranted confidence in reason.
   Nevertheless — paradoxically — some still nurture the illusion
   that science and technology enable us to control our destiny.

Current Tasks for Theology

92. Meeting the needs of our time,
    theology faces a double task:
       - renewing itself to serve evangelization more effectively;
       - looking to the truth that revelation entrusts to it.
    Though its methods are different
    this task challenges philosophy as well.
       To believe in a universally valid truth
       does not mean intolerance;
       it is the essential condition for a sincere dialogue.

93. Theology *provides an understanding*
    of revelation and faith,
       contemplating in the Scriptural texts
       and the living tradition of the church:
          the Triune God,
          the incarnation, passion, and death of the Son of God,
          his resurrection and ascension to the right hand of God the Father,
          and the sending of the Spirit
          that gives birth and growth to the church.

94. This bring us to the problem of meaning and truth.
    The texts to be studied transmit a meaning.
    This meaning presents itself as the truth about God,
    communicated by God in human language.
       This truth is not just the narrating of the story of some events.
       These texts rather relate a meaning
       that they have *in* and *for* the history of salvation.

This relationship between fact and meaning
— constituting the exact sense of history —
needs to be examined from a philosophical point of view.

95. The word of God is not addressed
to any one people or to any one period of time,
just as dogmatic statements
express an unchanging and ultimate truth.
This poses the problem
of how this universality of truth can be expressed
in formulas that are unavoidably conditioned by time and culture.
Human language, though historically and culturally conditioned,
can express truths surpassing those circumstances.
Truth is known in history,
but it also reaches beyond it.

96. This also helps us to understand the answer
to the problem of the enduring validity of Conciliar definitions,
a complex problem considering the meaning that words assume
in different languages and cultures.
The history of thought shows that certain basic concepts
retain their universal validity.
Were this not the case,
philosophy and sciences could neither communicate
nor find a place in different cultures.
Philosophy can be of great help in understanding
the relationship between language and truth.

97. In addition to interpreting its sources,
theology must deal with the understanding of revelation (*intellectus fidei*).
This understanding demands the contribution of philosophy.
The temptation to see the truths of faith
as mere rules of conduct always remains.
A Christology proceeding solely "from below"
or an ecclesiology solely based on the model of civil society
would be hard pressed not to avoid this danger.
The understanding of faith needs a new philosophy of being,
in harmony with the entire philosophical tradition,
viewing reality in its ontological, causal, and communicative structures,
reaching the One who brings all things to fulfillment.

98. All this equally applies also to *moral theology*.
As I noted before in my encyclical *Veritatis Splendor* (32),
the conscience of people is disoriented
because of the crisis of truth.
Moral theology, too, must turn to a philosophical ethics
that is neither subjectivist nor utilitarian

and is competent to tackle problems
like peace, social justice, the family,
the defense of life and the natural environment.

99. Theological work in the church is first of all at the service
of the proclamation of the faith and of catechesis.
    In order to form the person
    catechesis has to link teaching to living.
    The consequent philosophical implications
    should be studied.

CONCLUSION

100. A hundred years after Leo XIII's encyclical *Aeterni Patris,*
I felt the need to come back
to the relationship between reason and faith.
    Faith and reason "mutually support each other."

101. Theology has the duty
to recover its relationship with philosophy,
just as philosophy should recover
its relationship with theology.
    Philosophy will discover in theology
    not the thinking of a single person,
    but the wealth of a communal reflection,
    sustained by its *ecclesial context*
    and the tradition of the People of God.

102. Insisting on the importance of philosophy,
the church promotes
both the defense of human dignity
and the proclamation of the Gospel message
    to help people to discover
    their capacity to know the truth
    and the ultimate meaning of life.

103. Philosophy reflects the culture of a people.
Responding to theology's demands
and exploring the true, the good, and the beautiful,
the philosopher's task is part of the "evangelization of culture,"
one of the fundamental goals of the *new evangelization*
    and one of the challenges of the new millennium,
    especially in regions and cultures
    that have a longstanding Christian tradition.

104. Philosophical thought often is the only meeting ground
for dialogue with those who do not share our faith,

an understanding all the more vital today
considering that the issues facing humanity today
— ecology, peace, and the coexistence
of different races and cultures —
need the collaboration between Christians
and all others who have the renewal of humanity at heart.
A philosophy that contains even a glimmer of the truth of Christ
will provide the underpinning for the planetary ethics
which the world now needs.

105. In conclusion I am thinking particularly of *theologians*
and asking them to pay attention
to the philosophical implications of the word of God
and to be sure to reflect the breadth of theology
while in dialogue with contemporary philosophical thought.
I am also thinking of those *responsible for priestly formation.*
They must pay attention to the philosophical preparation
of those who will proclaim the Gospel today,
and even more so of those who will devote themselves
to theological research and teaching,
all in the light of the directives
laid down by the Second Vatican Council.

106. I appeal to *philosophers* and *teachers of philosophy*
to be open to the questions arising from the word of God.
I appeal to the *scientists,*
whose amazing work I admire,
never to abandon the *sapiential* horizon
and its philosophical and ethical values.

107. I ask *everyone* to look more deeply at the human being,
saved by Christ's love
and called to know and love God.

108. Finally I turn to the Blessed Virgin,
who gave up nothing of her human dignity and freedom
when she gave her assent to Gabriel's message,
resembling in that way
philosophy when summoned by the word of God.
May Mary, called of old
"the table at which faith sits in thought,"
be a sure haven for all in their search for wisdom.

Epilogue

*"... the human person is the primary and fundamental way
for the church."* (John Paul II)

It is a daunting task fully to understand the rich, complex thought of a person like Karol Wojtyla, Pope John Paul II. The temptation is to draw a general outline, to tell a "big" story, a reconstruction of thought and work, coming to a large and overarching view, with the risk of losing the person and his specific giftedness in such an approach.

That is why it might be better to stick to what John Paul II often did when explaining himself in the many autobiographic notes he wrote and in the information he gave to his biographers. It started where it begins in the lives of all of us, in some short stories, some little ones, some personal experiences — stories that according to him made him develop the way he did, when responding to the world around him and to the "signs of the times."

Most readers will know that Karol Wojtyla had a disturbed and difficult youth, growing up during wartime in Poland with its smoke of concentration and extermination camps, exiled from a university closed by the occupying Nazis. His mother died when he was ten and his only brother when he was twelve. When he was twenty-one, on February 18, 1941, he found his father dead in his bed, when he came back from fetching some food for him from a neighbor. He wrote: "I never felt so alone." No wonder that he, a very sensitive and artistic young man, felt lonely, depressed, and as counting for nothing.

In that predicament he profited greatly from his friendship with a layman, a tailor, he had met in February 1940, Jan Tyranowsky (1901–47). When all but one priest in his parish had been arrested, Tyranowsky had been asked to guide the parish's youth ministry. He had formed "Living Rosary" groups of fifteen youths each. Karol was a member of one of them. Noticing his depression, Tyranowsky advised him to read Teresa of Avila's *The Interior Castle* and John of the Cross's *The Ascent of Mount Carmel, The Dark Night of the Soul, The Spiritual Canticle,* and *The Living Flame of Love.*

Karol knew how to pray; Tyranowsky taught him to change his prayer into a means of becoming aware of God's presence in every aspect of his life. Jan helped him to *experience* concretely what he *knew* from his religious instruction in a somewhat abstract way.

Describing what Tyranowsky did for him, John Paul II later wrote that the main thing was: "to work on our souls in the full meaning of this term. He wanted to bring out the resources he knew existed in our souls, to reveal grace that becomes participation in the life of God." Jan Tyranowsky helped him to *live* the truths he knew from the catechism, from books, and from the sermons he had heard. Doctrine became flesh and blood, his flesh and his blood. It is in the light of this lived faith that Karol learned to read the signs of the times. Tyranowsky helped him discover *the presence of God* "in himself and in all others."

When John Paul II later wrote that Jan Tyranowsky was the most important influence in his life, he seemed to indicate where to find the key to his person and his understanding of his mission. Speaking to the cardinals and the Roman Curia in a Christmas address on December 22, 1986, he repeated to them his conviction that the "Holy Spirit is mysteriously present in *every* human heart" (emphasis added).

It is a kind of seed-truth in the life of the church, though it has not always been remembered. It was in a sense rediscovered and stressed in a new way during the Second Vatican Council especially in the documents on the relations of the Church to non-Christian religions (*Nostra Aetate*, 1965) and religious freedom (*Dignitatis Humanae*, 1965).

God's presence in each human being became a key theme for John Paul II. In his first encyclical, *Redemptor Hominis* (Redeemer of Humankind), of March 4, 1979, John Paul notes more than once, "the human person is the primary and fundamental way for the church" (RH 14, 18), a statement he repeats again and again in his other encyclicals. The human person is the primary route the church must travel in fulfilling its mission. The human person is a partaker in God's life (2 Pet 1:4); we are "the children of God" (Jn 1:12). And quoting the Second Vatican Council's document on the church in the modern world, John Paul II added that "through his incarnation the Son of God united himself to each one of us" (GS 2 and RH 13).

There is another, related theme that he expresses several times in his encyclicals: it is Christ who fully discloses human beings to themselves, revealing the Father's love (RH 8). When we look at Jesus we see ourselves as in a mirror. He would add that — consequently — everyone has the right to hear about Jesus.

In his second encyclical, *Dives in Misericordia* (On the Mercy of God), commenting on the parable of the prodigal son, he explains that this loving presence of God cannot be taken away from us.

When the prodigal son is coming to himself in the midst of a pigsty, he decides to return to his father and tell him: "I am no longer worthy to be called your son." He reasons that he has lost that dignity. But when he tries to say this, he cannot even finish because his father makes it very clear that he as father has remained faithful to the dignity of his son and to his life-giving parenthood (cf. DM 6). All of us are equipped with God's life-giving presence. When we sin we might close ourselves off from God, but God will never give up on us.

In his fifth encyclical, *Dominum et Vivificantem* (Lord and Giver of Life), John Paul II attributes that divine "life-giving" to the Holy Spirit. He sees the reality of the "presence of God" in every human being as the *axiom* to respond to the concerns of our age. That is what he means when he writes that "the human person is the primary and fundamental way for the church."

This presence of God in each one of us should not lead to a kind of transcendental individualism. The Spirit of God in all of us is at the same time binding the community together. It is this presence of the Spirit that makes the faithful live in fraternal communion of one heart and soul (Acts 4:32), "establishing fellowship from every point of view: human, spiritual, and material. Indeed, a true Christian community is also committed to distributing earthly goods, so that no one is in want and all can receive such goods 'as they need'" (cf. Acts 2:45; 4:35) (RM 26).

The different encyclicals explain in their respective fields of interest how this axiom of the presence of God's Spirit should be our guide when deciding on moral and social issues like, for instance, the rights of the worker or our respect for human life. It is the realization of the indwelling of the Divine Breath in us that should help us to overcome the emptiness of the world's materialism both in its communist and its capitalist forms. It is an approach that makes terms like "left" and "right," along with "conservatism" and "liberalism," out of date. It is an insight that should help us to respond to the spiritual/material concerns of our day, fostering personal sanctity, ecumenism and interreligious dialogue, peace, social justice, and the maintenance of the integrity of creation.

Under the influence of this new emphasis on God's presence in every human being, things are going to change. The "structures of sin" — a term John Paul II uses frequently in his encyclical *Sollicitudo Rei Socialis* (On Social Concerns) — are going to alter. According to the pope, structures do not determine persons; persons determine structures. It is the church's role to change the hearts of people. Individual persons created the structures that do not allow us to realize the justice and peace God's presence among us is asking for. He wrote: "... the indispensable transformation of the structures of economic life is [a road] on which it will not be easy to go forward without the intervention of a true conversion of mind, will, and heart" (RH 16). It is the church's role to change the hearts of people, as regards not only those global overall structures, but also the ones nearer to home. From 1979 till 1984 he gave 130 fifteen-minute catechetical instructions on sexuality and marriage under the title "Theology of the Body."

John Paul elucidates in his encyclicals that this axiom of God's presence in everyone is nothing new, though the church may not always have been sufficiently aware of it. Its reality was given to us as a seed, growing into a tree; as a pearl spotted, but still to be acquired; as a treasure found, but still to be dug up. In other words we are taken up in a process, in a development.

One of the great lessons of the Second Vatican Council was the renewed insight that the presence of the Holy Spirit works effectively even outside the visible church community: "The Spirit, therefore, is the very source of man's existential and religious questioning, a questioning which is occasioned not only by contingent situations but also by the very structure of his being" (RM 28).

Pope Paul VI had already pointed to one of the consequences of this insight when he wrote in his apostolic exhortation *Evangelii Nuntiandi* (On Evangelization of the Modern World, 1975) that we have to be faithful "both to a message whose servants we are and to the people to whom we must transmit it living and intact" (EN 4). He called this "the central axis of evangelization" (ibid). In other words we have to be faithful to the work of the Holy Spirit in us, enlightened by our relationship with Jesus Christ, and at the same time to the Holy Spirit at work and alive in the other.

Wherever John Paul II went during his world pilgrimages he has been faithful to this double task, but it often moved him to the cutting edge of God's reign in this world. All of us live under the same conditions according to the pope: we are alive thanks to tradition, and we are "framed" by it. Yet at the same time we are "in process."

Jesus himself pointed that out when he sent his disciples out on their mission, telling them, "I have much more to tell you, but you cannot bear it now" (Jn 16:12), and "Amen, amen, I say to you, whoever believes in me will do the works that I do, and will do greater ones than these" (Jn 14:12).

The "framework" of our tradition, however, remains open. Listening to those who live with the Spirit outside our tradition will be enriching and fruitful. In our ever more multicultural or, better, *diverse* world, interreligious dialogue — *and our witness to the Spirit of Jesus in us!* — have become essential to assure peace and justice with all its ramifications. Taking up this theme the Federation of Asian Bishops Conferences stresses constantly that a serious interreligious dialogue can be carried out only through solidarity and sharing with the poor.

In the encyclical *Redemptoris Missio* (The Mission of the Redeemer), John Paul II reacts to the fact that some thought that he went too far in this interreligious approach to the other. We noted above how he told the cardinals and the Curia in Rome in his Christmas address of 1986 of his conviction that the Holy Spirit is present in every human heart: He did that referring to a prayer meeting he had had that year in Assisi. Making it clear that he knew how he had been criticized, he wrote five years later: "Excluding any mistaken interpretation, the interreligious and multireligious prayer meeting held in Assisi was meant to confirm my conviction that 'every authentic prayer is prompted by the Holy Spirit, who is mysteriously present in every human heart'" (RM 29). Such a meeting had never taken place before. Each participant prayed in her or his own way. For some it had been too great a step.

Many wonder why the pope does not draw further conclusions from that same conviction. Again, the answer seems to be that we are in a process, we are not at the end of God's story with us. Saint Paul illustrates this dialectic when he wrote: "There is neither Jew nor Greek, there is neither slave nor free person, there is not male and female; for you are all one in Christ Jesus" (Gal 3:28), while also relegating women to a subordinate role and telling slaves to be submissive to their masters in other sections of writings attributed to him (1 Cor 15:34–35; 1 Tim 6:1–2).

In his short novel *The Actual* Saul Bellow describes how the hero of the story, Harry Trellman, rediscovers an old love of his, Amy. He looks in her face and in a moment of sublime revelation he sees her as a kind of miracle. "I stood back from myself, and looked into Amy's face. No one else on this earth had such features. This was the most amazing thing in the life of the world."

He discovered her personhood. How much more astounding should be the mutual discovery of God's presence in each other. And how decisive would be the consequences of this discovery, if actualized in our world, not only for someone like a pope, but for each one of us.

Index

abortion
 biblical texts and, 246
 the "contraceptive mentality" and,
  249–50
 the culture of death and, 190
 eugenic, 250–51
 forgiveness for, 288
 history of the church's position on,
  273–74
 movements against, 258
 population control and, 252
 resolving the conflict of civil and
  moral law over, 277–81
 responsibility for crime of, 272–75
 and the tragedy of democratic
  legality, 255
 Vatican II on, 231, 243
Aeterni Patris, 344
Africa, 165, 348
agnosticism, 327, 343
agricultural work, 64–65
AIDS, 284
Albert the Great, St., 339
alienation, 191, 192
Ambrose, St., 247
animals, 137, 190
Annunciation, the, 112–13
Anselm, St., 330, 338
arms race, the, 103, 133, 180
artificial insemination/reproduction,
  218, 250
Asia, 155, 157, 348
atheism, 7, 93, 103, 339–40
Athenagoras, Patriarch, 308
Augustine, St., 93, 208, 209, 337
autoeroticism, 218

baptism, 158–59, 296, 313
basic ecclesial communities, 160–61

behavioral sciences. *See* social/
  behavioral sciences
Bellow, Saul, 362
Benedict, St., 71, 308
Benedict XIV, Pope, ix
Benedictos (Orthodox patriarch of
  Jerusalem), 308
biblicism, 343
bioethics, 259
biomedical research, 285
birth control, 251–52. *See also*
  contraception
birth rate, 251–52
bishops
 ecumenism and, 316, 321
 mission and, 164
 moral teaching and, 240–41
 Paul VI and, 3
Bonaventure, St., 222

capitalism
 the church's social teaching and,
  140–41
 development and, 132
 environmental crisis and, 190–91
 labor and, 50–57
 misunderstanding of work by, 47–48
 the Third World and, 191–92
catechesis, 15, 167
celibacy, 18
charity, 163–64, 196
chastity, 287
children, 190, 265. *See also* young
  people
China, 348
church, the
 criticism of, 2–3
 on ecumenism, 293–305
 emphasis on the human person,
  9–10, 197–200

church, the (*continued*)
  firmness regarding the truth, 234–35
  the Holy Spirit and, 87–88, 105–6,
    107
  human destiny and the mission of,
    14–20
  human rights and, 13
  the kingdom of God and, 149–51
  Mary and, 117–21, 122–23
  mercy as the mission of, 35–40
  philosophy and, 341–46
  the poor and, 140–41
  on private property, 54–56
The Church in the Modern World.
    See *Gaudium et Spes*
cities, 155, 187
"civilization of love," 38, 137
civil law, 277–81
class struggle
  denial of God and, 177–78
  Leo XIII on, 174
  Marxism on, 51
  unions and, 62
Clement of Alexandria, 337
Cold War, the, 132–33, 179–80
collegiality, 3–4
Commission on Faith and Order, 314
communism
  the church's social teaching and,
    140–41
  on class struggle, 51
  the Cold War and, 180
  collapse of, 181–84
  development and, 132
  the magisterium's rejection of, 343
conception, 265–66
confession, 17
Congregation for the Evangelization
    of Peoples, 167
conscience
  abortion, euthanasia, and, 279
  ecumenical dialogue and, 303
  the Holy Spirit and, 92, 95–98
  mission and the formation of, 163
  moral theology and, 212, 213,
    221–24
  a new culture of life and, 287
  secularism and the eclipse of, 257
conscientious objection, 280–81

consequentialism, 228, 230
consumerism
  alienation and, 191
  the Cold War and, 180
  drugs and, 189
  enslavement of people by, 134–35
  the environment and, 189–90
  See also materialism
contraception
  to avoid abortion, 249–50
  moral theology and, 218
  Paul VI on, 231
  population control and, 252
  See also birth control
conversion, 158–59, 297–98
Coptic church, 120
creation, 66–67, 83–84
crime, 259, 271
cross, the
  the Gospel of Life and, 268–69
  the Holy Spirit and, 94–95
  Mary and, 117
  mercy and, 29–32
  reason and, 332
  work in the light of, 69–70
culture
  the Gospel's effect on, 348
  implanting the Gospel in Slavic,
    75–77
  mission and, 161–62
  the state and, 193–97
Cyril, St.
  background of encyclical on, 71–72
  biographical sketch of, 72–75
  ecumenism and, 298, 308
  influence of, 78–79
  process of building the Slavic church
    used by, 75–77
Cyrillic alphabet, 74

death, 103, 245–46, 249–52, 288
death penalty, 259, 271
debt, international, 132, 188–89
Declaration of Human Rights, 13, 133
decolonization, 180
Decree on Ecumenism. See *Unitatis
    Redintegratio*
democracy, 193–94, 254–55, 278–79

development
  dangers of, 11–12
  elements of an authentic human,
    134–37
  ethics and the rate of, 10–11
  guidelines for establishing authentic,
    140–42
  mission and, 163
  Paul VI's view of, 128–29
  peace and, 197
  survey of the state of, 131–34
  a theological reading of, 137–40
  See also progress
dialogue, ecumenical
  conscience and, 303
  disagreements and, 303–5
  the fruits of, 305–23
  local structures and, 302
  suggestions for carrying out, 301–2
dictatorship, 179. *See also* totalitarian-
    ism
Dignitatis Humanae, 13
dignity, 27–28, 242–43
Dimitrios I, Patriarch, 300, 308
disabled persons, 65, 274
dissent, 239–40
doctrine, 298–99, 304
dogma, 304
Dogmatic Constitution on the Church.
    See *Lumen Gentium*
dogmatic theology, 346
drugs, 189, 248, 284

Eastern churches
  Cyril and Methodius and, 78–79
  ecumenism and, 72, 307–12
  Mary and, 120
Ecclesiam Suam, 2
eclecticism, 352
ecology. *See* environment, the
economics
  current state of global, 130–34
  direct and indirect employers and,
    58–59
  disparity between the rich and poor
    and, 11–12
  work and, 47–48
  See also capitalism; labor

ecumenism
  background of encyclical on, 291–93
  the bishop of Rome and, 319–22
  the church's commitment to, 293–
    305
  continuing, 317–18
  contribution of the church to,
    318–19
  Cyril and Methodius and, 76
  and the Eastern churches, 72,
    307–12
  exhortation for, 323–24
  goal of, 322–23
  increase in, 144
  mission and, 160
  with other churches and ecclesial
    communities in the West, 312–14
  reasons to work for, 4–5
  results of, 305–7, 317
  the social question and, 199
elderly, the, 266–67, 286
embryos, 274
emigration, 65–66
employers/employment, 58–60
environment, the
  authentic development and, 137
  the Bible on, 264
  capitalism and, 190–91
  consumerism and, 189–90
  current severity of the crisis of, 248
  development and, 197
  materialism's effects on, 34
Ethiopian tradition, the, 120
Eucharist, the
  ecumenism and, 296, 309, 310, 313,
    316, 322
  effects of, 105
  Mary and, 123
  mercy and, 36
  penance and, 16–17
euthanasia
  biblical texts and, 246
  forms of, 251
  mass media on, 252
  movements against, 258
  prenatal diagnostic techniques and,
    274
  resolving the conflict of civil and
    moral law over, 277–81

euthanasia (*continued*)
  and the tragedy of democratic
    legality, 255
  Vatican II on, 231, 243
  as a violation of the law of God,
    275–77
Evangelii Nuntiandi, 3
evangelization, 157–64. *See also*
    mission; new evangelization
evil
  conscience and, 224
  the Holy Spirit and, 96–98
  intention and, 229–30
  intrinsic, 230–31
  moral duty regarding, 280
  moral theology on, 227–29
  natural law and distinguishing good
    from, 216–19
evolutionism, 343
existentialism, 343

faith
  background of encyclical on reason
    and, 325–28
  current task regarding reason and,
    350–57
  history of the relationship between
    reason and, 336–41
  and the interaction between
    philosophy and theology, 346–50
  the magisterium and, 341–46
  martyrdom and, 329–30
  revelation and, 328–29
  understanding and, 330–32, 333–36
Faith and Order. *See* Commission on
    Faith and Order
family, the
  the Gospel of Life and, 286
  human ecology and, 190
  a just wage and, 61
  work and, 50
farm workers, 64–65
fathers of the church, 336–38
fear, 10–11
feminism, 288
fetuses, 274
fideism, 342, 343
First World, the, 130–34
forgiveness, 37–39

formation, 357
Fourth World, the, 187
freedom
  the church's mission and human,
    8–9
  civil law on abortion, euthanasia,
    and, 278
  as a justification for attacks on life,
    252–55
  moral theology and, 211–21
fundamentalism, 194
fundamental theology, 347

Gabriella, Marta, 301
Gaudium et Spes, 127, 344–45
genocide, 243, 248
good
  conscience and, 224
  the Holy Spirit and, 97–98
  intention and, 229–30
  moral theology on, 227–29
  natural law and distinguishing evil
    from, 216–19
grace, 110–12, 236–37
Greek philosophy, 336, 337
Gregory of Nyssa, St., 227
Gregory the Great, Pope St., 319

health-care personnel, 284
hedonism, 256
hermeneutics, 352
historicism, 343, 353
holocaust, the, 179
Holy Spirit, the
  background of encyclical on, 80–81
  the church and, 87–88, 105–6, 107
  the inner person and, 102–5
  mission and, 151–53
  prayer and, 106–7
  and purification of the conscience,
    95–98
  and the reason for Jubilee Year 2000,
    99–102
  relation to the Father and the Son,
    81–87
  sin and, 88–93, 98–99
  as transforming suffering into salvific
    love, 93–95
  Vatican II and, 361

homelessness, 131–32
homosexuality, 218
Humani Generis, 343
humanism, 339–40
human rights
   church teaching and, 13
   contradiction of, 252–55
   development and, 136–37
   progress regarding, 133, 181
   the rights of workers and, 57–58
hunger, 248
hypostatic union, 100

idolatry, 138
illness, 266–67
Immaculate Conception, the, 109
immanentism, 343
imperialism, 139–40
inculturation
   in India, 348
   mission and, 161–62
   Paul and, 152, 347
   philosophy and, 345
   in Slavic countries, 75–77
India, 348
individualism, 64, 213, 256
infanticide, 251, 255, 274
institutes of consecrated life, 166
International Movement for Non-
      Aligned Nations, 132–33
interreligious dialogue, 145, 162–63,
      361–62. *See also* non-Christian
      religions
in vitro fertilization, 274
irrationalism, 354
Islam, 7

Japan, 348
Jesus Christ
   the Gospel of Life and, 259–69
   the Holy Spirit and, 81–87, 94–95
   Mary and, 110–17
   messianic message of, 23–24
   mission and, 148–51
   morality and, 203–10
   the mystery of redemption and, 5–9
   the purpose of mission and, 145–48
   relation to the modern human
      person, 9

as revealer of God's wisdom, 328–29
   work and, 67–70
Jews, 142, 179
John of the Cross, St., ix, 358
John Paul I, Pope, 2, 314
John Paul II, Pope
   autobiographical sketch of, 358
   main themes of encyclicals of, ix–x,
      359–62
   relation of his life to his encyclicals,
      ix
John XXIII, Pope
   on abortion, 274
   on Christian unity, 4
   on ecumenism, 298, 299
   the Orthodox Church and, 308
   on peace, 44, 199
   Redemptor Hominis and, 2
Jubilee Year 2000, 99–102, 109
Judaism, 7
justice
   limitations of, 34–35
   need for love as a complement to, 38
   the Old Testament on God's mercy
      and, 25–26
   wages and, 61
Justin, St., 337

kingdom of God, the, 148–51, 183
knowledge, 330–34

labor
   capitalism and, 50–57
   rights of, 57–66
   See also work
labor unions. *See* unions
laity, 144, 166–67
land, 186
language, 352, 354–55
law, 213–21
Leo XIII, Pope
   the apostles to the Slavs and, 71, 72
   on the balance of power, 193
   Centesimus Annus and, 173–77
   on private property, 185
   on the social question, 42, 126
   on social teaching, 198, 199
   on Thomas Aquinas, 344
Leo XIII, Pope, ix

liberalism, 54–55, 176, 217
liberation theology, 343
life
  background of encyclical on dignity
    of, 242–43
  catalog of current forms of attack
    against, 247–52
  the Christian message concerning,
    259–69
  foundations for a new culture of,
    281–90
  and holy law against killing, 269–81
  new threats to, 243–44
  personal freedom and attacks on,
    252–55
  secularism and attacks on, 255–57
  signs of commitment to, 257–59
linguistics, 352
liturgy, 76, 306
local churches, 159–60, 302
Lumen Gentium, 318
Lutherans, 314

magisterium, the
  on abortion, 271
  conscience and, 224
  ecumenism and, 304, 316
  the Eucharist and, 16
  moral commandments and, 240
  natural law and, 218
  philosophy and, 341–46
  theologians and, 15, 211, 214, 221
Marian Year, the, 124
martyrdom, 234–35, 318, 335
Marxism
  on alienation, 191, 192
  on class struggle, 51
  the Cold War and, 180
  collapse of, 181–84
  liberation theology and, 343
  the magisterium's rejection of, 343
  on private property, 54
  rejection of the church by, 193
  resistance to the Holy Spirit and, 103
Mary
  background of encyclical on, 108–10
  the church and, 117–21
  ecumenism and, 316
  the Gospel of Life and, 289–90

the Holy Spirit and, 100–101
  Jesus Christ and, 110–17
  as mediator, 121–24
  mission and, 172
  morality and, 241
  as mother of mercy, 32
  prayer to, 125
  as source of trust, 19–20
mass media, 156, 252
materialism
  and the eclipse of the sense of God,
    256
  harmful effects of, 34
  as ignoring the worker as subject,
    53–54
  resistance to the Holy Spirit and,
    103
  slavery of, 11–12
  the view of work based on, 47
  See also consumerism
means of production, 54–56
medical care, 62
medical science, 258
mercy
  the current world and, 32–35
  the incarnation of, 22–23
  the messianic message and, 23–24
  the mission of the church and,
    35–40
  in the Old Testament, 24–26
  the paschal mystery and, 29–32
  the prodigal son and, 26–29
  the revelation of, 21–22
Messiah, the, 84–85
messianic message, the, 23–24
metaphysics, 351–52
Methodius, St.
  background of encyclical on, 71–72
  biographical sketch of, 72–75
  ecumenism and, 298, 308
  influence of, 78–79
  process of building the Slavic church
    used by, 75–77
missiology, 169
mission
  background of encyclical on, 143–45
  the basis of, 8–9
  elements of, *ad gentes,* 153–57
  the Holy Spirit and, 151–53

the kingdom of God and, 148–51
methods of, 157–64
personnel and institutions involved
  in, 164–68
purpose of, 145–48
responsibility for, 168–71
a spirituality of, 171–72
missionary institutes, 165
Montfort, St. Louis Marie Grignion
  de, 124
morality
  evil laws and, 280–81
  Jesus Christ on, 203–10
  Mary and, 241
  technology and, 10–11
  See also moral teaching; moral
    theology
moral teaching
  background of encyclical on, 201–3
  bishops and, 240–41
  conflict with civil law regarding
    abortion and euthanasia, 277–81
  faith and, 233
  freedom and, 232–33
  grace and, 236–37
  martyrdom and, 234–35
  on the moral act, 227–32
  the new evangelization and, 237–38
  and the renewal of social and
    political life, 235–36
  on unchanging moral norms, 235
  See also morality; moral theology
moral theology
  conscience and, 221–24
  freedom of thought and, 213–21
  on the moral act, 227–32
  on mortal and venial sin, 226–27
  philosophy and, 346, 347
  role of, 238–40
  on sin, 224–27
  task of, 355–56
  tendencies in present-day, 210–13
  See also morality; moral teaching
mortal sin, 226–27
motherhood
  the Gospel of Life and, 283–84,
    288
  just remuneration for work of, 61
  Mary and, 115–16, 123

murder, 243, 247, 269–81
Muslims, 142

natural law, 205, 216–19, 223, 279
natural methods of regulating fertility,
  284, 287–88
nature
  consumerism and, 189–90
  development and, 137
  as revealing God, 331
  secularism and the distorted view of,
    256
new evangelization, the, 237–38
Newman, John Henry, 213
nihilism, 340, 353, 354
non-Christian religions
  firmness of belief of, 4
  John Paul II's response to criticisms
    of his emphasis on, 361–62
  mission and, 145, 162–63
  philosophy and, 356–57
  the social question and, 199
  Vatican II on, 7
nonviolence, 259
nuclear arms, 132–33. See also arms
  race
nuclear war, 52, 103, 180

On the Condition of Workers, 126
On the Development of Peoples, 126–27
On the Progress of Peoples, 60
ontologism, 342
Origin, 337
original sin, 90–93
Orthodox Church. See Eastern
  churches
ownership, 54–56. See also capitalism;
  private property

Pacem in Terris, 44, 57
Paul, St.
  on the Eucharist, 17
  on the flesh and the Spirit, 102–3
  on the fullness of time, 99
  on the Holy Spirit, 80
  on inculturation, 347
  on Mary, 108
  on mission, 152
  philosophy and, 336

Paul, St. (*continued*)
  on sin, 90
  on truth, 211
  on work, 68
Paul VI
  on abortion, 274
  on Christian unity, 4
  on a civilization of love, 38, 137
  on contraception, 231
  ecumenism and, 298, 314, 322
  on Mary, 19, 123
  the Orthodox Church and, 308
  on peace as development, 197
  Redemptor Hominis and, 2
  the social question and, 126–29
  on Thomas Aquinas, 339
peace
  development and, 142, 197
  ecumenism and, 315–16
  John XXIII on, 199
  progress toward, 133
penance, 16–17, 36
Pentecost, 87, 89–90, 117
personalism, 56–57
phenomenist claims, 343
philosophy
  current task of, 350–54, 356–57
  fathers of the church and, 336–38
  the magisterium and, 341–46
  modern, 339–40
  revelation and, 330, 335–36
  subject of, 326
  theology's relation with, 346–50,
    356
  Thomas Aquinas and, 338–39
  truth and, 334
Pius X, 343
Pius XI, 44, 274
Pius XII, 165, 274, 343
Plato, 337
Poland, 181
politics, 137–40, 183
pollution, 137
Pontifical Council for Justice and Peace,
    43
Pontifical Mission Societies, 170
poor, the
  basic ecclesial communities and, 161
  current severity of the crisis of, 248

current uneasiness in the world over,
    34
  development and, 11–12
  the early church and, 136
  Leo XIII on, 176–77
  Mary and, 120–21
  mission and, 156, 163–64
  population control and, 251–52
  social teaching and, 140–41
  solidarity among, 139
  survey of the global conditions of,
    131
population, 133, 251–52, 285
pornography, 189
postmodernism, 354
pragmatism, 353
prayer, 106–7, 168, 299–301
premarital sex, 218
prenatal diagnostic techniques, 274
priests
  celibacy and the vocation of, 18
  mission and diocesan, 165
  philosophy and, 345, 357
private property
  the church's view of, 55–56
  liberalism's view of, 54–55
  Marxism's view of, 54
  as under a social mortgage, 140–41
  and the universal destination of
    material goods, 185–93
proclamation, 158
procreation, 265, 287
prodigal son, the, 26–29, 359–60
progress
  dangers of, 11–12
  ethics and technological, 10–11
  the uneasiness of the modern world
    and, 33
  See also development
proportionalism, 228, 230
prostitution, 244
Protestant churches, 312–14

Quadragesimo Anno, 44

racism, 161
radical traditionalism, 342
rationalism, 342

reason
   background of encyclical on faith
      and, 325–28
   belief and, 330–32
   current task regarding reason and,
      350–57
   history of the relationship between
      faith and, 336–41
   and the interaction between
      philosophy and theology, 346–50
   as leading to understanding, 333–36
   the magisterium and, 341–46
   martyrdom and, 329–30
   revelation and, 328–29
redemption
   the church's mission and, 7–9
   the divine dimension of, 6
   the human dimension of, 6–7
   and humanity's situation in the
      modern world, 9–13
   the mystery of Christ and, 5
   as new creation, 5–6
Reformation, the, 312
relativism, 278, 327
religious orders, 166
Rerum Novarum, 42, 50–51, 173–77,
   178
resurrection, the, 29–32, 69–70, 86–87
revelation
   faith, reason, and, 328–30
   philosophy and, 335–36, 349
   of the Trinity, 82–83, 85
righteousness, 88–89
rights, 57–66, 136–37, 181. See also
   human rights
rhythm method. See natural methods
   of regulating fertility
Rus', 308, 309

sacraments, 306. See also specific
   sacraments
saints, 234, 238
salvation, 145–48
Satan, 92
Scholasticism, 345, 352
science
   crimes against life and, 244
   lack of ethics of, 353
   philosophy and, 345, 357

   as rejecting faith, 340
   truth and, 334
   the uneasiness of the modern world
      and, 33
scientism, 353
scripture
   ecumenism and, 316
   knowledge and, 330–34
   philosophy and, 354–55
   role in the church, 343–44
Second World, the, 130. See also
   communism
secularism, 233, 255–57
self-defense, 270–71
service, 18–19
sexuality, 218, 256–57, 287
sin
   ecumenism and, 303
   the Holy Spirit and, 88–93, 98–99
   moral theology on, 224–27
   the Old Testament on God's mercy
      and, 25
   structures of, 138, 190, 360
sisters, religious, 166
slavery, 244
Slavs
   background of encyclical on, 71–72
   biographical sketch of apostles to,
      72–75
   process of planting church among,
      75–80
social/behavioral sciences, 198, 212–13,
   239, 345
socialism
   as acceptable in some situations, 55,
      57
   alternatives to, 188
   Christian vision contrasted with,
      177–78
   on class struggle, 51
   Leo XIII on, 176
   social teaching of the church and,
      198
   true meaning of, 56
social question, the
   background of encyclical on, 126–27
   Leo XIII on, 42
   survey of the state of, 129–34
   work and, 43–44, 48

social teaching
    background of encyclical on, 173–77
    focused on the human being, 197–200
    the poor and, 140–41
    on work, 43–44
solidarity, 139–40
Solidarity Movement, 181, 183
South, the, 157, 163. *See also* Third
    World
spirituality, 66–70, 124, 171–72
state, the, 193–97, 277–81
sterilization, 218, 252
strikes, 63–64
structures of sin. *See* sin structures of
subsidiarity, 195
suffering
    the Bible on, 266–67
    current misunderstanding of, 251
    the Holy Spirit and, 93–95
    hope and, 288
suicide, 231, 243, 276
Synod of Bishops, 3

technology
    causing loss of sight of the human,
        340
    crimes against life and, 244
    moral ethics and, 10–11
    nuclear war and, 52
    philosophy and, 351
    the poor and, 141
    the uneasiness of the modern world
        and, 33
    wealthy countries and, 186
    work and, 45–46
    the worker as more important than,
        52–53
teleology, 227–28
Ten Commandments, the, 204–7
Teresa of Avila, x, 358
terrorism, 103
Tertullian, 273
theology
    on conscience, 221–24
    current tasks of, 357
    freedom and, 214–15
    on general moral norms, 221
    philosophy's relation with, 346–50,
        356

rationalism and, 343
revelation and, 330
role of, 15, 238–40
Third World, the
    capitalism and, 191–92
    cities of, 187
    the Cold War and, 180
    ownership of the means of
        production in, 56
    survey of conditions in, 130–34
Thomas Aquinas
    on faith and reason, 329, 338–39,
        344
    natural law and, 279
    on private ownership of capital, 57
    and the socialization of the means
        of production, 55
torture, 34
totalitarianism, 13, 193, 254
tradition, 55, 79, 221, 273, 304, 316
transnational companies, 58
tribalism, 161
Trinity, the
    creation and, 83–84
    the inner person and, 104
    revelation of, 82–83, 85
triumphalism, 2
truth
    background of encyclical on, 201–3
    the church as responsible for, 15–16
    conscience and, 221–24
    different faces of human, 334–36
    elements of the search for, 333–34
    freedom and, 232–33
    language and, 355
    the magisterium and, 341–46
    moral theology and, 212
    philosophy and, 351
    theology and, 354–55
Tyranowsky, Jan, 358–59

unemployment, 59–60, 132, 178–79
unions, 62–64, 175, 179, 188
Unitatis Redintegratio, 309, 310, 312,
    318
United Nations, 59
United Nations Organization, 13, 129,
    181

unity, Christian, 4–5. *See also* ecumenism
unmarried mothers, 284
utilitarianism, 256, 340

Vatican I, 321, 328, 342
Vatican II
  on abortion, 272, 274
  on collegiality, 3
  condemnation of attacks against human life, 243–44
  on the dependence of all created things on God, 215
  on disciplines besides philosophy and theology, 347
  Eastern churches and, 307–8, 310, 311
  ecumenism and, 291, 292, 294–99, 302, 309, 323
  on evil, 231
  on the Holy Spirit, 88, 101, 361
  on human rights, 13
  on Mary, 19, 110
  on mission, 144
  on moral theology, 211
  on non-Christian religions, 7
  on philosophy, 344–45
  on private property, 185
  on progress and its consequences, 33
  on Protestant churches, 313
  Redemptor Hominis and, 2
  on social concerns, 127
  on the supernatural character of God's revelation, 328
  Thomas Aquinas and, 344
  on work, 68, 70
  on the world as fallen in sin yet emancipated by Jesus, 89
venial sin, 226–27
violence, 247, 248, 269–81
Vladimir, St., 124, 308

vocations, 18–19, 168
voting, 280

wages, 60–61, 175–76, 179
war, 34, 197, 248
welfare state, the, 195
witness, 157–58
women
  abortion and, 288–89
  the Gospel of Life and, 288
  just wages and, 61
  Mary and, 123
  scripture on work and, 68
  in the Third World, 130
  violence against, 248
work
  capitalism and, 47–48, 50–57
  current changes in the nature of, 42–43
  defined, 41–42
  elements for a spirituality of, 66–70
  fair distribution of material wealth and, 192–93
  the family and, 50
  Genesis on, 44–45
  Leo XIII on, 174–77
  personal dignity and, 49
  and the rights of workers, 57–66
  social teaching of the church on, 43–44
  technology and, 45–46
  the worker as subject and, 46–47
  worker solidarity and, 48–49
  See also labor
workers, 192–93. *See also* labor; work
World Council of Churches, 313–14
World Day of Prayer in Assisi, 315, 361
World Mission Day, 168

young people, 156, 182, 287. *See also* children